TIMELINES

Wars and revolutions, economic crises and political conflict; these are the very stuff of modern history. This guide to the last 100 years of great power conflicts, social rebellions, strikes and protests gives us the essential history of the world in which we live. Based on the *Timeline* TV series, this is a fast-paced and accessible guide for those who want to know how power is exercised, by whom and for what purposes in the modern world.

From the rise and fall of great empires in the two World Wars and the Cold War through to the 'War on Terror' and the rise of China, *Timelines* describes the shifts in the Imperial structure of the world and it looks at the impact of those changes upon the conflict zones of the twenty-first century, including Afghanistan, Iraq and Iran.

Finally, *Timelines* looks at moments of popular resistance, from the Russian and Spanish revolutions to the fall of Apartheid in the 1990s and the ongoing socialist experiment that is Hugo Chavez's Venezuela. We live in turbulent times. These essays show us how we got here and outline the forces that are going to shape the history of the twenty-first century.

John Rees' books include *The Algebra of Revolution*, *Imperialism and Resistance*, *Strategy and Tactics* and *The People Demand a Short History of the Arab Revolutions* (with Joseph Daher). He is a member of the Editorial Board of *Counterfire* and a co-founder of the Stop the War Coalition.

TIMELINES

A political history of the modern world

John Rees

Routledge
Taylor & Francis Group
LONDON AND NEW YORK

First published 2012
by Routledge
2 Park Square, Milton Park, Abingdon, Oxon, OX14 4RN

Simultaneously published in the USA and Canada
by Routledge
711 Third Avenue, New York, NY 10017

*Routledge is an imprint of the Taylor & Francis Group,
an informa business*

© 2012 John Rees

The right of John Rees to be identified as author of this work
has been asserted by him in accordance with sections 77 and 78 of
the Copyright, Designs and Patent Act 1988.

All rights reserved. No part of this book may be reprinted or
reproduced or utilised in any form or by any electronic, mechanical,
or other means, now known or hereafter invented, including
photocopying and recording, or in any information storage or
retrieval system, without permission in writing from the publishers.

Trademark notice: Product or corporate names may be trademarks or registered
trademarks, and are used only for identification and
explanation without intent to infringe.

British Library Cataloguing in Publication Data
A catalogue record for this book is available from the British Library

Library of Congress Cataloging-in-Publication Data
A catalogue record for this book has been requested

ISBN: 978-0-415-69102-4 (hbk)
ISBN: 978-0-415-69103-1 (pbk)
ISBN: 978-0-203-12313-3 (ebk)

Typeset in Bembo
by Sunrise Setting Ltd

Printed and bound in Great Britain by the MPG Books Group

CONTENTS

List of figures — vii
Acknowledgements — x
Abbreviations — xii

Introduction — 1

1 The rise and fall of great powers — 7

The First World War — 7
The revolutions that made Russia — 11
The consequences of the First World War — 18
The rise of Fascism — 26
The Spanish Civil War — 34
The real history of the Second World War — 39
The Cold War — 54
The rise of China — 64
Obama and US power — 71

2 Empire and after — 80

Afghanistan — 80
The Iranian Revolution — 88
Palestine — 94
The Vietnam War — 102
The Iraq War and the Iraq Inquiry — 110

Ireland	117
A short history of immigration in Britain	126

3 The rulers and the ruled 135

Recessions and resistance	135
The Civil Rights Movement	144
1968: the year that changed the world	154
South Africa's struggle for freedom	160
Thatcherism	167
The revolutions of 1989	174
Hugo Chavez's Revolution	180
Student revolts	187

Conclusion: the first decade of the twenty-first century 194

Further reading	201
Index	207

FIGURES

1.1	The rival alliances in the First World War	8
1.2	The War on the Western Front	9
1.3	Imperial powers surround the Russian Revolution	17
1.4	The Ottoman Empire (with some modern borders indicated)	19
1.5	German marks vs. US dollar	22
1.6	Unemployment in the mid-1920s	23
1.7	The Great Slump revisited	24
1.8	German unemployment and Nazi vote share	29
1.9	Unemployment during the period 1928 to 1932	30
1.10	German election results, November 1932	31
1.11	Make-up of the International Brigades	36
1.12	Germany gains control of the Sudetenland, Czechoslovakia	41
1.13	The invasion of Poland, September 1939	43
1.14	The War on the Eastern Front	47
1.15	The Allied invasion of Italy	49
1.16	The Battle of the Bulge	51
1.17	The 'Iron Curtain' in Europe	55
1.18	The Cuban Missile Crisis, 1962	60
1.19	Gross external debt of the Eastern bloc, 1988	63
1.20	Annual growth since 2000 in China, the US and the UK	64

Figures

1.21	Opium trade between 1760 and 1880	66
1.22	The Long March, 1934 to 1936	67
1.23	Life expectancy in China, 1920 to 2000	69
1.24	Top 15 nations as ranked by military spending, 1999	73
1.25	US and 'threat States' ranked by military spending, 1999	75
1.26	NATO membership in Europe from 1990 to 2009	76
2.1	Make-up of the population of Afghanistan	81
2.2	Russian and US aid to Afghanistan prior to 1971	83
2.3	Iranian society, 2005	92
2.4	Palestinian and Israeli land, 1946	97
2.5	Palestinian and Israeli land, 1947	97
2.6	Palestinian and Israeli land, 1949	98
2.7	US military spending to foreign countries, 2008	100
2.8	French Indochina	103
2.9	Ho Chi Minh trail	108
2.10	The 'Red Line Agreement', 1923	112
2.11	Land ownership in Ireland, 1703	118
2.12	Ireland's exports, 1907	119
2.13	The North–South divide in Ireland	121
2.14	Immigration in Britain, 1951 to 2001	131
2.15	Asylum applications in Britain, 1993 to 2006	132
2.16	Migration to Britain, 1994 to 2004	133
3.1	Value of South Sea Company shares (log scale)	136
3.2	The stock market crash of 1929	138
3.3	Japanese industrial production, 1998 to 2009	140
3.4	Bank losses of all commercial banks between 2007 and 2010	141
3.5	US Wages/GDP between 1960 and 2005	142
3.6	US Real GDP	142
3.7	US GDP and total debt	143
3.8	Mississippi freedom rides	147

3.9	South African Land Act, 1913	161
3.10	South African economy, 1946 to 1990	163
3.11	Unemployment rate in South Africa, 1995 to 2009	164
3.12	Unemployment in Britain, 1975 to 1985	171
3.13	Average annual income gain in Britain, 1979 to 1990	172
3.14	Champagne shipments to UK between 1975 and 1990	173
3.15	Petroleum production in Venezuela	184
3.16	Overall spending of GDP in Venezuela, Sweden and France	184

ACKNOWLEDGEMENTS

The essays in this book are based on scripts that I originally wrote for the *Timeline* political history series shown on the Islam channel. I am grateful to the CEO of the channel, Mohamed Ali, for giving me the chance to make the programmes in the first place and for his continued commitment to the wider project of making politically committed programmes at the channel. All those I have worked with at the channel, both in the studio and in post-production, have been unfailingly helpful and supportive. In particular, Arfan Ali, the Head of Programming, has been an unswerving advocate of the *Timeline* project from its first moments. For most of the series, Aldo D'Andrea marshalled the camera operators and technicians at the studio; I am grateful to him and to them. The first series editor was Fatma Rivzi. I knew nothing about editing a TV programme when I worked with her, so I thank her for her patience and for what I learnt from her. It has been a pleasure to work with Kamran Khan who has edited the second and third *Timeline* series. The finished programmes are as much his work as mine. Karthik Raja has worked his magic on the graphics for the series. I am grateful to him for reproducing some of them for inclusion in this book and for providing the images for the cover. Selvan Sami has overseen post-production and I thank him for facilitating the no-doubt irregular methods by which Kamran, Karthik and I arrived at the finished product.

This is the third book that I have published with Routledge and I am happy once more to record the debt I owe Craig Fowlie both for his encouragement, professionalism and our occasional and enjoyable political discussions. I am grateful to Chris Nineham for the political discussions we have shared over many years that have advanced my understanding of the issues discussed in this book. Thanks are also due to Carmel Brown who first suggested that the scripts be made into a book and, as ever, to Lindsey German for reading the scripts and the book.

ABBREVIATIONS

ANC	African National Congress
AWB	Afrikaner Weerstandsbeweging Party (South Africa)
BNP	British National Party
CCP	Chinese Communist Party
CENTO	Central Treaty Organization
CIA	Central Intelligence Agency (US)
CND	Campaign for Nuclear Disarmament
COSATU	Congress of South African Trade Unions
CPSU	Communist Party of the Soviet Union
EU	European Union
FBI	Federal Bureau of Investigation (US)
GLC	Greater London Council
IRA	Irish Republican Army
ISI	Inter-Services Intelligence (Pakistan)
LAPD	Los Angeles Police Department
NAACP	National Association for the Advancement of Colored People (US)
NASA	National Aeronautics and Space Administration (US)
NATO	North Atlantic Treaty Organization
NF	National Front (UK)
NLF	National Liberation Front (Vietnam)
NUM	National Union of Mineworkers (UK)
OPEC	Organization of Petroleum Exporting Countries
PDVSA	Petróleos de Venezuela, S.A. (Venezuela)
RUC	Royal Ulster Constabulary
SAVAK	National Intelligence and Security Organization (Iran)
SEATO	Southeast Asia Treaty Organization
SNCC	Student Nonviolent Coordinating Committee (US)
SS	Schutzstaffel (Germany)
TGWU	Transport and General Workers' Union (UK)
TUC	Trades Union Congress (UK)

INTRODUCTION
The shape of modern history

What is 'modern history'? According to one commonly accepted definition the modern era, or at least 'the early modern era', has its beginnings in the seventeenth century. And there is some point to this, especially with regard to English history as this era saw the emergence of a more centralized National State, the first modern social revolution and the beginnings of a modern (as opposed to feudal) empire. For others, however, the modern world only really begins with the Industrial Revolution; first in Britain in the nineteenth century and then later in Europe and North America. Again, this dating has some virtues as both the recognizably Capitalist economies of the modern era, with their attendant state and military apparatuses, and the modern working class do indeed emerge in this period. Nevertheless, the essays in this book are mainly about the history of the twentieth century. Although, in some cases earlier events are recalled as essential context this is, in the main, an account of the last 100 years or so. So much of the world we know was fully established and still persists from within this timeframe. Globally competitive state systems, total war, nuclear weapons, fully developed means of mass communication, a truly international market, finance capital, multinational corporations, a world (rather than a metropolitan core) of Nation States, mass working class parties and stable Trade Unions all develop to their full stature within this period.

This book is, of course, a selective history which does not cover all these developments fully. The criterion on which selection was made has to do with the flash-points and fissures of contemporary politics. There is no reason why this book contains essays on Afghanistan and Vietnam, rather than, say, essays on Nigeria or Argentina, other than the fact that the former have become sites of crises in the modern Imperial system in a way in which the latter have not. But, selective as it is, the account that follows does give an overview of the shape of the modern world. It does so by delineating the shifting patterns of great power politics, and their effects on the fate of smaller nations, and the moments of resistance to these dominant powers by ordinary people, both in the metropolitan nations and in those they tried to dominate.

The first section of the book examines patterns of Imperial domination on a global scale. At the start of the twentieth century, the accumulated effect of the previous 100 years of industrial development in the core countries of the world economy was just impacting with its full force on the international State system. Industrial development in nineteenth-century Britain, America, Germany, France, Italy, Russia and the Austro-Hungarian Empire and other countries in the core of the system had transformed the nature of Imperial rivalry. The Colonial Empires of the major powers had spread with increasing speed through Africa, the Middle East, South America and the Far East. Rivalry between them had bred a series of limited military conflicts throughout the nineteenth century, but a decisive settling of accounts was not long in coming as the new century opened. When it did erupt in 1914 it was a very different kind of war than any before it, and not just because of its geographical extent. It was an industrialized form of war and it involved civilians to an unprecedented degree. The victors were, by and large, those States with both the most modern industries and the most modern State structures that retained the fewest semi-feudal remnants. Thus, Britain, the US and France were the major nations on the winning side and the Russian Empire, the Ottoman Empire and the Austro-Hungarian Empire were among the main powers on the losing side. Germany, though an empire, was a recently unified and industrialized State, but its political structure retained important pre-modern elements. The losers were the empires in a more archaic state than their conquerors. They were multinational conglomerations on an almost medieval basis, rather than the more monolithic States which became the norm in the twentieth century. They were also, by and large, less democratic in structure and the weight of the aristocracy and Monarchy was greater within them (although this should not be overstated, particularly as in France and Britain universal suffrage was a post-First World War development). For these reasons, revolution in the defeated nations attained greater force than it did in the nations who were victorious, though revolutionary pressure existed here as well, and in Russia,

Germany and in the Hungarian part of the Austro-Hungarian Empire it swept away the old State structure completely.

The First World War did, however, only lead to a partial rewriting of the Imperial order. The historian E. H. Carr was right to characterize the period from the First to the Second World War as a continuous period of Imperial rivalry which he called a new 'Thirty Years War'. This is an accurate designation if for no other reason than the fact that the major Imperial rivalry that stood at the heart of the First World War – between Britain and France on the one hand and Germany and the Austrian part of the old Austro-Hungarian Empire on the other – continued to dominate the post-War period and eventually resulted in the Second World War. But while the old powers of Europe positioned themselves to re-fight the old wars, two new powers were growing in strength. To the west the US was becoming the powerhouse of Capitalist development – although this was partially masked by the catastrophe of the Wall Street Crash and the depth of the slump that followed – whilst to the east post-revolutionary Russia was also undergoing unprecedented industrial growth – though this ascent was also partially masked from view, in this case by the brutalities and chaos of Stalin's counter-revolutionary regime. But during the Second World War itself, these nations were, militarily, the decisive forces. Indeed, the American economy was so strong that it became the foundation of victory in two wars: the European War against Germany and Italy and the Pacific War against Japan. Even more remarkably, the American economy's civilian production also expanded. This was unique and, by contrast, Russia's new power rested less on its economic growth, although this was also considerable from the 1930s to the 1970s, and more on the fact that its military forces had physically occupied Eastern Europe in their drive to Berlin.

So it is really the post-Second World War period that marks the second phase of Imperial rivalry in the twentieth century, the era of the Cold War. The previously dominant European powers were now only in the second rank, and over the next half-century even this position was only maintained by binding themselves together in ever-closer economic and, to a lesser extent, political unions. Instead, from 1945 until 1989 world politics was defined by the military and economic competition between the two superpowers and their attendant military alliances, NATO and the Warsaw Pact sect. Within their spheres of influence dissent was crushed either by the main powers themselves or by the local ruling classes or the client movements acting for them. This was true in Hungary in 1956 and Czechoslovakia in 1968 for the Russians. But it was also true in Iran in 1953 and Chile in 1973 for the US. On the political borders of the Cold War events sometimes threatened to, or actually did, turn into hot wars, as was the case in Korea, Vietnam, Cuba and Panama. In some places repression also failed, notably in Poland in the 1980s for the Russians and in Vietnam for the US in the 1960s and early 1970s. Both were Imperial turning points.

The Cold War was always as much about economic competition as it was about military competition. Indeed, military competition was largely a form of economic competition. It was about whether the US or Russia would last longest in the race to spend ever-increasing amounts of money on armaments without wrecking their own economies and provoking domestic unrest. The short and obvious answer to the question of who won seemed to be supplied by the revolutions of 1989 as the Russian bloc broke first. And in the obvious sense this is true. Russia and its allies were always smaller economies than the US and its allies and they broke apart first. But there is also a less obvious sense in which the US was a loser in the Cold War as well. The arms expenditures during the Cold War had sustained the post-Second World War economic boom which lasted from the late 1940s until the early 1970s, the longest sustained period of growth in the history of the Capitalist system. But the nations paying for the boom were not the only, or even the main, beneficiaries of the boom. The US and Russia might have been the largest economies, but they were not the fastest-growing economies. Arms expenditure limited their growth, while the money expended on it provided a growing market for their competitors. Germany and Japan grew faster, precisely because, as defeated nations, their arms expenditure was limited. But so did other economies not involved in the arms race in Europe, the Far East and South America. So it was that the US ended the Cold War militarily dominant but economically threatened in a way it had not been for most of the twentieth century. This has been made crushingly obvious by the rise of China, whose ownership of US debt in the world recession that began in 2008 is what stands between the US and bankruptcy.

It is this condition of US Imperialism – powerful militarily, but weakening economically – which has set the pattern for post-Cold War Imperial politics. The mismatch of US economic and military power predisposes the US to use force to overcome its economic weakness. It has attempted to win contracts with guns, or the threat of their use, rather than by economically competitive production. Nevertheless, the wars in Afghanistan, Iraq and Libya have proved the extremely limited efficacy of such a policy and created conditions in which rivals, from Iran to China, have prospered.

The second section of this book examines the process of Imperial competition from the point of view of the victims of Empire. It demonstrates that these people, so seemingly powerless compared to the forces ranged against them, have had a profound effect on the history of the twentieth century. They have disrupted the operations of Imperial powers and pointed out the limits of Colonial thought. From the start of the twentieth century up until the Second World War the metropolitan centres ruled their colonies directly, although always with the aid of local elites. The Cold War period was also a period of wholesale decolonization. One after another of the major powers were forced to grant independent Statehood to their former 'dependencies', as they were sometimes and revealingly called. The politics of independent, nationalist governments were varied, but whatever their ideologies – Nationalist, Socialist, religious, Capitalist – none have escaped the wider mechanisms of economic and politico-strategic dominance exercised by the major powers. Renewed revolutions have repeatedly challenged those ruling elites who have been too accommodating to the demands of the globalized market and the wishes of the Imperial powers. The latest and greatest of these revolts, the Arab Revolutions of 2011, have dramatized the fact that if revolution in the former Colonial World is to advance beyond replacing a dictatorial and exploitative elite bound to the Imperial powers with a 'democratic' and exploitative elite bound to the Imperial powers, it must deal with both the nature of the Capitalist system as well as the Imperialist system which grows out of it.

The final section of the book examines precisely this relationship between the rulers and the ruled in both its economic and political dimensions in some of the central conflicts of the twentieth century. Of course, these conflicts are rarely about pure and simple economic exploitation. In fact, the exploited and oppressed in the Capitalist system almost never experience the system as economic exploitation pure and simply. The mechanisms of class rule frequently involve a denial of democratic rights or discrimination on grounds of nation, race, gender or sexuality. So, when people resist they very frequently do so in the name of democratic rights, or justice, or equality as well as for economic reasons. This was certainly the case in the fight for civil rights in the US, in the struggle against Apartheid in South Africa and, for that matter, in the campaign against the injustice of the poll tax in Thatcher's Britain. It is also true for the Arab Revolutions of 2011. The task of the Left is to explain why these issues are rooted in the need of the Capitalist class to ensure continued economic exploitation and to relate these struggles to one another. The Left has often failed to raise itself to the level required to deal with this complexity because it treats struggles for democracy or equal rights as mere epiphenomena of a deeper, more central struggle. But however justified this might be at the level of social and economic analysis, it is not how struggles present themselves in the consciousness of those doing the fighting, or at least not at first. Where the Left has risen to this task, Socialist Revolution — the ultimate challenge to the Capitalist system — has become a live project. It became such in Russia in 1917, Germany in 1918, Hungary in 1919 and Spain in 1936. Likewise, although Socialist forces were weaker, a definite anti-system revolutionary potential also existed in Poland in 1980 and in South Africa in the early 1990s. In other places revolutionary minorities, while not able to realistically claim that they had a chance at taking power, were nevertheless important in shaping the critical struggles of their day, as was the case in the US Civil Rights Movement of the 1960s, for instance. But in only one of these cases was the Left actually successful in overthrowing the entire system — Russia in 1917. And so it is incumbent on the Left to address the questions that have arisen in the course of the tumultuous last 100 years in a more serious way and to develop a strategy which really does find an echo among the broad mass of people, enabling them to transform both the forms of oppression and the underlying exploitation which are characteristic of Capitalism as it enters the twenty-first century. This book will, I hope, contribute towards that project.

1
THE RISE AND FALL OF GREAT POWERS

The First World War

The First World War has scorched itself into our memory as perhaps the most futile war in history. The killing, the blood, the mud, the trenches, the shells and the poison gas lasted from 1914 until 1918. It was the world's first experience of total war and the world's first experience of industrial war. Yet, when the War began tens of thousands in every country rushed to join the armed forces. Famously, the propaganda said the War would be 'over by Christmas', but of course it was not and 15 million people never saw their homes again.

On 28 June 1914, the heir to the Austro-Hungarian Empire, Archduke Franz Ferdinand, and his wife, Sophie, were shot dead in the Bosnian capital of Sarajevo by a Nationalist Serbian student. It was literally the final trigger, but not the cause, of the First World War. The European Powers, most of them still monarchies, were glued together in two competing alliances; Britain, France and Russia formed one bloc, whilst Germany and the Austro-Hungarian Empire formed another bloc that dominated the heart of Europe. Each bloc had colonies around the globe and each was tied by diplomatic obligations to the smaller countries of Europe. So, when a month after the assassination of their Emperor, Austria declared war on Serbia, Russia began a countermobilization. Germany then declared war on Russia and France. Then, on 6 August 1914, Britain declared war on Germany. On the Western Front, the Germans advanced within a few miles of Paris, but were driven back by an Allied counterattack at Marne. The opposing sides then settled into trench warfare at the River Aisne. Meanwhile, on the Eastern Front the Russian advance was checked by the Germans at the Battle of Tannenberg in East Prussia.

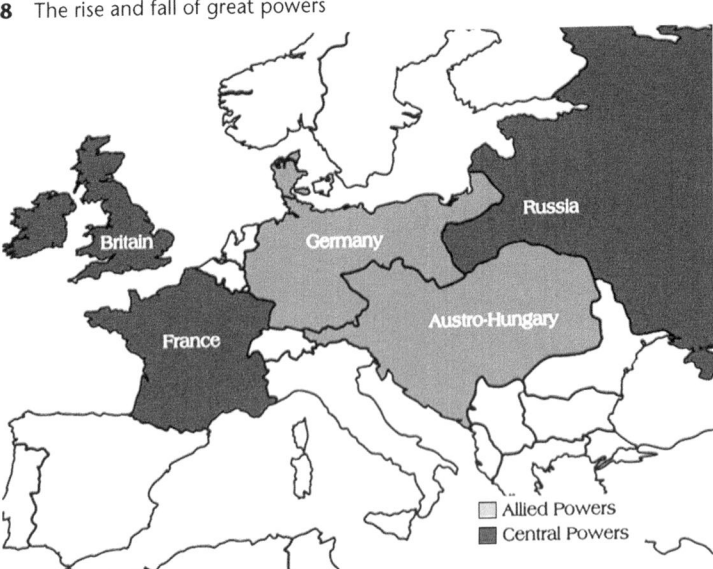

FIGURE 1.1 The rival alliances in the First World War

By 16 September 1916, all Germany's African Colonies had surrendered to Allied Forces. On 30 August 1916, Turkey entered the War on the German side and attacked Russia in the Caucasus Mountains. The territory of the countries now at war stretched from the Atlantic Ocean in the West to the Pacific in the East and from the Mediterranean in the South to the Baltic in the North. Furthermore, the European Colonial system meant that peoples with no direct interest in the struggle of the European powers were also drawn into the conflict.

The military leaders who went to war in 1914 were utterly unprepared for what the conflict would bring. The monarchs of Europe were bound together by ties of class and blood. Interested newspaper readers could see pictures of Britain's King Edward VII with Germany's Kaiser Wilhelm II, his nephew, just eight years before they went to war with each other. Like the monarchs of Europe, the Officer Corps of the rival empires had more in common with each other than they did with the ordinary soldiers under their command, but the rival industrial empires pitted them against each other in war just as rivalry for markets had

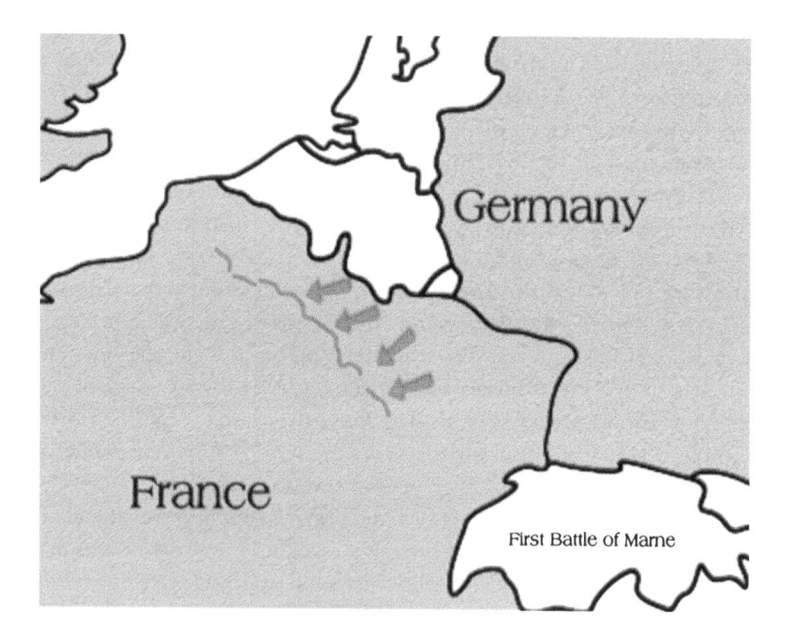

FIGURE 1.2 The War on the Western Front

pitted them against each other economically before the War. At first, workers enlisted in huge numbers as new popular newspapers transmitted a nationalist fervour from the political elite to ordinary citizens. However, the armies they joined still looked like they had done in the nineteenth century. The cavalry still wore breastplates and the uniforms were a gloriously outdated array of finery. The War turned into a very different struggle than the one the officers had imagined in their gentleman's clubs and military academies. The growth of industry had transformed war and mass artillery barrages, barbed wire, chemical gas, machine guns and, later, tanks dominated the battlefield. Massive battleships hunted by submarines transformed naval warfare, whilst Zeppelins rained bombs on civilians from the air. Perhaps the last stand of so-called 'noble' individual combat was taking place with the newest of weapons: the fighter plane with the 'aces' of the air counting their successes in terms of the number of individual kills.

Germany needed a quick victory in France to avoid fighting on both the Western Front and on the Eastern Front (against Russia). The plan for a swift advance through Belgium brought the Germans to within 50 miles of Paris, but it was halted in the Battle of Marne. Then a very different war began. In the second year of the War, the Western Front saw offensive after offensive. They all failed. Poison gas and chlorine were used for the first time during the battle for Ypres in Belgium during April and May 1915. On the Eastern Front, the Russians were driven back and Germany took Poland. In the Middle East, Britain attacked the Turkish in Mesopotamia, modern-day Iraq. They failed. And they failed again in the disastrous Gallipoli Campaign of Spring 1915. Italy entered the War against Austria, mainly because her politicians thought that this way she would end up on the winning side, but Bulgaria joined the Austrian and German side. 1916 saw some of the bloodiest battles of the War on the Western Front at Verdun and the Somme. Tanks were used for the first time. On 31 May, the Battle of Jutland, one of the greatest sea battles of the War, began.

In February 1917, however, a light began to glimmer in the East. The Tsar of Russia was overthrown in a revolution, but the Provisional Government of pro-Capitalist politicians, soon to be supported by moderate Socialists, vowed to keep Russia in the War. In April 1917 the US entered the War. The bloodiest battles of the War took place that year at Ypres and Passchendaele. They lasted from July to November. By October, it was all over for the Russian Army as the Bolsheviks swept to power and began the process of taking their War-weary nation out of the War. It was the event that, finally, meant that the carnage was nearing its end. On 3 March the Bolsheviks kept their promise to take Russia out of the War as Leon Trotsky signed the Treaty of Brest-Litovsk with Germany. On the Western Front, Germany began a final offensive, which was to see it reach the Marne by June. The Allied Forces countered at the battle of Amiens. Meanwhile, in Italy, at Vittorrio Vento, British and Italian Forces defeated the Austrians.

Then, suddenly, revolution spread from Russia to Germany. Naval mutinies in Kiel and other cities led to the abdication of Kaiser Wilhelm II and on 11 November 1918 the armistice was signed. The War started with workers rushing to the national flag, but it ended with the red flag flying in Russia and the Republican flag flying in Berlin. By the end of the War, age-old dynasties had vanished. Not only were the Romanovs gone from St. Petersburg and the Hohenzollerns from Berlin, but the Hapsburgs were gone from Vienna.

Timeline: the First World War

1914 (June): the Assassination of Archduke Ferdinand
1914 (July): Austria declares war on Serbia
1914 (August): Germany, France, Russia, Britain, Japan enter the war
1914 (August): Battle of Tannenberg
1914 (October): Turkey enters the War
1915 (April): poison gas used for the first time in Second battle of Ypres
1915 (April–August): Gallipoli campaign
1916 (February–November): Battle of Verdun
1916 (July–November): Battle of the Somme
1917 (April): US declares war on Germany
1917 (October): Russian Revolution
1917 (December): Bolshevik government takes Russia out of the War
1918 (November): German Kaiser overthrown
1918 (November): Armistice brings the War to an end

The revolutions that made Russia

The Russian Revolution of 1917 was one of the turning points of the twentieth century. Even after the 'fall of Communism' in 1989, the power of the Russian State still depended on the foundations laid by dictator Joseph Stalin in the 1930s and 1940s. But how did Stalin come to power? How could the freedom and hope that millions of Russians felt when the Tsar was overthrown in 1917 turn into the oppression and exploitation that was Stalin's Russia?

Russia was a ramshackle empire when it entered the First World War. The Tsar and the Russian aristocracy ruled over millions of peasants who tilled the land as they had done for centuries. But they were also faced with a small but growing working class concentrated in some of the largest factories in the world. And these workers were increasingly restive. There had been an attempt at revolution in 1905, but the Tsar had regained control. Nevertheless, the Revolutionary Movement began to regain its strength as the First World War approached. Famine, poverty and deprivation were a way of life for millions and the War only intensified their suffering. In its first battle of the War, Russia lost 30,000 killed or wounded, whilst another 90,000 were taken prisoner. After just five months of the War, 390,000 Russians had lost their lives. A year later, even the Ohkrana, the Tsar's secret police, were warning of 'the possibility in the near future of riots by the lower classes of the Empire enraged by the burdens of daily existence'.

The Russian Army was in retreat from 1915, short of arms and equipment. At home, food shortages and inflation led to lengthening queues and a strike wave in the factories. On the 23 February 1917, spontaneous food riots started the Revolution in Petrograd. Crowds chanting 'give us bread' were joined by striking women textile workers. The women struck partly to commemorate International Women's Day, but mainly to protest about the lack of bread. The Tsar told the Commander of the Petrograd Military District, 'I command you tomorrow to stop the disorders in the capital, which are unacceptable in the difficult time of war with Germany and Austria'. Some soldiers obeyed the orders to suppress the demonstrations, but many mutinied and joined the Revolution. The Government resigned and eventually the Tsar had to concede that his entire apparatus of political and military power had been overwhelmed by the Revolution.

On the 13 March, the Tsar abdicated, ending the 300 year rule of the Romanov Dynasty. Two bodies filled the power vacuum created by the abdication of the Tsar. One was the Provisional Government. Headed by Prince Lvov, it was at first dominated by the pro-Capitalist Cadet Party. It had the support of moderate Socialists who thought that the end of Tsarism would also be the end of the Revolution. The other body to fill the vacuum was the Petrograd Workers' Council, or, to use the Russian word for council, 'Soviet'. This institution had emerged in February as a delegate body of factory workers meeting to coordinate the strikes and protests against the Tsar, but as more and more factories, districts, army units and peasant villages began sending delegates to the Soviet it began to emerge as the most important focus of revolutionary activity. Subsequently, the Soviet model began to spread into the army and throughout Russia in both towns and the countryside.

These two institutions were bound to clash because they represented two fundamentally opposed constituencies with very different hopes for what the Revolution should deliver. The first crisis came in April. The Cadet leader Miliukov was determined to keep Russia in the War and made a speech saying that 'Russia would fight to the last drop of her blood'. As Miliukov spoke, Russian soldiers were, according to one British general, 'being churned into gruel until casualties in the firing line should make rifles available'. Meetings, riots, protests and street fights between pro- and anti-war crowds drove Miliukov from office. It was the end of the Cadet-led Government. In order to bolster its support among the increasingly militant population, the Cadet Government co-opted members from the moderate Socialist Party, the Mensheviks, and the pro-peasant party, the Social Revolutionaries. The moderate Socialist Alexander Kerensky became leader of the Provisional Government. But although there were new faces in the Government, there were no new policies. In the face of starvation and social breakdown peasants were seizing the land and workers were taking control of the factories. The Provisional Government opposed them all. Worse still, Kerensky continued Miliukov's pro-war policy, declaring that 'the inevitability and necessity of sacrifice must rule the hearts of Russian soldiers...I summon you not to a feast but to death'. But as one war-weary peasant soldier replied, 'what's the point of the peasants getting the land if I'm killed and get no land?' It was an argument of elemental power and it spurred tens of thousands of deserting soldiers to take the long trek back to their towns and villages in mid-1917. They simply walked away from the front.

By this point the Soviets were growing in power as an alternative source of governmental authority. This process of radicalization was accelerated when the leaders of the Revolutionary Left, many of whom had spent many years in prison and in exile under the Tsar, made perilous journeys across war-torn Europe to return to Russia. Leon Trotsky, one of the leaders of the 1905 Revolution, made it back from the US after being detained by Britain. Vladimir Lenin, leader of the Bolsheviks (the most radical Socialist Party), returned from exile in Switzerland in a train provided by the German Government, who hoped that he would help withdraw Russia from the War. As he stepped down from the train at Petrograd's Finland Station, Lenin surprised even his own supporters by insisting that the Left should not support the Provisional Government because it was a pro-Capitalist Government committed to continuing the War. However, Lenin's policy of 'Land, Bread and Peace' chimed exactly with what large numbers of workers, peasants and soldiers were beginning to think, and Lenin's demands were coupled with another slogan which explained exactly how to get these things: 'All power to the Soviets'. The struggle for power between the Provisional Government under Kerensky and the Soviet now began in earnest.

In July 1917, the anger at the Provisional Government was so great that it almost boiled over into a second revolution. Kerensky used Czech mercenaries to try and drive Russian soldiers to the front, but this simply fuelled popular anger. Huge armed demonstrations flooded through the streets of Petrograd. They burst into the session of the Petrograd Soviet, still under the leadership of the moderate Socialists. One worker, white with anger, leapt onto the podium and, shaking his fist in the face of the Chairman, yelled at him, 'take power... when it's given to you!' Nevertheless, the demonstrators were not quite ready for a revolution yet. The July Days were, Lenin said, 'more than a demonstration and less than a Revolution'. But as the demonstrations subsided the Government moved back onto the offensive against the Left. Kerensky created a special squad to hunt down Lenin, with orders to shoot him on sight. Lenin went into hiding disguised as a worker. Trotsky and other Bolsheviks were imprisoned; other less-fortunate Bolsheviks were murdered. The Party's offices and printing presses were also smashed.

Kerensky and the Provisional Government organized the anti-Bolshevik clampdown, but they were not its main beneficiaries. To the Right of the Provisional Government stood the big Capitalists of Russia — the old aristocracy and the officer corps of the Imperial Army. The abdication of the Tsar had been a blow to them, but they were still powerful and they dreamt of destroying the Left and imposing a military dictatorship. They were willing to use Kerensky and the Provisional Government, but only to deal with the Soviet. The leading figure of the reactionary Right was General Kornilov and from the moment he arrived in Moscow for a State Conference in August 1917, born aloft from his train by his officers, it was clear that a military coup was being prepared. Kornilov declared that he would 'not hesitate to hang all the Soviet members if need be'. Furthermore, he was utterly cynical about Kerensky, saying that after he had dealt with the Soviet, 'Kerensky and Co. will make way for me'. At first, Kerensky thought he could use Kornilov to crush the Soviet, but he soon realized that Kornilov meant to crush him too. Only then did he turn to the Soviet for help.

Not surprisingly, the Soviet delegates were losing faith in Kerensky and the moderate Socialists. Moreover, they did not trust the moderate Socialists to organize the defence of the Soviet against Kornilov's attempted coup. The Bolsheviks, their leaders still in prison, successfully organized themselves to defeat Kornilov. It was a shattering blow for the Right, but it was also a mortal blow for the moderate Socialists.

Kornilov was defeated at the end of August and on the 9 September 1917 the Bolsheviks won a majority in the Petrograd Soviet with Trotsky appointed its President. From that moment on, the Right and Centre were discredited and the Provisional Government was a fiction. Power was effectively already in the hands of the Soviet. The Revolution of the following month was about making that fact irreversible.

On the night of the 25 October 1917, the storming of the Winter Palace in Petrograd put an end to the Provisional Government and made the Soviet of Workers, Peasants and Soldiers' Deputies the new rulers of Russia. The Soviet kept it promises and it gave the land to the peasants. It gave control of the factories to the workers. Most importantly, it took Russia out of the First World War; it was a spectacular moment of liberation. On top of this, the first ever women Government Ministers anywhere in the world took their offices, whilst the oppressed nationalities of the old Russian Empire were offered, and took, their independence. Jews, who had been subject to Government-sponsored pogroms for generations, also experienced a new freedom from fear — after all, Trotsky, himself a Jew, was President of the Soviet. Officers were elected in the army and factories and farms came under the control of those who worked in them.

Nevertheless, the new Socialist Republic was an infant that was threatened from every side. The pro-Tsarist officers who had supported Kornilov began to form White Armies that threatened Petrograd and Moscow. They were joined by the armies of the major powers who invaded Russia in order to try and help the whites overthrow the Soviet Government. Britain, France, Japan, the US, Germany and Italy all sent troops to Russia. In fact, a total of 14 different foreign powers sent armed forces to assist in the crushing of the Russian Revolution. The white and foreign armies reduced the territory controlled by the Soviet Government to a small fraction of Russian land. In response, Leon Trotsky was made Commissar for War. He described the front in August 1918 as 'a noose that seemed to be closing tighter around Moscow...the soil itself seemed to be infected with panic...everything was crumbling. There was nothing left to hang onto. The situation seemed hopeless'. The economic situation was just as bad as the military situation as the First World War had wrecked the Russian economy. For instance, in 1918 Russia was producing just 12 percent of the steel that it had produced before the War. It was the same figure for iron, whilst sugar was down to under a quarter of its pre-war production level and coal was just 42 percent of the pre-war figure. Russia was a starving, broken country surrounded by enemies.

The Soviets had to rely on every last drop of enthusiasm from the workers and peasants to sustain themselves. Trotsky created a Red Army out of the ruins of the Tsar's Imperial Army. Propaganda trains toured the front to raise moral and cavalry rode with the first rank of riders wearing letter boards on their backs so that their fellow soldiers could learn their alphabet as they rode. Whole communities of Jews advanced and retreated behind Red Army lines so that they could avoid the pogroms carried out by the Whites. The White Armies were composed of old supporters of Tsarism, Capitalists and enemies of the Soviets; everywhere they ruled was a military dictatorship. But the severity and brutality of the Civil War also took its toll on the Red Army. Forced grain requisitioning became necessary to feed the towns, conscription was enforced to supply new soldiers and the Tsar was executed to prevent him becoming a rallying point for counter-revolution. Worst of all, in the long run, the towns were gutted of workers. Factories closed and in Petrograd grass began to grow through the deserted cobblestones.

By 1921, the White Army had defeated the counter-revolution and the last foreign armies were in retreat. But the cost of victory was high. The very workers who had made the Revolution – those who had been the delegates to the Soviets – had been wiped out as an effective political force during the Civil War. The Bolshevik Party and the Soviet apparatus were now suspended in mid air; the class that had given them life had disappeared. Inevitably, the State became bureaucratized. It became more and more divorced from the needs of society and increasingly driven by its own interests. Subsequently, there was a battle to stop the bureaucratization of the Revolution. Lenin fought against it until he died in early 1924 and Leon Trotsky formed a Left Opposition to try and stop the new bureaucracy from usurping power. By contrast, Joseph Stalin, a relatively minor figure in the Bolshevik leadership during the Revolution, embraced these changes and became the dominant figure in this rising bureaucracy.

By 1928, Stalin had defeated Trotsky and driven him into exile. Lenin and Trotsky's hopes for the success of the Russian Revolution had been based on their belief that it would spread to other countries in the wake of the First World War. These more advanced countries could then assist poor and economically backward Russia in their efforts to build a society which could meet the needs and desires of the

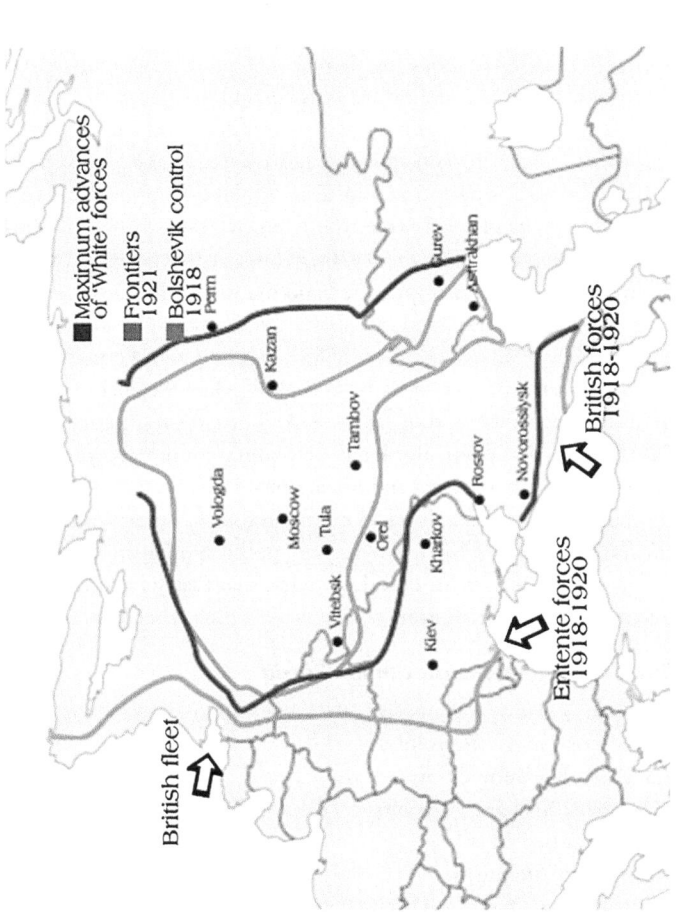

FIGURE 1.3 Imperial powers surround the Russian Revolution

workers and peasants. And, after the First World War, there was indeed an international wave of revolution; Germany overthrew the Kaiser in 1918, there was a revolution in Hungary in 1919, Italy went through the 'two red years' of 1919 and 1920 when strikes and factory occupations swept the country, there was a general strike in Britain in 1926 and in 1927 there was a revolution in China.

But Stalin abandoned hope in there being an international revolution. Instead, he began rebuilding Russian industry and agriculture by the most savage means. Workers were exploited with military brutality, farms were forcibly collectivized and the land taken back from the peasants. Political opposition was also ruthlessly suppressed. Most of the old Bolsheviks of 1917 were murdered by Stalin, some of them after grotesque show trials in the 1930s, whilst in the gulag of forced labour camps millions were imprisoned and many lost their lives. It was a counter-revolution that wiped out all the freedoms gained in 1917.

Finally, in 1940 an assassin sent by Stalin caught up with Leon Trotsky in Mexico, his new country of exile, and plunged an ice-pick into the back of his head as he sat working at his desk. The last great figure of the 1917 Revolution had been murdered by Stalin's counter-Revolution. Stalin had made Russia a great industrial power, but he had done it in the way that old rulers had always done these things, by exploiting the workers and peasants and by destroying any political opposition. Russia was a great power, but Stalin had done what the Tsarists had failed to do; he had killed the Revolution.

Timeline: the revolutions that made Russia

1917 (February): Tsar overthrown
1917 (July): crisis in the Revolution
1917 (August): Kornilov Coup
1917 (October): Socialist Revolution
1918: Civil War begins
1928: triumph of Stalinism
1930s: purges, show trials and industrialization
1940: assassination of Trotsky

The consequences of the First World War

The years between the First and Second World Wars were ones of crisis and instability. Economically, the world had barely recovered from

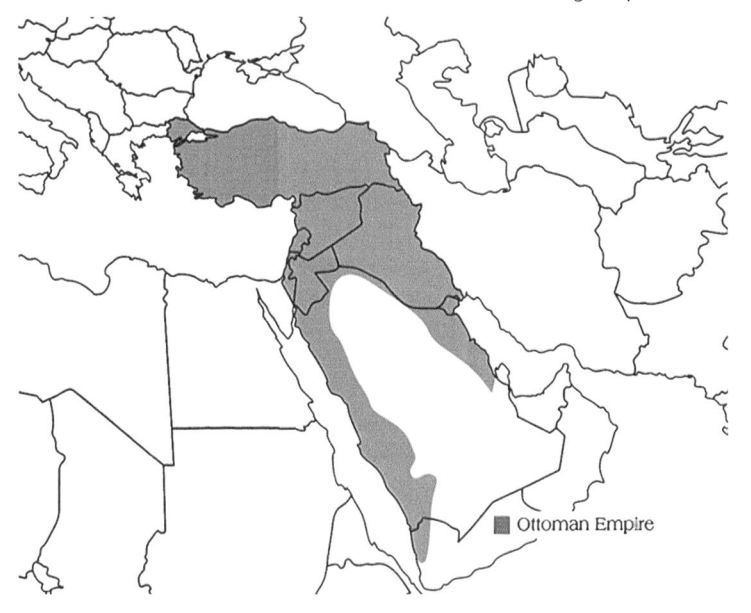

FIGURE 1.4 The Ottoman Empire (with some modern borders indicated)

the War before new recessions, deeper than ever, plunged millions into misery and despair. And from that misery grew the monstrous regimes of Mussolini's Fascists and Hitler's Nazis. Even before the shadow of the Second World War fell across the globe, local wars in China, Abyssinia and Spain disfigured the peace. It was the peoples of Europe who had finally put an end to the killing in the trenches of the First World War. In October 1917, the long-suffering peasants and workers of Russia were released from the murderous torment of the War when the Bolsheviks unilaterally declared peace. The following year, the German people overthrew the Kaiser and the War came shuddering to a halt. Two other empires had collapsed under the impact of the War. The Austro-Hungarian Empire, which had dominated Central Europe before the War disappeared, giving birth to a host of new and independent nations in the heart of Europe. The other was the Ottoman Empire which was overthrown by the Nationalist Young Turk Movement in 1908. Its disappearance left a power vacuum in the Middle East into which the European powers rushed to carve out their own spheres of influence.

One of the bitterest fruits of the First World War was harvested in the Middle East. In 1917, Arthur Balfour, the British Foreign Secretary, had declared Britain to be in favour of a national homeland for the Jewish people in Palestine. After the War, Palestine fell under the British Mandate and the declaration began to be made fact. We are still living with the consequences of the dispossession of the Palestinian people. The overarching peace treaty of the First World War was negotiated in Paris in 1919, though it has taken the name of the palace in which it was eventually signed: Versailles. Some 1037 delegates from 32 countries, supported by massed ranks of advisors and stenographers, gathered to negotiate the treaty. The sessions were secret, the very words of the delegates muffled by the Catherine de Medici Tapestries that hung on the walls of the conference hall. Woodrow Wilson, the US President, was the most powerful figure at the conference. He headed a nation whose economy had not been devastated by war. On the contrary, it had grown considerably. And although the US had not entered the War until very late, its contribution had been decisive.

Woodrow Wilson, a pious and convinced pacifist, used his authority to push through the creation of the League of Nations, an international body that was supposed to guarantee peace by threatening force against those that broke its injunctions. But the League was flawed from the start. Wilson himself could not get Congress to ratify US participation, whilst Russia also refused to participate. Italy, under Mussolini, soon also lost interest in the League. Of the major powers, that left Britain, France and Germany who was marginalized as she was supposedly the 'sole guilty party' in the First World War. Indeed, this phrase was written into the final treaty. France, meanwhile, was intent on exacting reparations from Germany on such a scale that she would remain a broken nation for years more, if not decades. Britain went along with France. As a result, Germany ceded territory to France, Belgium, Denmark and Poland, leaving eight million Germans under foreign rule. Germany also lost all her colonies to her enemies and her army and navy were reduced to nominal forces. On top of this, she was required to repay the cost of the War to the victors, produce coal for France, Italy and Belgium, build ships for the victors, pay for the cost of her own occupation and, on top of this, pay £1,000 million in reparations by 1921. No wonder that Lenin, the leader of revolutionary Russia, justified his country's absence from the League by describing it as a 'den of thieves'.

The breakup of the old empires had created a series of new, independent nations. Even a victor like Britain had had to let go of most of Ireland, resulting in the Irish Free State coming into being. But the Irish Free State was far from the only new nation to emerge. Modern Turkey also emerged from the rubble of the Ottoman Empire, headed by Kemal Ataturk. Austria and Hungary were independent countries created by the fall of the Hapsburg Empire. Czechoslovakia was born of the same implosion. Finland became independent and so did Latvia, Lithuania and Estonia, all free as a result of the anti-Imperial policies of the Russian Government. Poland also became an independent State for the first time since 1772. In other words, then, the Peace Treaty that was eventually signed, perhaps appropriately, in the Hall of Mirrors at the Palace of Versailles needed a miracle to survive.

The post-First World War peace received a further blow when Mussolini's Fascists took power in Italy in 1922. The workers' movement had been on the advance in Italy and strikes and factory occupations had swept the country. Inspired by the Russian Revolution, the Italian Communist Party had gained a mass membership. Italy's rulers were terrified and they cooperated with Mussolini's Fascist bands of de-mobbed soldiers to break up the Labour and Socialist Movement. The Fascist 'March on Rome' in 1922 was the establishment-aided coup that ended democracy in Italy for more than a generation. Mussolini stayed safe in Milan until the coup was over; his 'March' was made entirely in the sleeping car of the train that bore him south. Mussolini's regime was as aggressive abroad as it was repressive at home and soon the Imperial ambition of fascism would test the League of Nations to its limits.

The story of the inter-war years might have been different if the world economy had recovered from the devastation of the First World War. For some, economic prosperity did return, but the so-called 'Roaring Twenties' – the 'Jazz Age' or 'Dance Age' with its new cocktails, new dances and new movie industry – was an age in which the rich got richer and the poor got left behind. Inflation ripped through some economies, and in Germany the Government printed money to meet the debts extracted from them by the victors of the First World War. As a result, in 1914 $1 was worth 4.2 German Marks; in 1920 it was worth 40 Marks; and in 1923 $1 was worth 4,200 million Marks. Inflation like this meant economic ruin for whole swathes of German society, including its middle classes. Internationally, inflation also made nonsense of the reparations being exacted from Germany. But there was no pause for thought, France was determined to exact the full cost of the War. In 1923, French and Allied troops occupied the industrial heartland of Germany, the Ruhr. The British left Germany three years later but the French remained until the 1930s.

Even in the so-called 'boom years' before the Wall Street Crash, unemployment was high and in the mid-1920s unemployment averaged between 10 and 12 percent in Britain, Germany and Sweden, whilst in Norway and Denmark the average was 17 to 18 percent. Hunger marches took place in Britain in 1922 and in 1929 the marchers converged on London from all over the country. The most famous of the marches set out bound for London in 1932, only to be broken up by the police when it arrived. In 1926, in the middle of the 'Roaring Twenties', Britain's workers staged the General Strike. The immediate causes are not hard to identify; mines were in private hands and the owners, backed by the Conservative Government, demanded wage-cuts of between 10 and 25 percent plus a longer working day in order to increase their profits. The Miners' Union fought under the banner of 'not penny off the pay, not a minute on the day'. The Trades Union Congress (TUC) declared that the whole Trade Union Movement would stand behind the miners. The workers' response to the

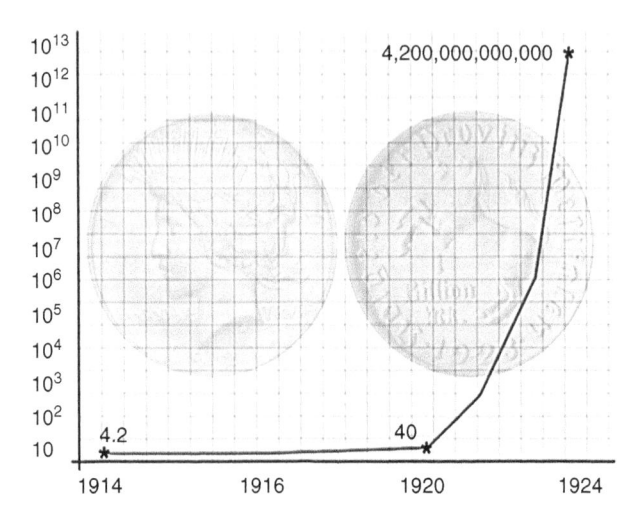

FIGURE 1.5 German marks vs. US dollar

strike call on the 3 May was immediate and overwhelming and some 1.75 million struck with an enthusiasm that took both the Government and the TUC by surprise. The strike grew in strength and there were more on strike on the last of its nine days than there were on the first day. But the TUC were terrified by the power of their own members, and when the courts lifted Union immunity for damages on solidarity strikes, the Union leaders collapsed without even getting a promise of no victimizations from the Government. It was a dark day that left working people in Britain disarmed in the face of the coming storm of the recession. That storm broke in 1929, the year of the Wall Street Crash.

The world economy collapsed in the wake of the Wall Street Crash. As financial speculation turned to full-scale economy-wide slump, unemployment figures reached new and terrifying heights. Nearly a quarter of Britons were on the dole in the pit of the slump. It was higher in the US and higher still at 31 percent in Norway and 32 percent in Denmark. Germany, already a victim of hyperinflation, now saw unemployment rates of 44 percent. Even the so-called 'economic recovery' after 1933 saw rates of unemployment of 16 to 17 percent in Britain and 20 percent in the US and Austria. The political effects were obvious and hideous. Hitler came to power in 1933. His militarized tyranny was the

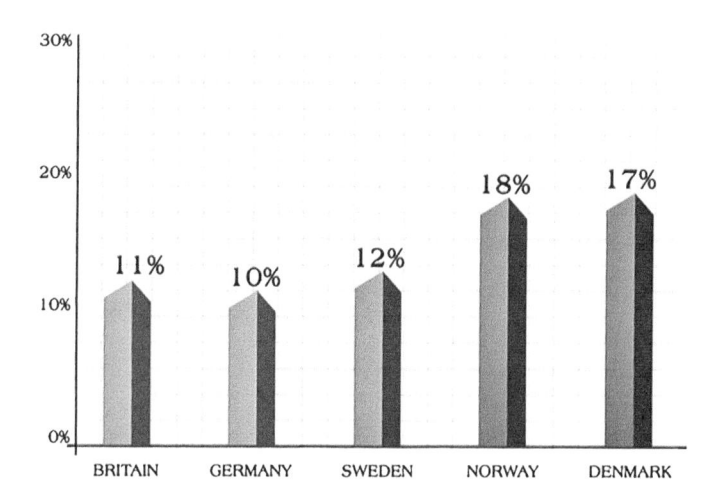

FIGURE 1.6 Unemployment in the mid-1920s

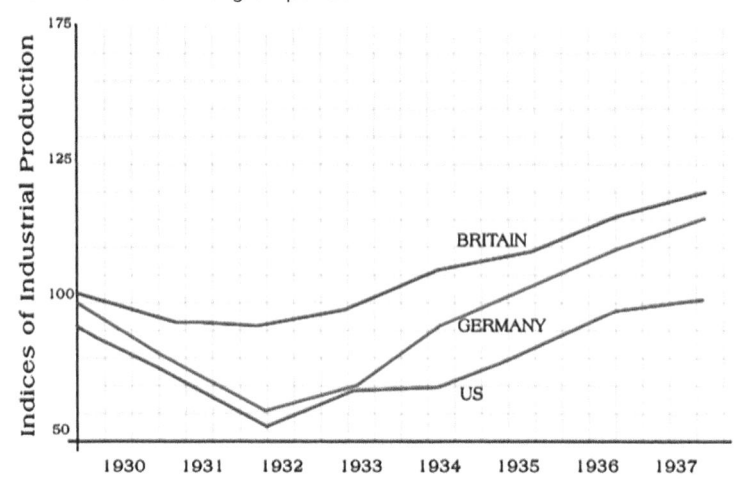

FIGURE 1.7 The Great Slump revisited
Source: League of Nations, world production and prices.

only regime in Europe that eliminated unemployment. Fascism was on the march and the prospect of a second global conflict was looming.

Vienna, capital of the new Austria, had been under a Social Democratic Government. They had built houses for workers and presided over a Welfare State well in advance of most countries. Yet, they were despised by the political Right who dominated the National Government and modelled themselves on Mussolini's Italy. In a four-day Civil War in 1934, the Chancellor of Austria, Engelbert Dollfuss, crushed 'red Vienna'. But Dollfuss had opened Pandora's Box. A few months later, Austrian Nazis broke into the Chancellery in Vienna and murdered him. Mussolini himself was now flexing his muscles on the international stage. In the year following the Civil War in Austria he invaded Abyssinia – modern Ethiopia – in a quest to build an African Empire. Haile Selassie, the Emperor of Abyssinia, appealed to the League of Nations to reverse the Italian invasion. He was jeered by Italian journalists as he made his speech at the League's Headquarters in Geneva. His appeal fell on deaf ears; the League was paralyzed by the major powers unwillingness to confront Mussolini and the Italian conquest of Abyssinia went on without effective opposition from the League. The failure to stop Mussolini meant that the League was finished as an effective barrier to Fascist territorial expansion. First Vienna, then Abyssinia; the world was on the road to war. But there was still one last chance to stop the Fascists: Spain.

Spain had only become a republic in 1931. Elections that year had given Republicans massive support and had triggered a potentially insurrectionary movement. As the country hovered on the brink of Civil War, King Alfonso abdicated. But Civil War was not avoided, merely postponed. In 1936, Monarchist Generals based in the Spanish Colony of Morocco invaded mainland Spain. Their leader was Francisco Franco. In the Civil War that followed Franco was supported by Mussolini and Hitler. The Italian air force and navy assisted Franco. In all, some 50,000 so-called volunteers came from Fascist Italy. Hitler sent 10,000 to fight in Spain, including the Luftwaffe's Condor Legion. Spain became the great dividing line in European politics, but the sides were not equal. Russia sent support to the Republican Government, but Britain and France stood by while the Fascists advanced on the Democratic Government of Spain. Ordinary people – Trade Unionists, Labour Party members, Socialists, Communists – tried to make good the studied absence of their governments. The International Brigades were volunteers who went to fight on the side of the Republicans. Altogether, some 40,000 from 54 countries formed Brigades named after democratic heroes: Lincoln, Garibaldi, Masaryk and so-forth. Among the volunteers were: Josip Broz Tito, better known as Yugoslavia's future leader Marshal Tito; Willy Brandt, who later became the German Chancellor; Klement Gottwald, who later became the Czechoslovakian President; Pietro Nenni, leader of the Italian Socialist Party; Hungarian writer Arthur Koestler; English writer George Orwell; and Jack Jones, future leader of the TGWU in Britain. Why did they go? Cecil Day Lewis, England's future Poet Laureate, tells us why:

> Tell them in England, if they ask
> What brought us to these wars,
> To this plateau beneath the night's
> Grave manifold of stars
> It was not fraud or foolishness,
> Glory, revenge or pay:
> We came because our open eyes
> Could see no other way.

But the International Brigades could not turn the tide. The War would ultimately be won or lost by Spanish forces, and here the Republican side had a fateful weakness. As George Orwell documented in his brilliant book, *Homage to Catalonia*, the Republican Government and its Stalinist supporters were too fearful of the revolutionary forces released by the Civil War to fully utilize the capacity of ordinary people to defeat Fascism. Eventually, in battle after battle, the Republican Government was smothered by Franco and his Fascist allies. The die was cast; as the Civil War in Spain drew to a close, Hitler began his triumphal march of conquest through Europe. In 1937, the Nazis annexed Austria; then Czechoslovakia; then Poland; then came the invasion of France. Only a world war could stop the Nazis now.

Timeline: the consequences of the First World War

1917: the Russian Revolution
1919: Versailles Conference
1921: Irish Free State established
1922: Mussolini takes power
1926: General Strike
1929: Wall Street Crash
1933: Hitler comes to power
1934: the fall of 'Red Vienna'
1935: Mussolini invades Abyssinia
1936: Spanish Civil War begins

The rise of Fascism

The instability in the State system which followed the First World War, the failure of the League of Nations, the fear among ruling classes of the spread of Communism and the economic instability of the 1920s and 1930s bore a terrible fruit: Fascism. European society emerged from the First World War in turmoil. There had never been death and injury on such an industrial scale before. Sir Edward Grey's mournful elegy to the old Europe, spoken as the First World War began – 'the lamps are going out all over Europe and we shall not see them lit again in our lifetime' – was coming true.

Revolution ended the Tsar's rule in Russia in 1917. Lenin's Bolsheviks came to power and effectively ended the First World War by withdrawing Russia from the conflict. The following year, the German Kaiser was overthrown and mass Socialist and Communist Parties became the most powerful popular political forces in Germany. In Italy the 'Biennio Rosso' ('the two red years'), which began as strikes and factory occupations, swept the country. In every European country labour militancy and Radical Left politics were giving voice to the discontent that had accumulated during the War. But there was a reaction from the Right, and at first it was most powerful in Italy.

Benito Mussolini, the future leader of Italian Fascism, began political life on the Left. But he was also an ardent Nationalist and he was insistent that Italy should not remain neutral during the First World War. Mussolini's nationalism and militarism, hallmarks of Fascism to this day, led to his expulsion from the Italian Socialist Party. He was an embittered Nationalist and a determined opponent of the labour unrest that looked set to create a revolution on the Russian model in Italy. Mussolini was not alone; the old ruling classes were down, but they were not out. Whilst the old aristocratic dynasties might have had to cede power to more parliamentarian forms of government, the industrialists and many of the middle classes were determined to defeat any further advances by the Radical Left. And, at the bottom of society, brutalized and demobilized soldiers and the growing mass of the unemployed were, like Mussolini, angry at the bitter fruits of war and the economic uncertainties of peace. Mussolini gathered these increasingly desperate men together in armed Fascist Squads, and the street thugs found support from the very top levels of society.

In 1920, the Minister of War offered four-fifths of their former army pay to ex-officers who joined the Fascists. In two years, more than 2,000 Fascist Squads were formed. They proceeded to attack Left-Wing communes and collectives using transport supplied by the landowners and paid for by the Capitalists. In 1921, street violence was transformed into electoral success when the Fascists won 35 parliamentary seats. But, again, they needed help from the political establishment as these electoral gains were made as part of an alliance with veteran Centrist politician and two-time Prime Minister Giovanni Giolitti. In what would become a familiar pattern for Fascist Movements, electoral success emboldened the Fascists in their street violence. In 1922 the Fascist Squads broke a general strike with incredible violence. It was a defeat that crushed the workers' movement and the Socialist Left for a generation. Mussolini immediately embarked upon his March on Rome. The March itself was more comic opera than a military operation, but with the workers' movement broken and the establishment desperate to ensure that it did not recover, Mussolini was enthroned at the head of an anti-Leftist Coalition.

Germany was the heart of Europe in the first half of the twentieth century. It was the largest country in Europe, it was (as it is again today) the crucial meeting point for Eastern and Western Europe, it was the critical western power facing Russia, it was Europe's greatest industrial power and it had the strongest Labour and Socialist Movement in the world. As a result, it took far stronger social convulsions to bring the Nazis to power in Germany than it did to bring Mussolini to power in Italy. And the German Nazis were, correspondingly, more brutal than their Italian allies.

Hitler was a former Non-Commissioned Officer in the German Army. He was ashamed of the defeat that Germany had suffered in 1918 and he detested the Trade Unions, the Socialists and Communists who had brought down the Kaiser. He had contempt for the parliamentary regime that had replaced the Monarchy. Before it became the badge of the Nazi Party, the Swastika was the symbol of the Freikorps, the bands of ex-soldiers, much like Mussolini's Fascist Squads, who fought the Left during the years of the German Revolution between 1918 and 1923. They were used by the parliamentary government to attack the Left and they were responsible for the murder of two of the most famous Socialists in Germany, Rosa Luxemburg and Karl Liebknecht. Inspired by Mussolini's March on Rome, Hitler first tried to mount a Nazi coup in Bavaria in 1923, but this infamous 'Beer-Hall Putsch' (so-called because the new regime was declared in a Munich beer-hall) failed. Hitler had the street gang, but he did not have the support of a section of the political establishment. Hitler rebuilt his forces; he rallied against the Socialists and Communists, and he developed a strand of nationalism and racism far more virulent than Mussolini's Fascism. In Hitler's creed, the Jews and the Marxists were closely connected. For instance, in 1924 he said:

> Should the Jew, with the aid of his Marxist creed, triumph over the people of this world, his Crown will be the funeral wreath of mankind, and this planet will once again follow its orbit through the ether, without any human life on its surface, as it did millions

of years ago . . . In standing guard against the Jew I am defending the handiwork of the Lord.

But Hitler was still unable to overpower the Left. Indeed, most of Germany's massive working class remained loyal to the Socialist and Communist Parties.

Three things finally gave the Nazis the conditions they needed to gain power. First, the economic situation deteriorated rapidly. Germany was hit hard by the 1929 stock market crash and the slump of the early 1930s. Unemployment rocketed from 1.4 million in 1928 to 5.5 million in 1932, the year that began the Nazis decisive push for power. Second, the Nazis got the backing they needed from the economic and political elites. In 1932 the Nazis actually suffered a reverse in the November elections – the Nazis won 196 seats, whilst the Socialists won 121 seats and the Communists won another 100 seats – but this lead for the combined Socialist and Communist vote over the Nazis only encouraged the aging President of Germany, Von Hindenburg, to offer Hitler the Chancellorship in January 1933.

In February 1933, some of Germany's wealthiest industrialists attended a meeting with Hitler and fellow Nazi leader Herman Goering where they were urged to contribute large sums to the Nazi's electoral

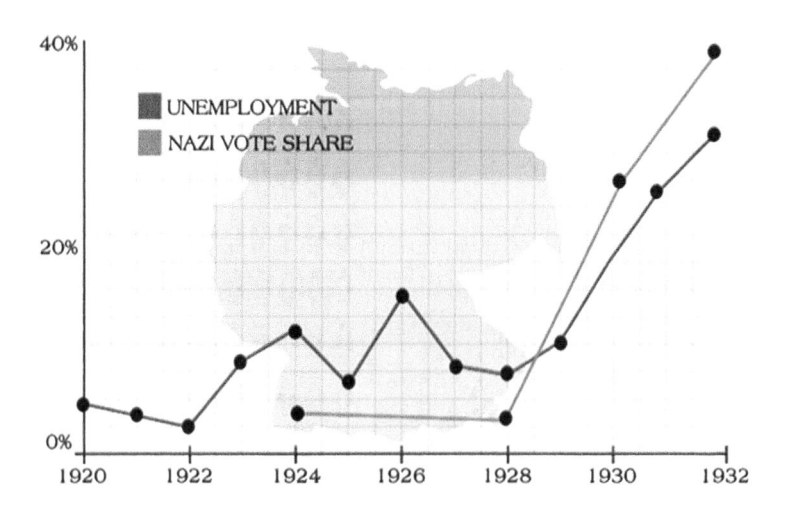

FIGURE 1.8 German unemployment and Nazi vote share

effort in the forthcoming March poll. Goering assured his audience that the financial sacrifices 'would be much easier for industry to bear if it realized that the election of 5 March will surely be the last one for the next ten years, probably even for the next hundred years'. As a sitting Chancellor and with the backing of big business, Hitler was set to take power. Before the election in March, the Reichstag, the German parliament, was burnt down. The arsonist had nothing to do with the Left, but Hitler's propaganda machine blamed the blaze on the Communists, creating an air of panic ahead of the vote. But even all this would not have been enough to bring Hitler to power had there not been a third factor at work. This was the disunity of the Left. Communists and Socialists combined were, until very late in the day, a more powerful force in German society than the Nazis. But for long periods they fought each other rather than combining to fight the Nazis. This division, this lack of unity, was their undoing.

When Hitler took power he established a brutal dictatorship within months. Trade Unions were suppressed, Communists, Socialists and all other parties but the Nazi Party were abolished, parliamentary government was destroyed and, as Goering had promised, there were no more elections. Churches were also subordinated to the State and the persecution of the Jews began its long and bloody path to the gas chambers of Belsen, Treblinka and the other concentration camps. Millions of Trade

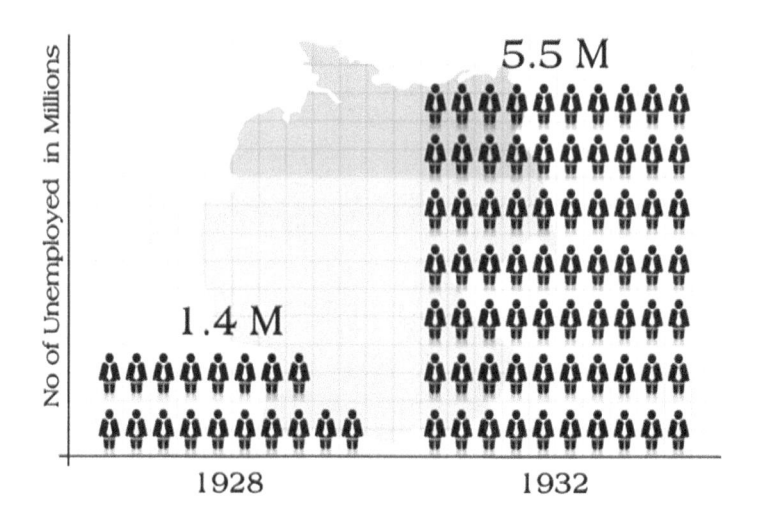

FIGURE 1.9 Unemployment during the period 1928 to 1932

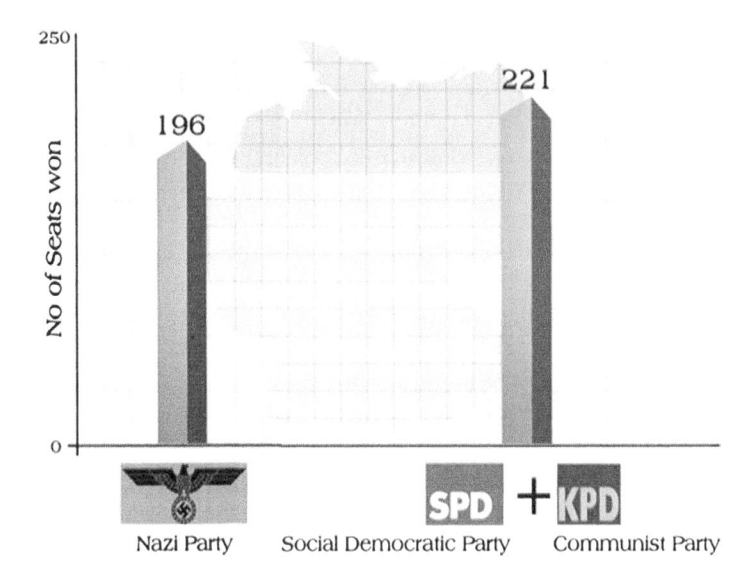

FIGURE 1.10 German election results, November 1932

Unionists, gypsies, Socialists, the disabled, Communists, Priests and Pastors were gassed, poisoned and burnt alongside them. The war the Nazis began just six years after taking power left millions dead, strewn across every corner of the globe.

Britain had its own Fascist Movement in the 1930s. It was launched in 1932, just as Hitler was making his final ascent to power. It was called the British Union of Fascists and Sir Oswald Mosley led it. Mosley was an establishment figure from an aristocratic background and he had been an MP for both the Tory and Labour Parties. His new Fascist Party attracted a lot of support from the lower middle classes – shopkeepers, farmers and small traders – and he also got some support from figures higher up the social scale. Lord Rothermere, the owner of the *Daily Mail* was one such supporter and in January 1934 he published an editorial headlined, 'Hurrah for the Blackshirts'.

But Mosley failed where Mussolini and Hitler succeeded. Why? Partly the economic crisis of the 1930s, while serious, was not as catastrophic in Britain as it was in Germany. But, crucially, the Left united against the Fascists in Britain, even though they sometimes had to ignore their leaders in order to do so. In 1934 the British Communist

Party, tiny compared with its German sister organization, led 5,000 demonstrators on a march to disrupt a Fascist rally at Olympia. The blackshirted Fascist stewards beat the anti-Fascist hecklers. The police refused to intervene, but the furore scared off some Fascist supporters like Lord Rothermere. Later that year, 100,000, anti-Fascists protested at a counter-demonstration when Mosley tried to hold a rally in Hyde Park. The official leaders of the labour movement had told protesters to stay away, but the demonstration was a great success, humiliating the mere 7,000 Fascists who had to beg the police for protection. Mosley tried to rebuild his support by dominating the streets of London's East End. Then, as now, the East End was a centre of immigration and in the 1930s Jews were the most numerous immigrants. With establishment support weak, the BUF increasingly relied on anti-Semitism as a recruiting tool. Mosley's blackshirts beat Jews in the streets, attacked their businesses and marched through the area chanting 'the Yids, the Yids, we've got to get rid of the Yids'. Neither the official leaders of the labour movement, nor the official leaders of the Jewish community, were prepared to support a militant mobilization against Mosley, but the Communist Party, the Independent Labour Party, sections of the Jewish ex-servicemen's organization and the Jewish youth were prepared to resist. In October 1936 a massive 100,000 mobilized at Cable Street in the East End to stop Mosley marching. The Fascists and the police tried to force their way down Cable Street. Barricades and fierce resistance ensured that they did not succeed; Mosley was defeated.

The Fascist organizations of post-1945 Britain are the direct ideological descendants of the European and British Nazis of the 1930s. In 1967 a former member of Mosley's British Union of Fascists, A.K. Chesterton, founded the National Front (NF). The recession of 1973 to 1975 gave the NF an opportunity at electoral success. So did the increasing racist tone of establishment politics. This was dramatically signified by former Tory Cabinet Minister Enoch Powell's speech in 1967 that predicted 'rivers of blood' if immigration were not stemmed. By 1977, the NF were capable of getting 119,000 votes in the Greater London Council elections. Even more seriously they were mounting physical attacks on black and Asian people and those on the Left. They were increasingly set on repeating the tactics of the 1930s Fascists by organizing street demonstrations aimed at intimidating immigrant communities and their political opponents.

In a repeat of the Cable Street experience, the NF were confronted with opposition when they tried to march through Lewisham, South London, in the summer of 1977. A quarter of London's police force, armed for the first time with riot shields, were mobilized to ensure that the march could go ahead. But thousands of protesters mobilized by the Socialist Workers' Party alongside locals from the black community broke through the police lines and cut the NF march in two. In the aftermath of Lewisham, the Anti-Nazi League was launched and its carnival in Victoria Park, headlined by the Clash, drew 100,000 people. The Fascists were not finished yet, but they were defeated and isolated. John Tyndall, the former leader of the NF, formed the BNP at the end of the 1980s. It started campaigning on the slogan 'Rights for whites' in East London. In 1990 the European Parliament's Committee on Racism and Xenophobia described the BNP as 'an openly Nazi Party'. Tyndall himself, who had been pictured in Nazi uniform during his NF days, said 'many who feel that Hitler was right do not believe it is yet safe to state such views openly; but times will change'. The BNP has tried to present a more respectable image to the electorate. In this it is modelling itself on some European Fascist and Far-Right parties, like Jean Marie le Pen's National Front in France, who hope to build up their support electorally before they try to gain control of the streets. The failure of establishment political parties and the growing cynicism that many feel towards official politics is giving the BNP fertile ground in which to grow.

However, since the attack on the World Trade Center in September 2001 the anti-Islamic attitudes displayed by some mainstream politicians have allowed the BNP to speak of Muslims as their 1930s precursors once spoke of Jews. And in the current recession, the BNP hope that working class people afraid that they will lose their jobs and their houses can be persuaded to blame their neighbours, as Germans once blamed the recession of the 1930s on the Jews who lived among them. The Fascists are not yet as strong as they were in the 1930s, the Trade Unions and the Left have not been defeated as they were then, parliamentary institutions are not as weak as they were then and anti-racist sentiment is still strong in many parts of society. But, in unstable and uncertain times, events follow on one another with dizzying speed. Today's certainties can vanish tomorrow. Fascist solutions appeal in societies where the centre ground disappears and progressive forces fail to provide an alternative. That is the warning of history.

Timeline: the rise of Fascism

1917: Russian Revolution
1918: end of the First World War
1922: Mussolini's March on Rome
1929: the Wall Street Crash
1933: Hitler comes to power
1936: Battle of Cable Street
1977: Battle of Lewisham

The Spanish Civil War

The Spanish Civil War was one of the decisive conflicts of the twentieth century. It was the last moment when the rise of Fascism could have been halted before the Second World War and it was a moment of revolutionary upheaval as millions of Spanish workers took the destiny of society into their own hands. Hundreds of thousands of volunteers from across Europe rushed to their aid. There has never been anything like it, before or since.

In the late 1920s, the military-backed Government of Spain was in economic trouble. Unemployment was high, the rich refused to pay higher taxes and inflation was out of control. In 1930 the Prime Minister resigned and in 1931 King Alfonso XIII agreed to democratic elections. It was the first time in 60 years that Spaniards had been able to participate in a free vote. They voted overwhelmingly for a republic and Alfonso's only chance of avoiding an insurrection was to leave the country. He went into exile in April 1931. In the General Election that followed in June the same year the Socialist Party and other Left Parties won a huge majority.

The new Government introduced land reform measures and legislation in favour of local autonomy for Catalonia and the Basque country. They also survived an attempted military coup in 1932, but lost the election to the Right in 1933. The Right-Wing Government started undoing the reforms of the previous Administration, triggering a general strike in 1934. The strike was accompanied by an armed insurrection in the Asturias Region. Clearly, Spanish society was split down the middle. On one side were the Socialists, Communists, Anarchists, Trade Unionists, Liberals and Democrats, although they were far from in agreement with one another. On the other side, were the Monarchists,

Army Generals, the Catholic Church, the Fascists of the Falange Party, the employers, the landlords and the rich.

In February 1936, there was another General Election in Spain. The main Left organization was the newly formed Popular Front, an alliance of Socialists, Communists and Republicans. Opposing them were the National Front alliance of Right-Wing parties and Monarchists, supported by the Catholic Church and the Falange. The Anarchists stood aside from the electoral contest. Nearly ten million Spaniards voted and the Popular Front won the contest by just 1.1 percent of the poll. The new Government resumed the land reform programme, granted autonomy to Catalonia, and banned the Falange Party. Spain's rich began to drain money from the economy, precipitating an economic crisis. Even more worryingly, four Generals, including Francisco Franco, began plotting against the Government. In response to the economic crisis, workers began to take action. From March to May street riots and strikes grew to revolutionary proportions. Workers began taking over the economy and running it themselves. The English writer George Orwell described the scene in Barcelona, the capital of militant Catalonia, when he reached there a few months later:

> It was the first time that I had ever been in a town where the working class was in the saddle. Practically every building of any size had been seized by the workers and was draped with red flags or with the red and black flag of the Anarchists; every wall was scrawled with the hammer and sickle and with the initials of the revolutionary parties . . . Every shop and cafe had an inscription saying that it had been collectivized; even the bootblacks had been collectivized and their boxes painted red and black. Waiters and shop-walkers looked you in the face and treated you as an equal . . . And it was the aspect of the crowds that was the queerest thing of all. In outward appearance it was a town in which the wealthy classes had practically ceased to exist . . . Practically everyone wore rough working-class clothes, or blue overalls, or some variant of the militia uniform. All this was queer and moving. There was much in it that I did not understand, in some ways I did not even like it, but I recognized it immediately as a state of affairs worth fighting for.

This was a situation that the Right-Wing and the Generals were not willing to tolerate. In July, there were military uprisings in the Spanish colony of Morocco and some parts of mainland Spain. The Government dissolved the regular army. On 19 July 1936 Franco took command of the army in Morocco. From the start, the leaders of the military coup had help from Mussolini's Fascist State in Italy and Hitler's Nazi Regime in Germany. Indeed, it was German and Italian planes that airlifted Franco's Army to the Spanish mainland.

In August 1936, the First International Brigade volunteers arrived in Spain. They were supported by Stalin's Russia, although it was not until October that the first aid from Russia arrived for the Republican Government. The International Brigades were astounding phenomena. Some 2,000 British came, 2,800 Americans, 3,350 from Italy, 5,000 Poles and Ukrainians, 5,000 Germans and Austrians, and 10,000 French. In all, some 40,000 young people from over 50 nations came to fight Fascism in Spain. The International Brigades were thrown into action immediately. Franco's forces were contained in isolated areas at first, but they drove against Madrid in October 1936 and the International Brigades played a significant role in repulsing them. But the forces of the Right had more powerful backers than the volunteers who came to fight for the Republic.

In September, a military junta named Franco as Head of State and Commander in Chief of the armed forces of Spain. In November,

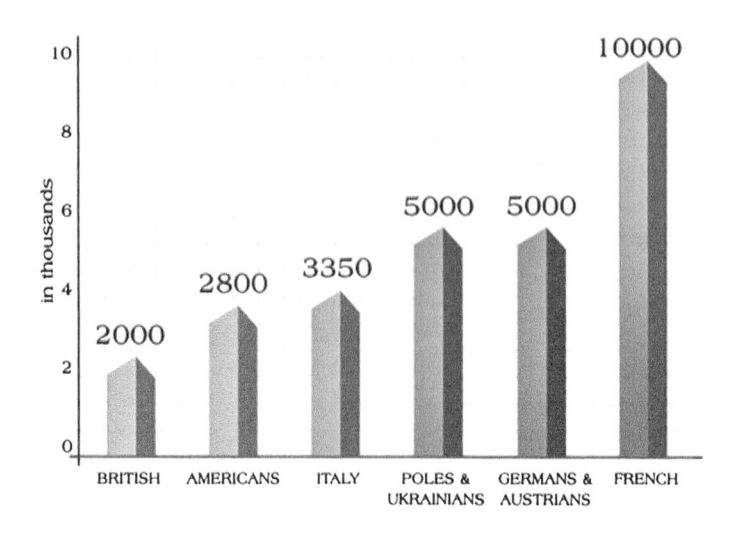

FIGURE 1.11 Make-up of the International Brigades

Germany and Italy recognized Franco as head of Spain's Government. In February 1937, Franco started another major offensive against Madrid. The International Brigades played an important part in resisting this offensive. Perhaps, the atmosphere among Republicans at this time was best captured by black American singer Paul Robeson. Robeson was a world famous artist. He rushed to Spain to perform for Republicans and was given honorary membership of the Abraham Lincoln Brigade of volunteers. His song about the defiance of Madrid, 'The Four Insurgent Generals', captures all the passion and anger of the Republican cause.

Franco was under pressure from Hitler and Mussolini to gain a quick victory by capturing the capital. In March, he launched an attack on Guadalajara 40 miles north-east of Madrid. He had the assistance of 30,000 of Mussolini's Italian 'volunteers', but his forces were defeated. As they retreated, Republicans captured documents proving that the Italian volunteers were really Mussolini's soldiers. The League of Nations refused to accept the evidence of Italian support for Franco, but it did ban all volunteers going to fight for the Republic. This was in line with the French, US and British policy of non-intervention in Spain. What this policy really meant was that Hitler and Mussolini went on supporting Franco while the Western democracies left the Republic to fight on without aid, except from Stalin's Russia. The result of this was felt in the next two months. In April, Hitler's Condor Legion of Heinkel bombers destroyed the town of Guernica. Immortalized in Pablo Picasso's painting, which bears the town's name, the event remains a by-word for the destruction and loss of civilian life in modern warfare. In the same month, Franco forced all the Right-Wing forces to unite in a single Falange Party. Giant posters appeared all over Spain with the slogan, 'One State! One Country! One Chief! Franco! Franco! Franco!' It was, of course, a direct imitation of Hitler and Mussolini.

With Stalin as its only supporter, the Republican Government found it harder and harder to resist the influence of the Spanish Communist Party. And the Spanish Communist Party did not want a full-blooded revolution in Spain because this would cause a rift between Russia and Britain and France; and it was in this alliance that Stalin's hopes of resisting Hitler lay. In May, this disastrous foreign policy had a decisive effect on the Spanish struggle. Under Communist pressure, the Popular Front Government moved to put a stop to the social revolution that had seen workers take effective control of Barcelona. Communist Party death squads hunted down supporters of the Anarchist Trade Unions and the opposition United Marxist Workers' Party. There was fighting in the streets of Barcelona as the Communist Party struggled to suppress the Revolution. It succeeded, but the standing of the Popular Front Government was never the same again and morale plummeted among the Republic's supporters. By the summer of 1937, the Francoists were on the advance. In June, the strategic city of Bilbao fell to them. In August, the Vatican recognized Franco's regime.

By April 1938, Franco's forces had driven a wedge through the Republican forces from one side of the country to the other. Republican Spain was now split in two. The following month, Franco declared that the Republicans must unconditionally surrender. In July, the Republican Army began to collapse after the Battle of the Ebro. The International Brigades were withdrawn and sent home. They had suffered heavy losses; among the dead were 2,000 Germans, 1,000 French, 900 Americans and 500 British. The Republican Army that remained was constantly bombed by the Condor Legion and by artillery. In January 1939, the proud working class experiment in popular control that was revolutionary Barcelona fell to Franco. The workers' movement was so demoralized by the Communist Party's attack on it in 1937 that there was barely a fight.

It was now only a matter of time before the Republic was defeated. In February, Britain and France, who had done nothing to save the Republic from Fascism, recognized the legitimacy of Franco's Government. In March, defiant Madrid surrendered to Franco. The following month the Republic surrendered unconditionally. Franco had an estimated 100,000 Republican prisoners executed after the War. Another 35,000 Republicans died in concentration camps in the years after the War. Hitler and Mussolini celebrated Franco's victory. Democrats and Socialists everywhere waited in fear to see the consequences of what the Western powers had allowed to happen in Spain. They did not have to wait long; by the end of the year the world was at war.

George Orwell came back from Spain and wrote what is perhaps his best book, *Homage to Catalonia*. But he also wrote another essay called 'Looking Back on the Spanish War'. He wrote it in 1942 in the midst of the worldwide war that might have been prevented had the Fascists been beaten in Spain. He wrote then that he remembered 'the Italian militiaman, who shook my hand in the guardroom, the day I joined the militia'. Orwell said that this man's face,

Which I saw only for a minute or two, remains with me as a sort of visual reminder of what the War was really about. He symbolises for me the flower of the European working class, harried by the police of all countries, the people who fill the mass graves of the Spanish battlefields and are now, to the tune of several millions, rotting in forced-labour camps... The question is very simple. Shall people like that Italian soldier be allowed to live the decent, fully human life which is now technically achievable, or shan't they? Shall the common man be pushed back into the mud, or shall he not? I myself believe, perhaps on insufficient grounds, that the common man will win his fight sooner or later, but I want it to be sooner and not later – sometime within the next hundred years, say and not sometime within the next ten thousand. That was the real issue of the Spanish war, and of the present war, and perhaps of other wars yet to come.

Timeline: the Spanish Civil War

1931: birth of the Republic
1936: victory of the Popular Front
1936: Franco revolts
1937: battle for Madrid
1938: the fall of the Republic

The real history of the Second World War

The Second World War was the greatest conflict in human history. Estimates of the number who died vary, but it was not less than 50 million, and may have been more than 70 million. It is a conflict that has burnt itself into popular memory. Politicians and governments constantly try to use the memory of the Second World War for their own ends. The 'Dunkirk spirit' or the 'spirit of the Blitz' are frequently invoked in Britain to bolster 'national unity' in times of crisis. New wars have been justified by describing foreign enemies – from Egypt's President Nasser during the Suez conflict of 1956 to Saddam Hussein during the invasion of Iraq – as 'the new Hitler'. However, the truth about the Second World War is not so simple.

The period from the outbreak of the First World War in 1914 to the end of the Second World War in 1945 has been described by the historian E. H. Carr as the 'Thirty Years War'. What Carr was getting at is the fact that throughout this whole period the major powers – Britain, Germany, the US, Italy, Japan and Russia – were locked in a struggle for global supremacy. Ultimately, it took two global conflicts and the international slump of the 1930s to settle this conflict. At the start of this period, the British Empire ruled supreme, but by the 1920s and 1930s, both the US and Germany were outstripping Britain economically. Germany was the outstandingly successful economy on the Continent. But she had also been the loser in the First World War, and in 1918 the German Kaiser had been overthrown by revolution. Hitler represented an attempt by Germany to redraw the power relations of Europe to her advantage. This would not just represent the triumph of German industrial growth, but would also avenge the humiliation that had followed defeat in the First World War. But, crucially, Hitler was also able to do battle with the working class movement. The German Revolution of 1918–1923 had almost swept away the entire ruling class, as well as the Kaiser. Soviet Russia was a living example of what could happen. Moreover, the German Communist and Socialist Parties had millions of supporters. For the German ruling class, then, Hitler was a bulwark against revolution.

Hitler came to power in 1933 and through rearmament helped pull Germany out of depression. In other parts of Europe, Fascism was on the march. Mussolini had already been in power in Italy for more than a decade, whilst Franco's Fascist forces were set to win the Spanish Civil War that had begun in 1936. The major exception to this trend was France, where a Popular Front Government led by Socialist Leon Blum came to power in 1936. But even this had the contradictory effect of pushing many of the French upper and middle classes into sympathy with Fascism out of fear of Socialism. This was the European landscape within which Hitler's programme of territorial expansion began.

In March 1938, Hitler's forces walked into Austria and annexed it to Germany. The 'Anschluss', as it was called, was preceded by a Nazi coup in Vienna to prevent the Austrian Chancellor from holding a referendum on whether or not Austrians wished to join the Third Reich. Consequently, the German Army entered Austria without firing a shot. They were welcomed by pro-Nazi crowds. In a Nazi-organized plebiscite the following month, 99.73 percent of voters were said to have agreed with the annexation. There were only muted protests from Britain; many in the Government wanted to avoid conflict with

FIGURE 1.12 Germany gains control of the Sudetenland, Czechoslovakia

Europe's rising power. But the full depths of Britain's appeasement of Hitler only became clear in September 1938 when Prime Minister Neville Chamberlain signed the Munich Agreement with Hitler. At Munich, Britain and the major powers agreed that Hitler could annex the German-speaking Sudetenland areas of Czechoslovakia. Czechoslovakia was not even invited to attend the conference at which her territory was given away to the Nazis; the Western powers simply tore up the previous agreements to defend Czechoslovakia's independence. Neville Chamberlain returned to Britain clutching the piece of paper signed by Hitler and claimed he had secured 'peace in our time'. In fact, he had taken an enormous step on the road to war.

In March 1939, just a year after the Anschluss, Hitler invaded the rest of Czechoslovakia. The whole command structure of Germany's armed forces had been opposed to the invasion. They sent agents to Britain who told the Government that Admiral Canaris, the Head of German Intelligence, and Graf von Helldorf, the Berlin Police Chief, were willing to arrest Hitler. There was just one precondition: Britain and France must threaten war over the invasion of Czechoslovakia. Chamberlain and the French leader Daladier did not take the information seriously and refused to react to the betrayal of the Munich Agreement. The plan to arrest Hitler collapsed. Czechoslovakia's fate was sealed and within months Hitler was ready to invade Poland.

Britain was not the only power which thought it could serve its own interests by making a deal with Hitler. So did Russia. After Munich, Stalin feared that the West would remain neutral if Russia were attacked by Hitler. The Hitler–Stalin Non-Aggression Pact was the direct result. The Pact also led to the carve-up of Poland, Finland and the Baltic States between Russia and Germany. Stalin assisted Hitler in the invasion of Poland. Indeed, just a month after the Hitler–Stalin Pact was signed, Russia invaded Poland from the East as Germany invaded from the West. Just a week before German troops invaded Poland, Hitler made a speech to his Generals. It revealed exactly what he thought of the British and French Governments and of the Munich Agreement: 'The enemy did not expect my great determination. Our enemies are little worms, I saw them at Munich.... Now Poland is in the position I wanted...I am only afraid that some bastard will present me with a mediation plan at the last moment.' But even in the minds of the British and French Governments, further appeasement was no longer an option. On the 1 September 1939, Hitler invaded Poland without even bothering to declare war. On the 3 September, Britain and France declared war on Germany. The Second World War had begun.

Why did the British Government appease Hitler? Why did they allow him to build a European Nazi Empire without serious opposition? The most fundamental reason is that in the inter-war years Britain was past its peak as a great power and it was fearful of the economic damage that another war might cause. Importantly, it was also terrified of losing its Empire, which was now even more extensive than it had been under Queen Victoria. Germany was a rising power. To the majority of British politicians it seemed as if the best way to hang on to what they had was to appease Hitler. Moreover, there was considerable sympathy for the Nazis among Britain's rulers. And it came right from the top. King Edward VIII was a supporter of appeasement and an admirer of Hitler. After his abdication in 1936 – a result of his decision to marry an American divorcee – he and his new wife visited Hitler. During the widely publicized visit Edward gave full Nazi salutes. Hitler was certainly saddened by Edward's abdication: 'If he had stayed, everything would have been different. His abdication was a severe loss for us.' But

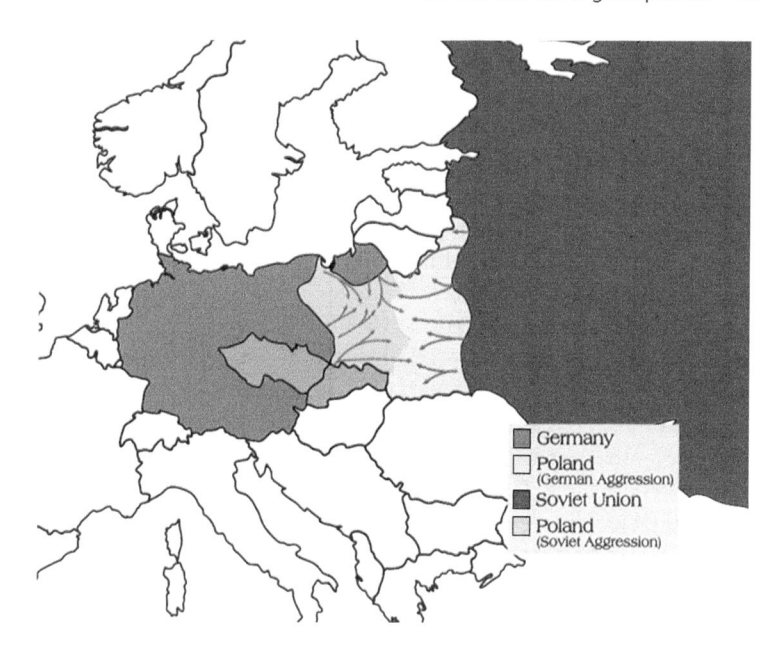

FIGURE 1.13 The invasion of Poland, September 1939

pro-Nazi sympathies ran much more widely among Britain's rulers. The 'Cliveden Set', so-called because they met at Cliveden, the home of Tory MP Lady Nancy Astor, were famously pro-Nazi. They included Foreign Secretary Lord Halifax and the Editor of *The Times*, Geoffrey Dawson. While Dawson edited *The Times* it was forbidden to make any mention of anti-Semitism in Hitler's Germany.

Labour MP Hugh Dalton accused the wealthy, Tories and members of the Peerage of being the main supporters of appeasement. In 1940 Michael Foot, the future leader of the Labour Party, and two other journalists, Frank Owen and Peter Howard, issued a pamphlet entitled 'Guilty Men' under the penname 'Cato'. It called for the resignation from public life of 15 public figures, including Chamberlain and his predecessor Stanley Baldwin. W. H. Smith and other major wholesalers refused to distribute the book and it was sold from news stands and barrows. It sold more than 200,000 copies in a few weeks. Appeasement was dead for the majority of people in Britain. There was one notable opponent of appeasement in the British elite: Winston Churchill. The Churchill myth is now so powerful that it is hard to recall how he appeared to his contemporaries, but the truth is that Churchill was a maverick even among the elite. Although he had been at the forefront of politics for decades, he was far from popular. Many working class families remembered him as the hardline Home Secretary who had deployed the soldiers who shot at striking miners in Tonypandy, South Wales in 1911. They remembered too that he had masterminded the Government response to the General Strike in 1926. Among his own class he was remembered for his advocacy of the Gallipoli Campaign in the First World War – a disaster which cost him his job as First Lord of the Admiralty. His decision to set the value of the Pound to that of gold (the so-called 'Gold Standard') in 1925 seriously weakened the economy and was one of the causes of the General Strike. Churchill was an unashamed champion of the British Empire, and it was this unreconstructed nationalism that brought him to see more clearly than others the threat Hitler posed to British interests. From this lonely position, Churchill opposed appeasement and correctly predicted that Munich would lead to war. Churchill replaced Neville Chamberlain as Prime Minister in May 1940. This was practically the last card that a disgraced political elite had left to play. Although the wider truth about the Wartime Administration is that it depended on Labour Party figures, it was just as reliant upon longer-standing figures of the British elite.

Appeasement, however, had already done its worst. On 10 May 1940 Hitler invaded France, outflanking the massive defensive fortification of the Maginot Line. German armoured units pushed through the Ardennes Forest and cut off the Allied forces who had taken forward positions in Belgium. At the end of May, the remnants of the British Expeditionary Force in France had to evacuate from Dunkirk. Every last ship and boat, Royal Navy or privately owned, was used to get the defeated British Army off the coast of France. Mussolini's Italy declared war on France on 10 June. On 14 June, the seemingly impossible sight of the Nazis overrunning Paris was captured on newsreel. The Swastika was hoist up on the Eiffel Tower; Hitler's forces were the masters of Continental Europe. Hitler was now set to invade Britain. There was very little to stop him; he had the capacity to get an army across the English Channel and the British Army had been all but destroyed in France. But there was one thing that Hitler's invasion needed and which he did not yet have: air superiority.

In the summer of 1940 the Battle of Britain began. The RAF Spitfires and Hurricanes attempted to break up the German bomber formations protected by the Messerschmitt 109es. The battle was a very close run thing. The fighter planes were almost exactly equal in speed, manoeuvrability and armament. At the time both sides massively exaggerated their successes, but post-War analysis shows that the RAF shot down 2,698 Germans planes (against 1,023 lost to all causes), although Luftwaffe fighters claimed 3,198 RAF aircraft (against total losses of 2,087). But, there can be no doubt about what happened on the critical day of 15 September 1940. Two massive waves of German attacks were decisively repulsed by the RAF. The total casualties on this critical day were 60 German and 26 RAF aircraft shot down. The German defeat caused Hitler to order, two days later, the postponement of preparations for the invasion of Britain. In the end, the daylight raids by the Germans could not be sustained and the RAF had done enough damage to halt the threat of imminent invasion. The effect on morale was as important as the military victory. The seemingly invincible Nazi War Machine had been beaten for the first time. Hitler was far from finished, however. In September 1940 the Axis powers – German, Italy and Japan – formally declared their alliance.

The Battle of Britain may have been over but the nighttime bombing of British cities was not. The Blitz began with 57 nights of consecutive raids on London. One of the most devastating raids was on Coventry on 14 November 1940. Hour-after-hour of bombing induced near-panic and destroyed the City Centre. By the time the Blitz ended in May 1941, some 43,000 civilians had been killed, half of them in London. The Government feared that a 'shelter mentality' would develop if people were provided with deep shelters in central London. Instead, they encouraged people to construct weak and shallow 'Anderson Shelters' in their back gardens. The rich faced no such problems. One American journalist went to the Dorchester Hotel where he discovered that the management had converted the cellars into expensive luxury shelters. Nine peers slept there each night; one of them was Lord Halifax, the Foreign Secretary. Throughout the night he was well-supplied by a waiter serving his favourite brand of whisky. Ordinary people started taking matters into their own hands. In some places, those taking refuge published their own magazines, such as the *Hampstead Shelterers' Bulletin* and a network of contacts throughout London grew up. In November 1940, a conference was held. A total of 79 delegates from 50 shelters decided to form the London Underground Station and Shelterers' Committee. They elected two implacable Socialists, Harry Ratner and Alfie Bass (later to become a well-known television comedian), as Secretaries. The authorities in London, after being put under very considerable pressure from public opinion, did make subsequent use of about 80 underground stations to shelter about 177,000 people.

A similar political battle was being fought on the airwaves. J. B. Priestley was a nationally known novelist, columnist and playwright when the BBC offered him a Sunday evening radio programme entitled 'Postscripts'. Priestley developed the vision of a 'People's War', championing not only the military conflict against Hitler and the Nazis, but also the struggle to build a society where the 'festering sores on the body of a diseased world' would not return. At the programme's peak, about 40 percent of the population tuned in to hear Priestley's broadcasts. The message was not welcomed by Winston Churchill. He argued that Priestley's message was a diversion from the need to focus on the military effort. Other leading Tories were angered by his 'Socialist ideas'. The BBC booted Priestley off the slot after only six months. A second series in early 1941 lasted for just eight broadcasts.

In 1941, Hitler was the conqueror of Europe. Despite the fact that the Nazis had failed to mount an invasion, it was clear that Britain could not win the War alone. In June 1941 Hitler tore up his Pact with Stalin and the Nazis began Operation Barbarossa, the invasion of Russia. Operation Barbarossa is still the largest military operation in human history. The Nazi invasion became the site of some of the largest battles, deadliest atrocities, highest casualties and most horrific conditions for Russians and Germans alike. It was a massive gamble, but at that moment there was no 'Western Front' and Britain was in no condition to create one. The US had also still not entered the War.

At first, the Nazi invasion of Russia swept all before it. Nazi forces drove thousands of miles into Russia, surrounding and capturing city after city. It was clear that Hitler could only be defeated if the US declared war. Initially, the US elite were sceptical that Britain would survive. Joseph Kennedy, father of the future US President John F. Kennedy, had been US Ambassador in London. When he returned to report to President Franklin D. Roosevelt at the outbreak of war, he said Britain was likely to be defeated. Roosevelt, encouraged by the outcome of the Battle of Britain, was more hopeful, but he still kept the US out of the War. Only the Japanese attack on Pearl Harbour, Hawaii, in December 1941 changed that. The attack was a military triumph for Japan; they suffered just 65 servicemen killed or wounded

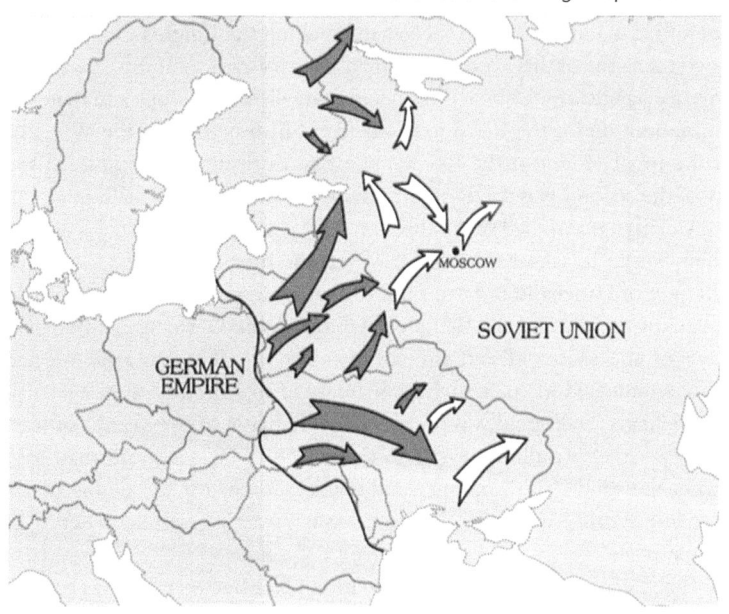

FIGURE 1.14 The War on the Eastern Front

and lost just five midget submarines and 29 aircraft. By contrast, the US lost four battleships, three cruisers, three destroyers, one mine layer and 188 aircraft. Some 2,402 US personnel were also killed and another 1,282 injured. But the attack was a strategic and political disaster for the Axis Powers. As the surprise attack on the US fleet took place, Hitler also declared war on the US even though no treaty required him to do so. The US was now engaged in the Pacific and European theatres of the Second World War. It was to be the tipping point of the conflict.

Britain was still isolated and embattled, even after the US entered the War in the closing days of 1941. German U-boats (small submarines) were determined to sink the Atlantic convoys supplying Britain from the US. Britain's large Empire had made her highly dependent on imported goods. Without convoy supplies she could not survive. The Battle was the longest continuous campaign of the War. But the Allies had the upper-hand after a series of convoy battles in the first half of 1943. Victory had depended on the increasing involvement of the US, the Allies use of radar and the British success in breaking the Enigma Code, which gave them the ability to read German military radio transmissions. The victory against the U-boats was decisive in allowing troops and material to be built up for the invasion of mainland Europe later in the War. But if the involvement of the US was the first critical turning point in the War, the second was the Russian victory in the Battle of Stalingrad.

German troops had swept through Russia with amazing speed despite their failure to take Moscow. However, the city of Stalingrad stood in the way of Hitler's attempt to seize the oil producing area of the Caspian Sea. At times during the Battle of Stalingrad, the Germans held 90 percent of the shattered and ruined city. But the Russians held on and counterattacked in an encircling manoeuvre that destroyed the German Sixth Army. Stalingrad was the most deadly battle in the history of warfare. Over two million people lost their lives. That is more than four times the total British military and civilian deaths for the whole of the Second World War. Still, Stalingrad was Hitler's first major defeat of the War.

The Second Battle of El Alamein took place between the 23 October and the 4 November 1942, whilst the Battle of Stalingrad was raging. The war in North Africa had been swinging back and forward between the Allies and the German and Italian Forces since the start of the War. The First Battle at El Alamein had stopped the Axis advance led by the charismatic General Erwin Rommel. The Second Battle threw them back decisively. It also paved the way for the Allied invasion of Italy the following year. But the North African Campaign was important to Churchill for other reasons. For Churchill, the Middle East and the Mediterranean were vital because they were part of an Imperial vision and because the Suez Canal was the gateway to India, Britain's foremost Imperial possession. Churchill certainly wanted to defeat Hitler, but he was at least as determined to save the British Empire. Churchill was quite open about this with US President Franklin Roosevelt, telling him:

> Mr. President, I believe you are trying to do away with the British Empire.... But in spite of that, you constitute our only hope. You know it. We know it. You know that we know that without America, the British Empire won't stand.

This Imperial obsession led Churchill to make military priorities out of theatres of war that were not central in the struggle to beat Hitler,

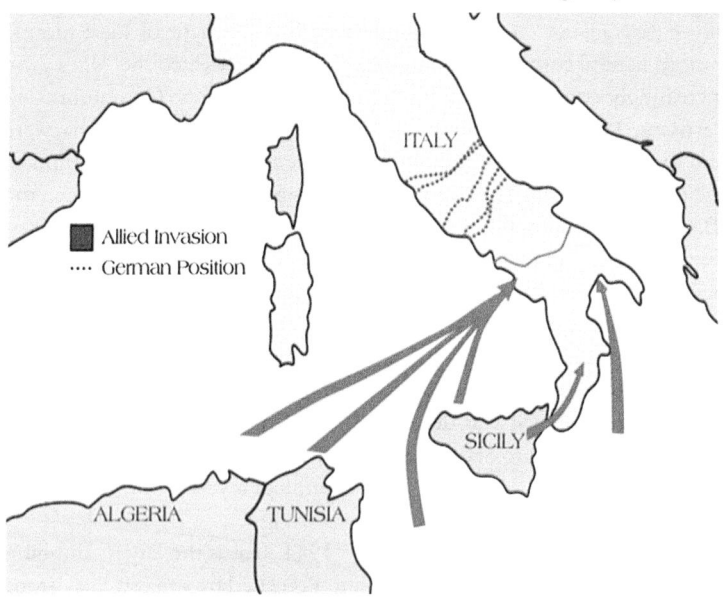

FIGURE 1.15 The Allied invasion of Italy

but were vital to the continuance of the British Empire. This tension surfaced in the most acute disagreement in the relationship between the Allies: the Second Front Controversy. Despite desperate Soviet demands to open the Second Front as soon as possible, the Western Allies only launched a massive cross-Channel operation in June 1944. This left the Russian's bearing the brunt of the War effort. In 1942 there were just 27 German Divisions left to defend France while 190 were fighting Russia. Some 24 million Russians died in the Second World War, 14 percent of the entire population (compared with 0.3 percent in the US). One great understated truth about the Second World War is that, more than any other Nation, it was won by the Russian people.

Meanwhile, Churchill was insisting on an invasion of Italy, supposedly the 'underbelly' of Fascist Europe. But Italy was to prove very far from a soft option. Italian fascists only surrendered on the 29 April, just 48 hours ahead of the final surrender of the German army on 1 May 1945. The long slog up the boot of Italy, exemplified by the costly Battle of Monte Casino, wore down the Allies. Even after Mussolini fell and the Allies had the assistance of Partisan Forces, the fighting was never easy against German defenders with the benefit of ideal mountainous natural barriers. In fact, as the Germans retreated the Allies were increasingly concerned to marginalize the power of the Communist-led Partisans. Left-Wing Partisans in France, Greece and Yugoslavia were also to discover that they and the Allied elite had very different visions of the post-War world. The Second Front was only finally agreed when the 'Big Three' – Stalin, Churchill and Roosevelt – met at the Tehran Conference at the end of 1943. Roosevelt gave Stalin the pledge that he had been waiting for since June 1941: that Britain and the US would open a Second Front in France in the spring of 1944. Churchill had to abandon the idea of a joint British, US and Commonwealth Forces initiative through the Mediterranean to secure British interests in the Middle East and India. Roosevelt was determined to break up the British Empire, and the concessions to Stalin served this purpose. The struggle for power in the post-War world had already begun, half a year before the D-Day landings.

D-Day began at 6:30am on 6 June 1944. It was the largest amphibious military operation ever undertaken. Preceded by a massive paratroop drop of 24,000 soldiers, some 175,000 infantry poured onto five Normandy beaches codenamed 'Sword', 'Juno', 'Omaha', 'Gold' and 'Utah'. At first, Hitler would not release armoured divisions for a counter-attack. When he did, elements of the Twenty-first Panzer Division drove into the gap between the British and Canadian Divisions at Sword Beach and Juno Beach. They almost reached the sea. The landings might have failed, but British anti-tank gunners stopped that happening. By the end of August 1944, all of Northern France was liberated and the invading forces reorganized for the drive into Germany, where they would eventually meet with Soviet forces advancing from the East to bring an end to the Nazi Reich. But the Nazis still put up fierce opposition to the Allied advance, and the Allies were to suffer some serious reverses.

In mid-September 1944 the Allies attempted to shorten the War by outflanking the German line of defence. The objective was to secure the bridges across the Rhine River in the Netherlands and encircle the industrial Ruhr Region. Operation market Garden, as it was called at the time, was to be carried out by paratroopers and was the largest airborne offensive of all time. But it was 'a bridge too far' (as the 1977 movie version of the event famously put it). By the end of nine days of fighting, it was clear that the Allied landings had not been in sufficient

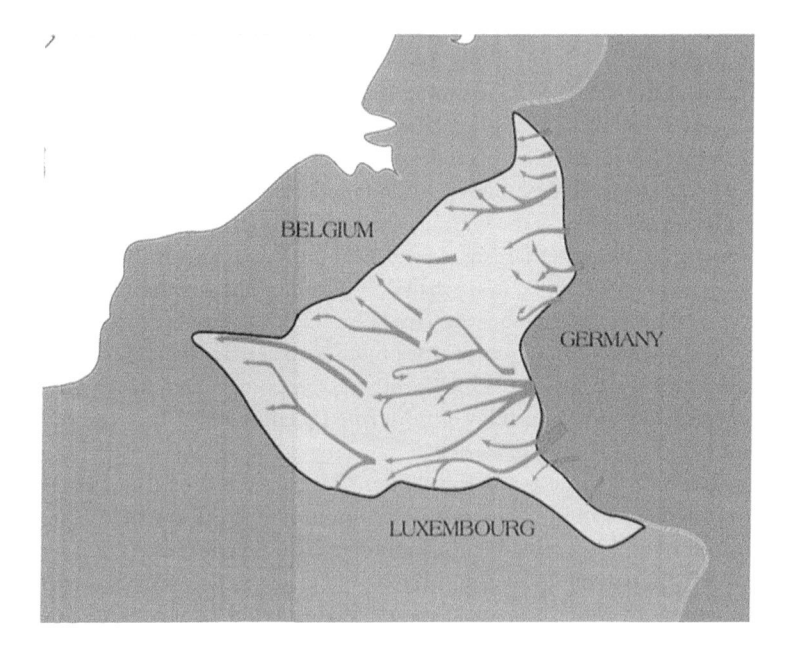

FIGURE 1.16 The Battle of the Bulge

force. The German resistance was much greater than had been expected. The Allies took at least a third more casualties than the Germans and were forced to retreat. It would be another six months before the Allies took these Rhine bridges. The Allies still moved forward, but at the end of 1944 the Germans struck back in a last attempt to break the line of advance. The Germans attempted to break through and divide the US and British forces with a massive thrust through the mountainous and forested Ardennes region of Belgium, France and Luxembourg. The Allies were taken by surprise, and the Germans were able to force their line back, creating, on the maps of the day, the bulge from which this 'Battle of the Bulge' takes its name. The Allies were outnumbered and outgunned on this weak section of the advancing front. Fought in snow-covered forest in the dead of winter, the Battle was the largest and bloodiest in which US forces were engaged during the War. But the offensive cost the Germans more casualties and, eventually, in January 1945, the bulge was pushed back and the Allies resumed their advance. The last of the German reserves were now gone, the Luftwaffe had been shattered and the remaining German forces in the West were being pushed back.

Just as the Allies were resuming their advance on the ground, they also began an aerial bombing campaign which demonstrated that the Germans had no monopoly on dealing death to civilians from the air. In February 1945, Allied bombers pounded the German city of Dresden, the Baroque Capital of the German State of Saxony, in what remains one of the most controversial Allied actions of the War. In four raids, 1,300 heavy bombers dropped more than 3,900 tons of high-explosive bombs and incendiary devices on the city. The resulting firestorm destroyed 15 square miles of the city. The death toll is uncertain, but it is not less than 25,000, and may be as high as 40,000. By comparison, the rightly-reviled German raid on Coventry during the Blitz killed between 600 and 1,000.

In the final battle for Berlin, Hitler had only the last SS and Hitler Youth Units to resist. They were overpowered in street-by-street fighting in May 1945. By that time, Hitler had already taken his own life in his bunker in Berlin. Allied soldiers moving towards Berlin uncovered the full horror of the Nazi regime. They liberated the concentration camps where six million Jews and another five million Trade Unionists, Socialists, Communists, gays, gypsies, Catholics, Freemasons, Jehovah's Witnesses, prisoners of war and the disabled had been exterminated. Some 60,000 prisoners were discovered at Belsen by the British Eleventh Armoured Division. 13,000 corpses lay unburied. The British forced the remaining SS Guards to gather up the dead bodies and bury them in mass graves. Some 10,000 of those who survived died of illness and malnutrition in the following weeks. Could the Allies have done more to stop the genocide? Jewish leaders had requested that the US bomb the rail lines to the camps in the summer of 1945. The US War Department refused, even though, on 7 July a fleet of 452 Fifteenth Air Force bombers flew along and across the five deportation railway lines on their way to bomb oil refineries nearby.

The conflict in the Pacific went on until August 1945. The Japanese surrendered after the US dropped nuclear bombs on Hiroshima and Nagasaki. The nuclear bomb 'Little Boy' killed 70,000 in Hiroshima in an instant on the 6 August. Another 70,000 died in the days that followed. As they were dying the nuclear bomb 'Fat Boy' killed another 80,000 in Nagasaki three days later. It was a totally unnecessary act of mass murder. We now know that the US had signals intelligence which told them that the Japanese were trying to surrender. They wanted to use the nuclear bombs in order to intimidate Russia, not because they wanted to shorten the War, the reason given at the time. In the same month that the Germans were retreating from the Battle of the Bulge and the city of Dresden was being bombed, the Allied leaders were meeting at Yalta in the Crimea. It was the second and last time that the Big Three were to meet. The shape of the post-War world was emerging. Roosevelt and Stalin took the lead; Churchill was more marginal. By the time of the conference, Marshal Zhukov's Russian forces were 65 km from Berlin. Stalin's position at the conference was so strong that he could dictate terms. A US delegation member commented, 'it was not a question of what we would let the Russians do, but what we could get the Russians to do'. The Cold War and the partition of Europe were already emerging from the fog of war.

There is one other story that shows that perhaps the Governments that fought against Hitler were not so committed to anti-Fascism as the ordinary people that they governed. The German rocket programme for the V1 and V2 unmanned flying bombs was technologically far in advance of anything in the US. Shocked US Officials decided they should just take Wernher von Braun and his team of German rocket scientists to the US and set them to work. Operation Paper Clip was the name given to this programme. President Truman agreed to the programme, but insisted that no one with a Nazi past should be allowed into the US. In response, the military and the intelligence services expunged the Nazi records of von Braun, who was an SS member, and his fellow scientists and simply gave them new pasts and identities. These were paper-clipped to their files; hence the name of the operation. The Nazi rocket scientists became the absolutely essential core of the NASA space programme and in 1975 von Braun was awarded the US National Medal of Science. Without them there would not have been a man on the moon. Among other things they contributed to the US military was the stealth technology that was developed into the US stealth bombers and fighters of the twenty-first century.

Fortunately, the ordinary people who fought the War took its democratic and egalitarian aims more seriously. Everywhere in the West, returning troops were determined that there would be 'no return to the 1930s', meaning no return to unemployment and poverty. Troops in North Africa mutinied and held their own 'parliament' in Cairo to discuss what sort of world they wanted to build after the War. Western

Governments had to struggle everywhere to keep Communists and Socialists, who had played a central role in the resistance movements, out of power. But they could not resist the demands for better jobs, welfare, homes, healthcare and education. Perhaps this mood was most obvious in Britain. Churchill was swept from power the moment the War ended and Labour came in with a landslide in the election of 1945. The NHS was founded. Council houses were built. Education was opened up in a way it never had been before. For an all too brief moment, the lives of working people became easier and more peaceful.

Timeline: the real history of the Second World War

1938 (March): Austrian Anschluss
1938 (September): Munich Agreement
1939: the fall of Czechoslovakia
1939 (August): the Hitler–Stalin Pact
1939 (September): the fall of Poland; Second World War begins
1940: the fall of France
1940 (May–June): Dunkirk evacuations
1940 (July): Battle of Britain
1940 (September): the Blitz begins
1940–1942: North Africa campaigns
1940–1943: Battle of the Atlantic
1941 (June): the Nazi invasion of Russia
1941 (December): Pearl Harbour attack
1942 (July): Battle of Stalingrad begins
1942 (October–November): Second Battle of El Alamein
1943 (September): invasion of Italy
1943 (November): Tehran Conference
1944 (June): D-Day
1944 (September): Operation Market Garden
1944–1945: Battle of the Bulge
1945 (February): bombing of Dresden; Yalta Conference
1945 (May): end of Battle for Berlin
1945 (August): Hiroshima and Nagasaki bombings; Japan surrenders

The Cold War

The Cold War lasted more than 40 years. It began almost as soon as the Second World War was over and by the time it ended the US had

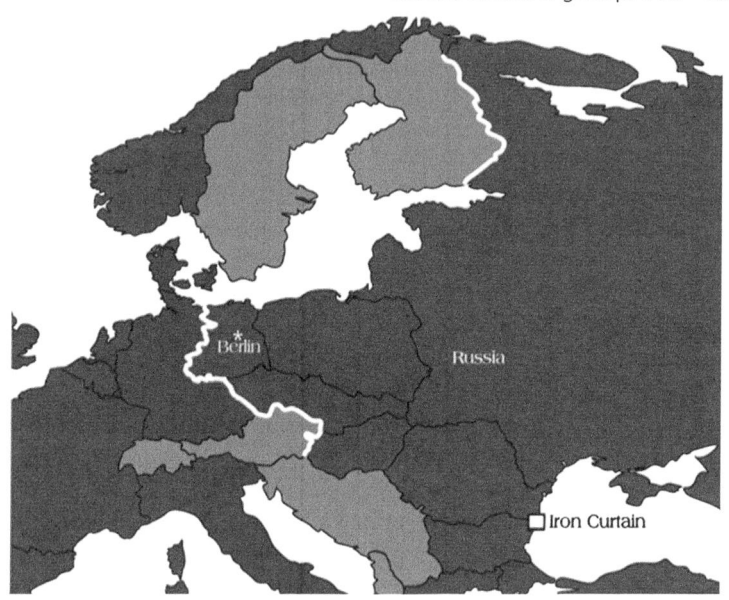

FIGURE 1.17 The 'Iron Curtain' in Europe

military alliances with 50 States and had 1.5 million troops stationed overseas in 117 countries. On occasions, the nuclear armed stand-off almost turned into a hot war as, for instance, in the Cuban Missile Crisis of 1962. And, although nuclear war was avoided, shooting wars in Korea and Vietnam still cost millions of lives. The victors of the Second World War – the US, Britain and Russia – barely remained united. The so-called Big Three met at the Yalta and Potsdam Conferences at the end of the War with the aim of dividing the globe between them. They had very different hands to play. The US was by far the strongest. Economically and militarily it had grown enormously throughout the War and it had suffered little of the war damage that devastated Europe and Russia. Britain was exhausted, so weak that bread rationing had to be introduced after the War, even though it had never been necessary during the War. Britain was incapable of sustaining its Empire. Russia had contributed more to the Allied War effort than any other country. The loss of life and material that she had incurred was gigantic. But her troops had swept across Eastern Europe and had reached Berlin first. In doing so Russia had annexed an empire.

The tensions between the US, Britain and Russia were so obvious that writer George Orwell had already coined the term 'Cold War' in 1945. The following year, Winston Churchill speaking in Fulton, Missouri, first used another phrase that came to describe the Cold War; there was, he said 'from Stettin in the Baltic to Trieste in the Adriatic' an 'iron curtain' descending across Europe. Churchill's speech came shortly after one of the architects of post-War US policy, George Kennan (then stationed in Moscow), sent his so-called 'Long Telegram' in which he predicted that the US would have to take an increasingly hard line in order to contain the spread of Communism. The conflict between the Allies existed, the words had been found; the Cold War had begun. It would be a different kind of conflict because in the same year that the great powers were meeting to discuss the post-War world a new and terrible weapon was used. On the 6 August 1945, the first nuclear bomb was dropped on Japan by the US. It was hideously destructive. The shadow the bomb cast was a long one; it hung over the whole Cold War and it hangs over us still. And, of course, the weapon spread. Russia had its own soon after. So too did Britain, France and China. The Cold War was the era in which people first learned to live with the threat of nuclear annihilation. This was the first generation to live with the knowledge that the weapons they possessed could end life on the planet. Even their limited use could return us to the Stone Age.

1947 was the year the Cold War really came of age. In that year, US President Harry Truman enunciated the doctrine – the 'Truman Doctrine' – that would bear his name. It called for $400 million to be allocated to help Greek Monarchists win the Civil War against Greek Communists, a role that the US was taking over from the cash-strapped British. He framed the conflict as part of the global struggle of Democracy against Totalitarianism. The Marshall Plan, an extensive package of economic aid announced the same year, was directed at restoring the European economies, although its creator, Secretary of State George Marshall, insisted that its benefits would not be extended to any country that voted Communists into power. A great deal of money was about to be spent by the US and a great deal of the justification for it was that it was necessary to fight Communism. However, the Eastern bloc did not seem bent on expansion. True, Stalin tightened his control by imposing one-party rule on Czechoslovakia – previously the only country in Eastern Europe permitted to retain democratic institutions – but the split between Stalin and Yugoslav leader Josip Tito weakened the Communist bloc. The first trial of strength came in the following year, 1948, and it came in Germany.

Germany was still effectively an occupied country divided into zones controlled by the US, France, Britain and Russia. The US and Britain, and later France, merged their zones, introduced a new currency – the Deutschmark – and pumped Marshall Aid money into the economy. It was the beginning of the creation of the West German State, with its capital in Bonn. Russia, the main victim of Nazi aggression in the Second World War, did not want Germany rebuilt. Stalin controlled the whole of East Germany, and although Berlin was divided between the four powers it was situated deep within East Germany. Stalin used this geographical anomaly to hit back at the West by blockading all land access to Berlin. The blockade was countered by a massive airlift of supplies to Berlin by the US, Britain, France and their allies. Two million people lived in Berlin and they needed 4,000 tons of supplies every day. They did not always get it. But the airlift built up and on its peak day in April 1949 aircraft landing every 62 seconds delivered a total of 13,215 tons of material in one day. The blockade was broken. This should have shown the West that although Stalin was keen to hold onto the East European Empire he had occupied at the end of the War, he had neither the economic nor political capacity to export Communism by force of arms. Instead, from this point on an awful irregular symmetry was the hallmark of the Cold War. Whichever side acted first, the other retaliated in some way. Neither could, nor even seriously tried to, overwhelm the other. But still, it was a dangerous game.

In 1949, the West created the North Atlantic Treaty Organization (NATO), which bound together the US and the countries of Western Europe in a military pact. The Senior Officer of which was always an American. The pact was said by its supporters to be defensive, but unifying nearly all the Western powers into a single military alliance was bound to look threatening when viewed from Moscow. Six years later, in 1955, the Warsaw Pact military alliance of East European countries was formed as a counter to NATO. But before this, in 1949, other reinforcements arrived in the Communist World: Mao took power in China. Russia's Red Army had overrun Manchuria in the last month of the Second World War and occupied the Korean Peninsula as far as the 38th Parallel. In 1950, the local Communist Government under Kim Il-Sung invaded South Korea. The US headed an international military force under UN auspices which fought North Korea to a standstill. One impact of the War was to hasten the development of the military structure of NATO. The Korean War was to continue for three years, its end coinciding with the defeat of the French in Vietnam.

Meanwhile, in Europe, Berlin was once again the centre of attention, only four years after the Berlin Airlift. In 1953, workers in the old German capital revolted against Stalinist rule. The tanks went in and the workers were ruthlessly suppressed. The Marxist playwright and poet Berthold Brecht, living in East Germany at the time, perfectly captured the idiocy of a so-called 'Workers' State' shooting down its own workers:

> Some Party hack decreed that the people
> had lost the government's confidence
> and could only regain it with redoubled effort.
> If that is the case, would it not be simpler,
> If the government simply dissolved the people
> And elected another?

The tanks restored order in East Berlin, but they could not make the system stable. Stalin died in the same year as the Berlin Rising and only another three years went by before there was an even more profound shock to the Stalinist system.

1956 was a year of change. The new Russian leader Nikita Khrushchev made a secret speech to Party apparatchiks in Moscow. The content was explosive, a full-scale denunciation of Stalin as a brutal and repressive tyrant. And the speech did not stay secret for very long. Khrushchev's regime was more liberal than Stalin's, but that is not saying very much. The real test came when the Hungarian Government took the new mood coming from Moscow as the cue for its own more far-reaching liberalization. On 23 October 1956 a huge demonstration clashed with the hated security police in Budapest. Statues of Stalin were toppled and revolutionary committees were set up throughout Hungary. Imre Nagy, recently expelled from the Communist Party in a dispute with the Stalinist leadership, was recalled and formed a coalition government. George Lukacs, the legendary Marxist philosopher and member of the short-lived workers' government of 1919, joined the Administration. The Russian Army in Hungary tried to put down the revolt but after five days of fighting were forced to scurry out of Budapest. But on 4 November, the Russian Army was back in force. Some 25,000 Hungarians died. Imre Nagy was arrested and executed. 200,000 Hungarians fled abroad. The repression in Hungary ought to have handed the Western powers a huge propaganda victory, but the Suez Crisis of the same year meant that they had troubles of their own. Egypt's President Nasser nationalized the Suez Canal and, in response, Israel, France and Britain invaded Egypt. It was hard to make denunciations of Russian Imperial behaviour in Eastern Europe look convincing while the Western powers were engaged in a colonial adventure of this sort in the Middle East. Moreover, the miserable defeat suffered the Suez War did not even make the West look strong. The net effect of 1956 was that both sides in the Cold War looked ugly. Many on the Left found that they could not stomach Western Capitalism or Russian so-called 'Socialism'. Tens of thousands left the Western Communist Parties and combined with others to create the New Left. In the Third World many decided to back the 'non-aligned movement' that tried to walk a radical path between the two Cold War blocs. In 1955 the Bandung Conference, in Indonesia, had already brought them together in a loose international alliance.

The Cold War, however, was about to escalate in an even more frightening direction. In 1957 the Russian's launched the first spacecraft to orbit the earth. Sputnik, as the craft was called, instantly became a household name on both sides of the divide. Four years later another Russian name became internationally famous: Yuri Gagarin, the cosmonaut who in April 1961 became the first human being to travel in space. The following month, in a speech to Congress, US President John Kennedy gave the NASA Space Agency and the Apollo Programme the goal of landing a man on the moon by the end of the decade. Behind all the talk of human exploration, the 'Space Race' had a very real military objective. Each new success in space proved that the nation that achieved it had the more sophisticated intercontinental ballistic missile launch rockets – the very same rockets that carried nuclear warheads. In this sense, the Space Race was a proxy nuclear war. Fortunately, it was a war without casualties, unlike the wars still being fought with conventional weapons. The Vietnam War was the most destructive of the Cold War conflicts and its history will be dealt with more fully later in this book. But here we need to place it in the context of the Cold War. From the early 1960s onwards, US troops were increasingly fighting and dying

FIGURE 1.18 The Cuban Missile Crisis, 1962

in Vietnam. China and Russia aided North Vietnam and the Viet Cong Guerrillas. But US aid to South Vietnam was far greater. By the time the Vietnam War was over, nearly 60,000 US soldiers had died. So too had nearly two million Vietnamese. The Communists took over the South and reunited their divided country. The US was humiliated; but there was no 'domino effect', as the hawks in the US predicted. No other nations 'fell to Communism'. All that happened was that the Vietnamese peoples' long suffering under colonialism came to an end. But there was a lot more road to travel in the Cold War before that could happen.

The 1962 Cuban Missile Crisis was one of the classic tit-for-tat episodes of the Cold War. The US had stationed missiles in Turkey, a frighteningly short flight time from Moscow. Cuba, meanwhile, had been liberated from the pro-US dictator Batista by forces led by Fidel Castro and Che Guevara in the 1950s. In 1962 the new Cuban

Government agreed to Russian missiles being installed on the island. The US responded with an air and sea blockade of Cuba. Khrushchev told Kennedy that this 'constituted an act of aggression propelling humankind into the abyss of a world nuclear-missile war'. The war of words, even at the UN, was frantic and frightening. The Cuban Missile Crisis is often regarded as the moment during the Cold War when the world came closest to nuclear war. That was averted when the Russians agreed to withdraw the weapons from Cuba. Less well known is that the deal also involved the decommissioning of US missiles in Turkey. After the crisis a 'hotline' between Washington and Moscow was installed which was a tacit admission of how near to nuclear war the crisis had brought the two superpowers.

By the end of the 1960s the world that had produced the Cold War was beginning to disintegrate. The year that proved this beyond doubt was 1968. That year, like 1956, marked a crisis on both sides of the Cold War divide. It began with the shock of the Tet Offensive in Vietnam. North Vietnam and the Viet Cong mounted an attack which took the US completely by surprise. The US project in Vietnam never really recovered from the political blow that the Tet Offensive delivered, even if they did eventually regain military control. The anti-war movement in the US and around the world reached new peaks of involvement and militancy. Just as the West was reeling from the debacle in Vietnam, the East faced a revolt in Czechoslovakia that was as serious as the Hungarian Revolution the previous decade. Yet again, the Russian tanks had to roll in to restore Moscow's rule. Then the revolt came to the West again. The student revolt was an international phenomenon, but in France it combined with a general strike which threatened the very existence of the French State. There were barricades in the Paris streets and behind them were people who had learnt that they should rely on their own self-activity to achieve political change, people who had seen that it was unwise to look to either Moscow or Washington for inspiration. But 1968 was only the beginning of the end, not the end itself.

The Cold War stayed with us for another 20 years, although there was a lull while the US came to terms with its defeat in Vietnam. In 1972, US President Richard Nixon visited China to meet Chairman Mao and try to normalize relations between the two countries. He and Henry Kissinger, the Secretary of State, thought this would weaken Russia. And with the cost of both the Cold War and the Vietnam War weakening the US's economic standing, Nixon also tried to bargain down the number of weapons that the two superpowers maintained in the Strategic Arms Limitation Treaty. At the end of the decade the Russian invasion of Afghanistan was putting detente, as this new period of reduced tension was called, under strain. By the start of the 1980s, with Ronald Reagan in the White House and Margaret Thatcher in 10 Downing Street, a new Cold War was underway. Reagan began a new arms race: new nuclear weapons on computer guided cruise missiles were deployed in Europe; the Star Wars space weapons programme was begun and new Imperial adventures in Central America and the Middle East were given the green light. The 1983 Able Archer nuclear exercise in Europe was sabre-rattling of a very dangerous and aggressive kind. The US seemed determined to show that it was willing to contemplate using its new 'battlefield' nuclear weapons. Reagan's arms expenditure was a gamble. It weakened the US economy. But it was an even bigger strain on the East European and Russian economies which, smaller to begin with, could not compete in this new round of military competition. The Eastern bloc was cracking again.

The free Trade Union Solidarity erupted onto the scene in 1980. Less a strike and more a revolution, it was the greatest of all the East European revolts. This time the revolution was too great and Russia too weak to send in the tanks. Solidarity was driven underground by the Polish military, but it was not utterly crushed as previous East European revolts had been. And the refusal of Russia to intervene in Poland indicated that something fundamental was changing. In 1985 Mikhail Gorbachev became the new leader of Russia and two years later he announced the policy of Perestroika, or 'openness'. Gorbachev intended to reform and modernize the East European system, but others flung wide the door he had only meant to open a crack. In Poland, Solidarity reemerged and could not be suppressed a second time. With the threat of military intervention from Russia removed, Hungary and Czechoslovakia also began to dismantle the old system. It was still a trickle of reform, mostly choreographed by the old elites, but in 1989 the trickle became a torrent as masses of ordinary people took the streets and cast the old system aside. Finally, that enduring symbol of the Cold War, the Berlin Wall, was pulled down in 1989.

The Cold War was a superpower stalemate. Russia and the US, and their respective allies, killed millions and spent billions trying to wrestle one another into submission. The myths and lies which supported the War on both sides are now easier to see for what they were. But

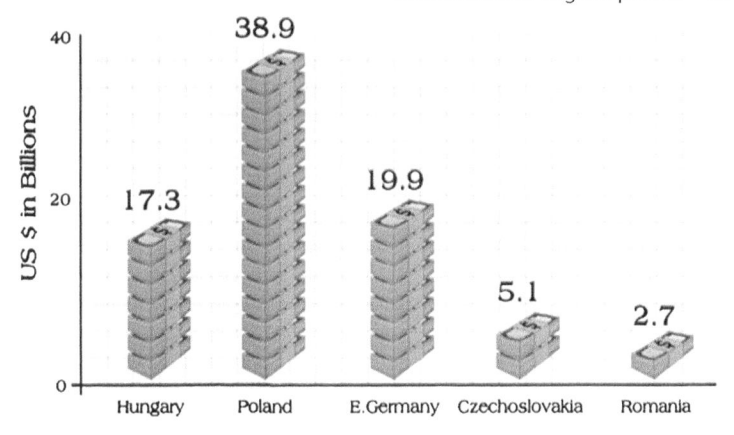

FIGURE 1.19 Gross external debt of the Eastern bloc, 1988

the Cold War has left a bitter legacy. Huge nuclear stockpiles remain, able to obliterate humanity in a few minutes. The US was weakened economically at the end of the Cold War, but militarily it seems more willing than ever to try and order the world according to the needs of corporate business. In this New World Order, as US President George Bush senior called it, we should remember that the Cold War was finally ended by the mass mobilization of ordinary people. In our dangerous times they may need to mobilize again.

Timeline: the Cold War

1945: Yalta and Potsdam Conferences
1947: Truman Doctrine; Marshall Plan
1948: Berlin Airlift
1949: NATO treaty signed; Mao comes to power
1950: Korean War
1953: Berlin Uprising
1956: Khrushchev's secret speech; Hungarian Revolution; Suez Crisis
1955: Bandung Conference
1957: Sputnik and the space race
1959–1975: Vietnam War
1962: Cuban Missile Crisis

1968: Prague Spring; Tet Offensive; France in revolt
1972: Nixon in China; Strategic Arms Limitation Treaty I
1980: Reagan elected US President
1980–1981: Solidarity Revolt in Poland
1985: Gorbachev becomes General Secretary of the CPSU

The rise of China

China is one of the oldest civilizations on earth. Yet, for much of its history, its ruling dynasties came and went without the West paying much attention. Today it is different. If China's phenomenal economic expansion continues it will become the largest economy in the world by the mid-twenty-first century. And with economic power comes military might. China is a nuclear power and it has developed a space programme. It recently shot down a satellite in Earth's orbit. Here we examine how China rose from a nineteenth-century empire overrun by Western Colonial powers to the fastest growing economy on the globe.

China is a massive country, but in the nineteenth century it was a feeble giant. The industrializing powers of the West, foremost among them Britain, used their economic and military superiority to run rough-shod over the Chinese Emperor and his people. Nothing illustrates this

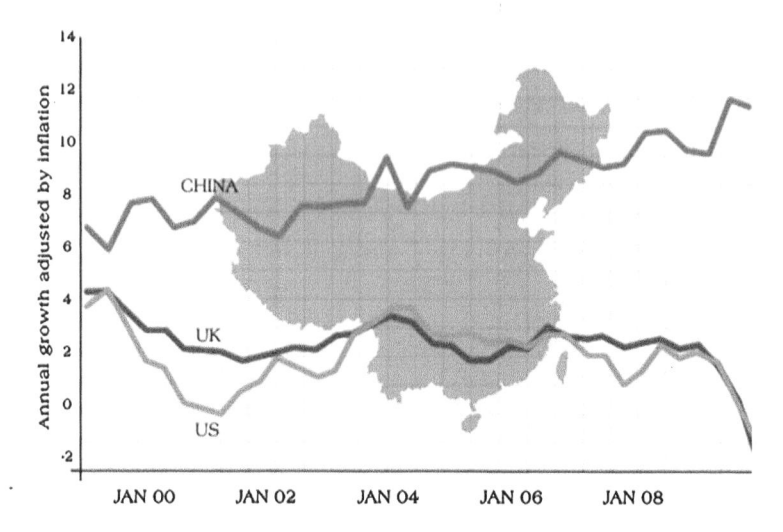

FIGURE 1.20 Annual growth since 2000 in China, the US and the UK
Source: Bureau of Economic Analysis.

situation more clearly than the series of Opium Wars fought by Britain in China in the nineteenth century. The British had been importing opium from India to China since the end of the eighteenth century and the trade became massively profitable in the nineteenth century. Opium was measured in chests and each chest equalled 140lbs. In the 1760s, the trade was 1,000 chests imported per year; these were smuggled into China because the importation of opium was outlawed by the Chinese. In 1800, the trade rose to 4,000 chests. In 1824, the figure was 12,000 chests. In 1830, that rose to 19,000 chests. In 1835, some 40,000 chests, or 2,500 tons of opium, were being taken to China. In the 1860s, the trade rose again to 60,000 chests and then it rose again to 100,000 chests in the 1880s. The Chinese resisted this trade and struggled to outlaw the importation of opium. In response, the British fought a series of wars to force opium into China and eventually succeeded in so humiliating the Chinese Government that they agreed to legalize the trade. The British massacred and plundered their way through the First Opium War of 1839–1842, taking Hong Kong as a prize. The British Foreign Secretary Lord Palmerston declared that the War 'would form an epoch in the progress of the civilization of the human races'. But one British Officer in China more accurately summed up this war for drugs when he said: 'the poor Chinese had two choices . . . [either] . . . submit to be poisoned, or be massacred by their thousands for supporting their own laws in their own land.' The Chinese did resist. The Taiping Rebellion, hailed by Karl Marx as 'the Chinese Revolution', began in the early 1850s and was only finally crushed in the Second Opium War of 1856–1860. In a manoeuvre that must rank high in the annals of British treachery, the British Army fought both against the Chinese Emperor and with the Emperor's Army against the Taiping Rebels!

In the next major revolt, the Boxer Rebellion of 1900–1901, the Rebels fought both against the Emperor and against the British and other foreign powers. The Boxers, or to give them their proper name the Righteous Fists of Harmony Movement, gained their name from their practice of martial arts. The Emperor became so embattled that he relented on his persecution of the Boxers and began to issue his own calls for the foreigners to leave China. Britain joined an eight nation alliance, that included the US, Russia and Japan, to crush the Rebellion. They succeeded and the reprisals were bloody. But the end of both the Empire and the foreign presence was near at hand. The Wuchang Uprising of 1911 began the Chinese Revolution and it ended a year later with the abdication of the Emperor. The Revolution did not result in a stable democratic government. Instead, it set up a weak Provisional Government that presided over a country which remained politically fragmented. The Monarchy was briefly and abortively restored twice and there was a period of military rule. Warlords fought each other. This weak republic was rocked by a huge outburst of revolutionary activity took place again between 1925 and 1927. The Nationalist Kuomintang Movement, led by Chiang Kai-Shek, massacred the Chinese Communist Party preventing the Movement from transforming Chinese society. The struggle between the Communists under Mao and the Nationalists continued after 1927 and included the legendary 'Long March' of 1934–1936. This was actually a series of marches by different groups in which Communist Forces escaped encircling Kuomintang Armies by marching into the north and west of the country. The most famous of the marches was led by Mao Zedong and it marked the start of his ascent to power.

China's Second World War began early. In the 1930s there was a conflict with Japan, whose forces captured Shanghai in 1932. In 1937, Nationalists and Communists temporarily suspended their Civil War and combined to resist the invader. However, the conflict with Nationalist Forces reignited with the end of the War, and only ended with the

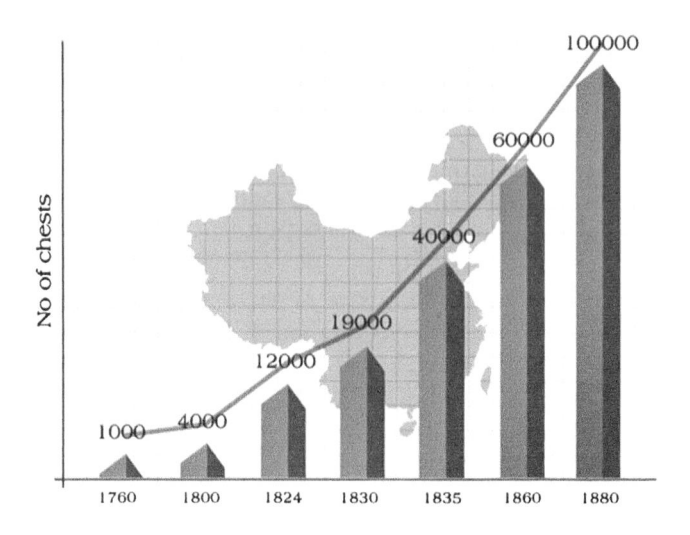

FIGURE 1.21 Opium trade between 1760 and 1880

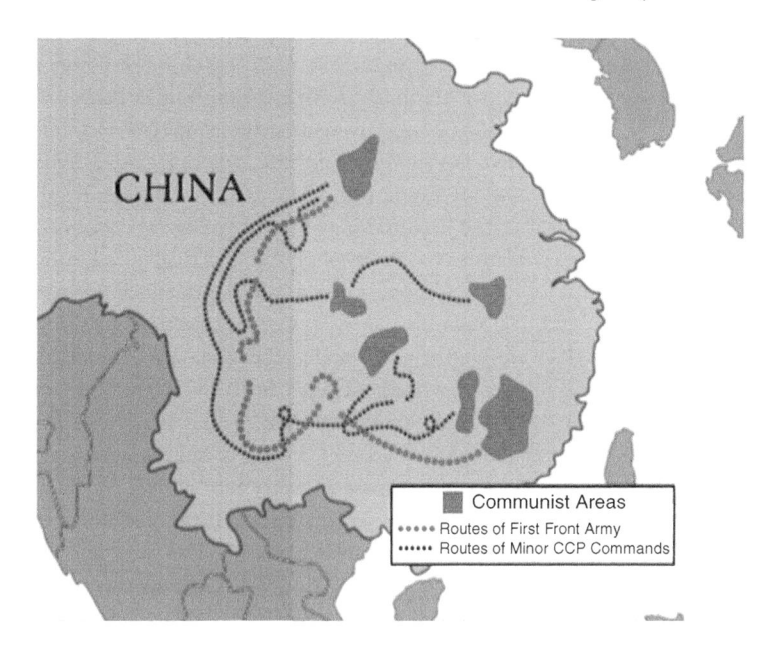

FIGURE 1.22 The Long March, 1934 to 1936

establishment of the People's Republic of China in 1949. Chiang Kai-Shek fled to the island of Taiwan and set up his own republic. This was recognized by the US in preference to the giant Communist State to the East. It remains a flashpoint in international relations to this day. Millions of Chinese lost their lives in the struggle for national independence and in the Civil War. Millions more were to lose their lives as Mao's Communists attempted to create an industrial base for the economy in the midst of a hostile State system and a competitive world market. They did so by cutting China off from the rest of the world market and using the State to try and force through industrial development. This was a strategy that was attempted by many Third World countries in the 1950s and 1960s in an attempt to emulate Stalinist Russia. The Great Leap Forward launched in 1958 meant trying to force through an industrial revolution that had taken decades in the West in a matter of years and it required a furious attack on the peasantry. The strategy was a disaster, a great leap backward. Land went untilled as labour was thrust into industry. Official figures say that 14 million died of starvation; the real figure may be more than twice as high. But while its people were dying in their millions, the State still had the resources to make China a nuclear power. From this period on, the Chinese Communist Party was in turmoil as political factions fought to manage the economy and suppress dissent. The so-called 'Cultural Revolution', which began in 1966 and ran for a decade, was an attempt by Mao to keep control of this process. The upheaval of the Cultural Revolution paralyzed economic activity and produced chaos in the political system. Political persecution became as endemic as it was unpredictable. Only the death of Mao in 1976 brought an end to instability.

The Chinese had suffered greatly under the State-led model on industrialization. But after the death of Mao little about the level of political repression by the State was diminished. There was, however, a change in economic policy. Instead of a State-led isolationist model of economic development, the Chinese Government adopted a strategy of using all of its formidable power to open up the economy to the market. First, an internal market was licensed. This was initially most effective in the countryside. Then, the State opened the economy, including industry, to the forces of the global market. However, the State was still politically repressive and it still intervened heavily in the economy. But now its economic intervention was aimed at competing on the world market, attracting foreign investment and, therefore, being more accommodating to the West. This policy had begun when Mao was alive with Richard Nixon's historic visit to China in 1972. But it became much more pronounced as China instituted its 'open door' policy to the West in the 1980s. This 'Coca Cola Communism' has produced a huge level of industrial development in China. But industrial revolutions also cause huge levels of exploitation and social dislocation. The Tiananmen Square Revolt in 1989 was a product of these tensions; and it showed just how the Chinese State intended to deal with demands for democratic freedom. It was clear from this moment on that the introduction of so-called 'free-market Capitalism' did not mean that there would be any greater political freedom in China.

The long-suffering Chinese people are now carrying the burdens of this industrial development. Their displacement in the countryside as millions head for the towns, displacement in the towns as whole neighbourhoods are bulldozed to make way for factories, pollution and mass-unemployment and poorly paid labour. As always in rapidly-industrializing societies, ethnic and Nationalist conflicts are becoming

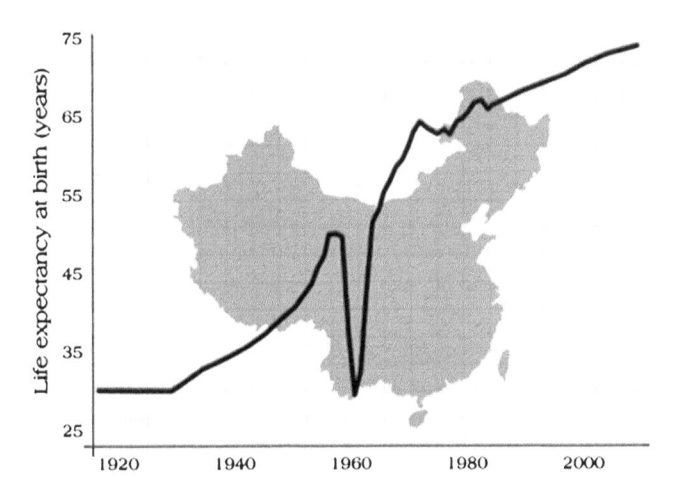

FIGURE 1.23 Life expectancy in China, 1920 to 2000

inflamed. But on the back of this suffering, China's political elite are creating a great power. China's trade is now central to the US economy and China is now the world's third biggest exporter. Since the 1991 Gulf War, China's military spending has increased by between 275 percent and 560 percent, depending on which estimate you accept. China is also becoming more assertive in its international strategy and military policy. In 2001, leaders of China, Russia and four other Central Asian States launched the Shanghai Cooperation Organization. It is a direct challenge to the expansion of NATO into Eastern Europe. In 2005, China and Russia also held their first joint military exercises. China also has an active space programme and in 2003 it launched its first manned spacecraft. Reports also claim that in 2007 China carried out a missile test in space, shooting down an old weather satellite. The US, Japan and others have expressed concern at China's military build-up. And although China cannot yet challenge the US as a global power, it does aim to assert its power in the East. And that alone would upset US relations with Japan, both North and South Korea and the developing economies of South East Asia.

China's rise to independent nationhood involved more than a century of bloody and destructive conflict in which millions of Chinese died in war and from starvation. Millions more lost their lives as brutal rulers struggled to turn an independent State into an industrialized economy. If we compare industrial development in China and Britain from 1800 to the present day, we see that, as Britain went through its industrial revolution in the 1800s, it became richer and its citizens lived longer. But, in the same period, China actually went backwards. Life expectancy remained lower than 35 years and wealth per-head actually fell. This is the era in which the Opium Wars were fought. China only began to advance once it attained independence and got rid of the Emperor. But then the Great Leap Forward and the Cultural Revolution thrust the economy and life expectancy back in a way that has few parallels in economic history. The rapid decline in Britain during the First World War is small in comparison. But, since the 1970s, China's economy has raced forward and is now rapidly catching up with those in the West. Yet, in all these turbulent decades, the mass of Chinese have only ever known democracy in brief moments of revolutionary upheaval. The emergence of China as a world power will not end this history of struggle. In fact, every industrial revolution always brings with it greater social tensions as agricultural and urban workers try to defend themselves against those who wish to strengthen the State and the private owners of capital at their expense. This resistance is taking place today in China and it is intimately connected with the struggle for democracy just as it was in Britain during the Industrial Revolution of the nineteenth century. It will be these developments which also shape how the rise of China affects military competition between China and the West.

Timeline: the rise of China

1839–1842: First Opium War
1856–1860: Second Opium War
1900–1901: Boxer Rebellion
1912: China becomes a republic
1925–1927: Chinese Revolution
1937–1945: China–Japan War
1949: Mao comes to power
1958–1961: Great Leap Forward
1966–1976: Cultural Revolution
1976: death of Mao; introduction of free-market policies
1986–1990: 'open door' policy to the West
1989: Tiananmen Square Uprising

1998: the Asian financial crisis; thousands of State-owned enterprises are restructured
2001: leaders of China, Russia and four Central Asian States launch the Shanghai Cooperation Organization
2003: launch of China's first manned spacecraft
2005: China and Russia hold their first joint military exercises
2007: reports say China has carried out a missile test in space, shooting down an old weather satellite
2008: the Government announces a £370 billion economic stimulus package
2009: Russia and China sign $25 billion deal to supply China with oil for next 20 years

Obama and US power

When Barack Obama was elected President of the US there were more hopes resting on his shoulders than on those of any American President since John F. Kennedy was elected in 1960. He was the first black man to become President in a country founded on slavery and still scarred by systemic racism. He was opposed to the Iraq War and had promised in his election campaign to end the US occupation of Iraq. But now the question being asked of Obama's Presidency is, 'why didn't he deliver?' The answer lies in the history of America as the world's major power.

It was the Second World War that made the US a global superpower. The US military effort was decisive in securing an Allied military victory. But the economic power of the US also expanded during the War. In every other combatant country, War production ate into civilian industrial production, but not in the US. In the US, military production and the civilian economy both expanded during the War. In 1945, US industrial production was double what it had been in the late 1930s. For example, at one point during the War, the massive US industrial engine was launching merchant ships faster than the German U-boats in the North Atlantic could sink them. At the end of the War, US manufacturing accounted for half of world manufacturing. In 1953, US manufacturing exports were five times greater than Germany and 17 times greater than Japan. The US dollar was so powerful it became the international means of economic exchange. International institutions were set up under US leadership to implement the US's economic priorities –

the IMF, the World Bank and the Bretton Woods Agreement. At the end of the War, the European economies, in both the defeated and the victorious nations, were wrecked. But the US economy was so strong that it could launch the Marshall Aid Programme of economic assistance, which aimed to put the European economies back on their feet.

The US was as powerful militarily as it was economically. The North Atlantic Treaty Organization, NATO, grouped the countries of Western Europe together in a military pact whose senior officer was always an American. Other pacts – SEATO in South East Asia and CENTO in the Middle East – followed. In the years since the Second World War, the US has used its military might in dozens of interventions in many areas of the globe. But there were still areas of the globe that the US did not dominate. Russia, Eastern Europe and China were chief among these. They were State-dominated economies and strategic rivals of the US. The Cold War was the expression of this economic and political rivalry. It lasted from the late 1940s to the revolutions in Eastern Europe in 1989. Every conflict that took place in this period – whether in Korea, Cuba, Vietnam, Africa or the Middle East – was seen through the lens of the Cold War. The rival systems vied for allies, and for economic and political advantage in every corner of the globe. And not just the globe; the space race, an extension of the arms race, took the competition between the US and Russia off the face of the planet and into outerspace.

The period from the end of the Second World War to the 1970s was the longest sustained economic expansion in the history of Capitalism. But important changes took place among the major powers during this time. The US bore the greatest costs of the arms race. By contrast, Japan, Germany and other European economies spent less on arms and began to rebuild their economic strength. The US built more tanks, but its rivals built more cars. As the world market recovered from the Second World War, these rival economies began to grow faster than the US economy. US manufacturing fell from 50 percent of the world total at the end of the Second World War to 31 percent in 1980, and now stands at 20 percent. Today, the US is still the world's biggest economy, but its competitors have grown at its expense. Moreover, at the same time as the US was facing increased economic competition, it also faced its most serious military defeat in the post-War era. The US had been committing greater and greater numbers of troops to the war in Vietnam ever since they had replaced the French as the dominant Imperial

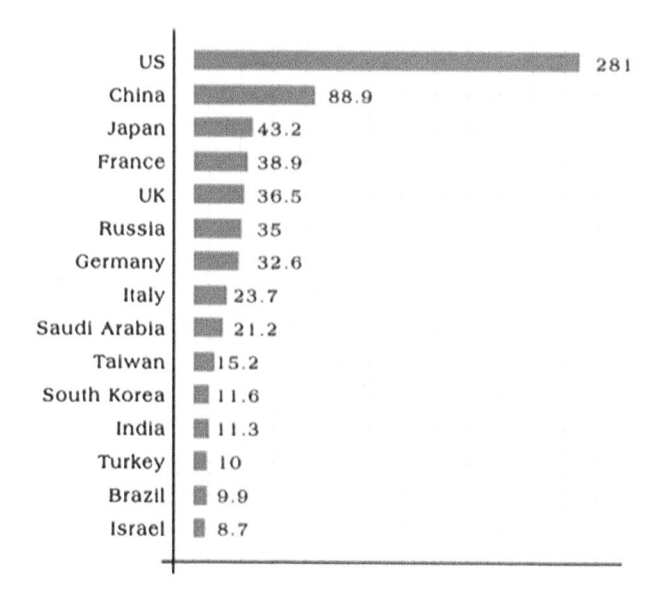

Country	Spending
US	281
China	88.9
Japan	43.2
France	38.9
UK	36.5
Russia	35
Germany	32.6
Italy	23.7
Saudi Arabia	21.2
Taiwan	15.2
South Korea	11.6
India	11.3
Turkey	10
Brazil	9.9
Israel	8.7

FIGURE 1.24 Top 15 nations as ranked by military spending, 1999
Source: truthandpolitics.org.

power in the area in the early 1960s. But just as the long post-War boom was faltering, it became increasingly clear that the US was going to be defeated in Vietnam. The Vietnamese Resistance enjoyed the support of the population and they were not going to stop fighting. The Civil Rights Movement in the US had also developed in to an anti-war movement that was destroying domestic support for the War; and it was becoming an international movement destabilizing politics in countries allied to the US. By the time the last US troops left Vietnam in 1972, the US was still a giant, but a humbled giant, weaker than it had been economically, humiliated militarily and weakened ideologically at home and abroad. Nothing very much improved for the US during the 1970s, as the decade ended with Revolution in Iran. This deprived the US of a key ally in the Middle East and created an Islamic Republic with which the US has still not come to terms.

One thing that did help the US's standing after Vietnam was the end of the State-dominated Communist Regimes in Russia and Eastern Europe. Japan, Germany and other allies might be catching up with the US economically, but its major enemies were not. Russia and the other State-dominated economies had originally grown faster than the US after the Second World War, even though they were smaller to start with. But as the world market from which they were excluded grew in the 1950s and 1960s, and as they had to devote larger and larger sums to the arms race, they began to fall behind the US. By the 1980s, they were indebted and stagnating. Unable to compete militarily and economically in the new arms race launched by Ronald Reagan, they faced increasingly restive populations. In 1989, the damn finally burst and they were swept away in a series of dramatic revolutions. It should have been a moment of triumph for the US, but the victory was ambiguous. US military power is certainly greater today than all the military might of the so-called 'threat States' (Iran, Syria, North Korea, etc.) added together. Indeed, the US is still the most powerful military power on earth; its arms expenditure in 1999 was even greater than that of all the other major nations added together. The stealth bomber, alone, was the most expensive plane in history; each one is worth three times its own weight in gold. But the economic power of the US in the world was lower than at any time since the Second World War. This paradox – great military power yet declining economic power – is driving US foreign policy more than any other single factor, including that of the views of the man who sits in the Oval Office. The end of the Cold War should have ushered in a unique period of peace and prosperity, but the imbalance in US power means that the most powerful nation on earth is now predisposed to use its continuing military might to compensate for its declining economic strength. The US seeks to use its military muscle to achieve what it can no longer afford to buy in the world. The successive conflicts that have followed the end of the Cold War are testimony to this fact.

The Neo-Conservatives Dick Cheney, Condoleezza Rice, Donald Rumsfeld and Paul Wolfowitz who came to dominate George W. Bush's Administration first rose to prominence during the 1990s before Bush was elected President. They embodied the new aggressive post-Cold War stance of the US State. In 1991, the First Gulf War began the business of trying to make Iraq a stable pro-Western, pro-business base for US operations in the Middle East. But although Saddam Hussein's Iraq was beaten, it did not become the ally the US wanted. Indeed, the War actually destabilized relations with Saudi Arabia, another key US ally in the region. In 1999, the US-led NATO Alliance went to war in the Balkans. This was NATO's first 'out of area' conflict since

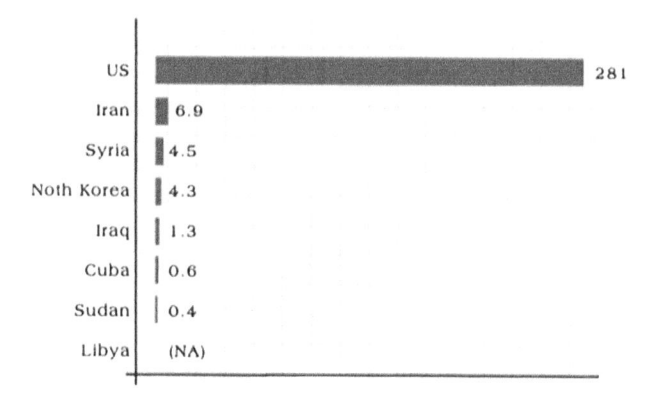

```
        US  ████████████████████████████████████  281
      Iran  █ 6.9
     Syria  █ 4.5
Noth Korea  █ 4.3
      Iraq  | 1.3
      Cuba  | 0.6
     Sudan  | 0.4
     Libya  (NA)
```

FIGURE 1.25 US and 'threat States' ranked by military spending, 1999
Source: truthandpolitics.org.

the Second World War and the first war on European soil since 1945. It began in the very month that NATO enlarged its membership to include three former East European countries, Poland, Hungary and the Czech Republic, starting the process of encircling Russia with Western military bases. In 2001, in the wake of the attack on the World Trade Center in New York, a US-dominated NATO force invaded and still occupies Afghanistan. In 2003 the US and Britain provided the only significant numbers of troops for the invasion and occupation of Iraq. This war policy, signalled by the rise of the Neo-Conservatives during the eight years of George Bush's Presidency, eventually became known as the 'War on Terror'. It has been a failure even for the US foreign policy elite. It has failed to get the US what it wanted in Iraq, and it has weakened the standing of the US internationally.

Barak Obama has been given the task of clearing up the mess that George W. Bush created. Obama may have wanted to end what are seen as the 'excesses' of the Bush era, but he still wants to find a way of maintaining the international power of the US. He wants to end the costly nuclear arms stand-off with Russia, a relic of the Cold War which no longer serves the military needs of the US in this era of 'hot wars'. This is actually an old policy from the Reagan–Gorbachev era that Obama has revived. Neither Russia nor the US believe that there is going to be an intercontinental nuclear war any time soon and so they are both interested in doing a deal. Obama wanted an end to the

FIGURE 1.26 NATO membership in Europe from 1990 to 2009

disaster in Iraq and to reduce the US troop numbers to a still substantial 50,000; low enough, he hoped, to shift the main fighting and killing onto Iraqi forces and get the US out of the immediate spotlight. But the Iraqi Government refused to agree the Status of Forces Agreement that would have sanctioned this and the US forces were obliged to withdraw in 2011. This left behind an Iraqi Administration sections of which were politically sympathetic to Iran. The reverse in Iraq has left the US with a huge problem. Because it has not managed to get a stable base for operations in the Middle East, the aftermath of the War has left Iran as a much-strengthened regional power. This is unacceptable to the US, but after Iraq they are in no state to initiate a direct attack on Iran.

This is why Obama began his Presidency by signalling his willingness to talk to Iran and to halt the threats of military action. But this element of policy has given way to traditional belligerence and an ever-tightening sanctions regime against Iran. There was, however, always a 'Plan B' for dealing with Iran's growing influence in the region. This involved allowing a US proxy in the Middle East to attack what the US sees as an Iranian proxy in the Middle East: the Lebanese Resistance Movement, Hezbollah. In this way, the US hoped to weaken Iran, but the Lebanese

Resistance defeated the Israeli invasion in 2006. This only strengthened Iran, the very opposite of the US's plan. In early 2009, Hamas, also seen as an Iranian ally, withstood the Israeli invasion of Gaza. So, one legacy of the Bush Presidency is that the issues of Iran and Palestine are more closely linked than ever before. Neither problem is likely to be solved without a solution to the other, but no US President has been able to propose a viable solution to the Palestinian issue. Barak Obama does not look as if he is going to break with the traditions of the US foreign policy elite over Palestine. His first appointment as Chief of Staff, Rahm Emmanuel, has served as a member of the Israeli Defence Force and Vice President Joe Biden and Secretary of State Hilary Clinton are both noted for their pro-Israeli stance.

In Afghanistan, there is nothing but continuity between the Bush and Obama Administrations. Indeed, Obama actually oversaw a surge in troop numbers and recent withdrawals have only reduced the number of troops to the same level they were before Obama's surge. This has been coupled by even more hawkish attempts to spread the conflict over the border and into Pakistan, symbolized by the assassination of Osama Bin Laden in 2011. Barak Obama also faces some problems that George Bush did not have to face. China's growing economic and military power had only just started to impose itself on the Bush Administration's agenda, but it will become an increasingly important issue during the Obama Presidency. A major power that emerges as an economic and strategic rival to the US will raise the question, as the reassertion of Russian power has begun to do, of whether we will once again see conflicts between great powers. The post-Cold War conflicts have so far been conflicts between great powers and much smaller states like Afghanistan and Iraq. But with major power rivals to the US emerging, the prospect of a direct conflict between them cannot be ruled out, a prospect already signalled by the Georgia conflict last year.

Obama's Presidency has also been overshadowed by the recession gripping the world economy. The economic crisis is likely to heighten international tensions. It has already raised the problem of protectionism, as each State rushes to protect its own economy at the expense of others. This is, essentially, the explanation behind the successive European bailouts of Ireland, Greece and Portugal. When Iceland's bankrupted financial houses refused to pay back British depositors, the British Government used anti-terror legislation to seize their funds. We can expect more such tensions as the recession and its consequences unfold. For the US, the recession poses an especially big problem. The recession began in the US and it has been badly affected by the downturn. Moreover, the US–British model of 'free-market' deregulated Capitalism is blamed by many for worsening the crisis. Whether or not this is true, it further weakens the US's standing around the globe at a time when it has already been undermined by the Iraq War. The narrowly avoided prospect of the US defaulting on its debt, a sizable proportion of which is owned by China, dramatized this fact in 2011. The deal which avoided this unprecedented default destroyed Obama's domestic spending programme, an outcome forced on him by jubilant Republicans and accepted by demoralized Democrats. Barak Obama had political capital when he came to power. Some of that capital came simply from not being George Bush. The US foreign policy elite needed that capital to try and extract themselves from the disasters of the Bush years, but Obama and the wider elite have now all but drained it dry.

In any case, it has always been true that US foreign policy is not solely determined by the character of the individual in the White House. John F. Kennedy and his successor Lyndon Johnson were the two most liberal Presidents in post-War US politics, but they also presided over the disaster of the Vietnam War. They, like Obama, were subject to the influence of a wider US governing elite that is not divided by Democratic or Republican Party loyalties. This elite has common goals and it is certainly not the case that all the hawks are Republicans and all the doves are Democrats. The leading figures in the Bush Administration were, like their President, closely linked to some of the most powerful corporations in America: Dick Cheney to Haliburton, Condoleezza Rice to Exxon and so on. But so too are key figures in the Obama Government, like Richard Holbrooke – former Vice Chairman of Credit Suisse First Boston and Managing Director of the recession casualty Lehman Brothers and now central to US diplomacy since his service in Vietnam – who oversaw NATO enlargement for Bill Clinton and became envoy to the Balkans. He is now Obama's representative in Afghanistan and Pakistan. The shape of US policy is determined by how this elite sees the long-term strategic needs of the US. These are, in turn, affected by the US's relative economic decline since the height of the Cold War. The specific predication for armed conflict is a result of the way in which this economic weakness has combined with a post-Cold War world in which the US enjoys an overwhelming superiority in arms.

Barack Obama has played these cards because an intractable, recession-wracked world will not do the US's bidding otherwise. The US elite will be content that he has played these cards more carefully than George Bush. This may indeed be a necessity given the failures of the Bush Era. But the forces opposed to the US, and the unpredictability of the world in this new era, have narrowed the options open to Obama and thus produced a policy much more consistent with the Bush Era than many hoped would be the case in the heady days of his election campaign.

Timeline: Obama and US power

1948: Berlin Airlift, Cold War begins
1955: first US military advisors sent to Vietnam
1962: Cuban Missile Crisis
1972: last US troops leave Vietnam
1979: Iranian Revolution
1989: East European Revolutions
1990: Balkan War; NATO enlarged
1991: first Gulf War
2001: invasion of Afghanistan
2003: invasion of Iraq
2008: Barak Obama elected US President

2
EMPIRE AND AFTER

Afghanistan

Imagine a barren land of desert and mountain, its people among the poorest in the world. Imagine feudal lords, kept safe behind the walls of their forts, who have ruled them for centuries. Imagine too that this destitute scrap of land has been soaked in blood as three major powers – Britain, Russia and the US – have fought to control it. The country you are imagining is Afghanistan. Thousands of US and British troops have been sent here to kill and be killed. Why? What is the history of a country the West only knows as a battleground?

The modern Kingdom of Afghanistan was founded in 1747. In that year, the lords, or khans, of the Pashtuns – the largest ethnic group in this multi-ethnic area – elected the adventurer Ahmed Shah as their king. At that time, Afghanistan covered a larger area than it does today. It included the fertile plains of Peshawar and Sindh and the Valley of Kashmir, areas all now in India and Pakistan. These areas provided the surplus on which the new State depended. But a series of dynastic wars tore the Empire apart and these areas declared their independence. In the 1830s the Afghan King, Amir Dost Mohammed, asked the British in India to help retake Peshawar. Nervous that this would cause instability in India, the British refused. So the King turned for help to the Russians to the North. The British panicked at the prospect of growing Russian influence and they invaded Afghanistan for the first time in 1838. They installed a former king in place of Amir Dost Mohammed and began the practice, current to this day, of handing out bags of gold to subdue opposition from the landlords and local leaders. It worked at first, but then the East India Company realized it was paying out more in subsidies than it was gathering in revenue. It cut subsidies to border tribes and local khans. This fuelled resentment towards the large British armies camped in Kabul and Kandahar. And, although the Afghans were divided ethnically and linguistically, they nevertheless shared an Islamic faith. This bound them together against the British. The khans plotted, the border tribes attacked and the mobs in the towns rioted. The Afghan resistance wiped out all but a few of the 20,000 strong British Army during its retreat from Kabul. The British returned briefly to 'teach the Afghans a lesson' – that is to burn, sack, loot and rape – but they could not hold the country. They left and Dost Mohammed retook the throne.

Although the British Army had gone, British money remained. Both Dost Mohammed and his son after him were paid a subsidy by the British. But, by 1878, the British were again fearful of growing Russian influence in Afghanistan. An Ambassador with 300 troops was sent to intervene. They were not immediately attacked because the Afghan Army, unpaid for months, believed that the British would make good their wages. Some of them marched all the way from Herat to present themselves, unarmed, at the British Embassy expecting pay. The British

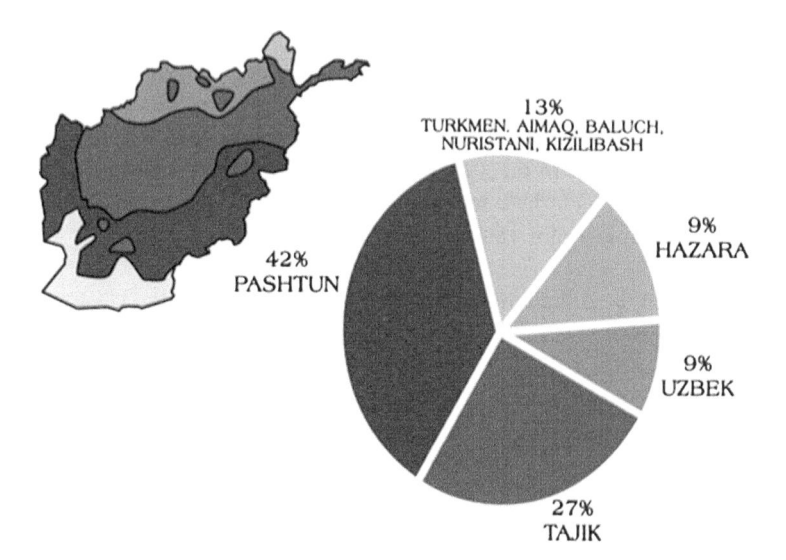

FIGURE 2.1 Make-up of the population of Afghanistan
Source: CIA Word Factbook 2006, UNDP.

refused. The soldiers went back to their barracks and got their guns. They then wiped out the British force. The Second Afghan War had begun. The British invaded with extreme force and brutality, but at a decisive battle near Kandahar they were defeated and left Afghanistan for a second time. They covered their retreat by leaving a new king, Abdur Rahman, on the throne. As before, he received a British subsidy, often amounting to a quarter of the State's annual revenue. Abdur Rahman used some of the money to restore the Presidential Palace that the British had razed to the ground. He also enjoyed the sole right to import new repeater rifles through India, ensuring that he could defeat any internal, musket-armed, opposition. The British loved the 'Iron Amir', as they liked to call him, and he continued to be paid by the British until he died in 1901. His son was also paid until he was murdered in 1919. The next in line to the throne was Abdur Rahman's third son, Amanullah Khan. He led Afghanistan into its third war with the British. Exhausted by the First World War, the British were defeated and ended their subsidy. Afghanistan was independent, but desperately poor after decades in which any hope of economic advance had been crippled by the Monarchy's dependence on the British subsidy. Without the subsidy the Afghan rulers could not pay the army, and as each one reached this crisis they fell to be replaced by another king equally unable to stop himself being toppled for the same reason. Beneath the kings, the landlord class, the khans survived each change of monarch and the age-old relations of expropriation in the countryside endured into the twentieth century. In the 1930s Afghanistan was almost unique, being a country in which there had been almost no significant economic or social development for 150 years.

The Cold War provided a bonanza for the Afghan State, if not for the Afghan people. Aid poured in from both the Russians and the US as the superpowers bid for influence. In the 1950s and 1960s Afghanistan was receiving one of the globe's highest rates of aid per-head of the population. Indeed, aid represented as much as half the country's budget, even higher than the British subsidy in the nineteenth century. And then there was military aid. This sustained an army of 150,000 conscripts with modern tanks and an air force. The planes were Russian-made MIGS, but some of the pilots were trained in Texas. This level of aid and military assistance created a modernized Afghan State machine more powerful than ever before – more powerful, for the first time, than the local khans. Partly, the Government did this by favouring one powerful lord

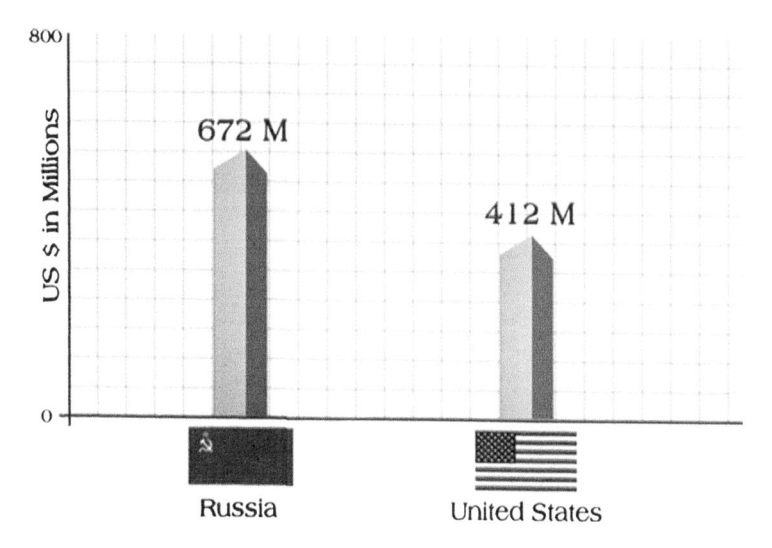

FIGURE 2.2 Russian and US aid to Afghanistan prior to 1971

from among many, raising him above all the other khans. It was a kind of modernized, State-led feudalism. So, although there was little economic progress, some things did change. Education was expanded for a layer of the younger middle classes. These students later joined in the worldwide student revolt of the 1960s, protesting for democracy, against censorship and for women's rights. Some were also looking forward to jobs very different to those of their parents in the growing State sector.

But just as the students were demonstrating, the US was getting into trouble in Vietnam. They cut their subsidy to Afghanistan, leaving the Russians as the largest suppliers of aid. As ever in Afghanistan, power followed the aid money. Those sections of the ruling elite who were pro-Russian began to gain power at the expense of those who were pro-American. King Zahir's cousin and brother-in-law, Mohammed Daoud was the focus of the pro-Russian elements in the elite. In a bloodless coup in 1973, Daoud overthrew his kinsman, but the Russians did not reward Daoud by increasing their aid and, in a pattern now depressingly familiar, he was overthrown in a coup just five years later. Those who came to power in 1978 were from tiny 'Communist' organizations with their roots in the student movement of the 1960s. As such, they were less like tightly disciplined mass Communist Parties and more like circles of like-minded radicals operating in a country where the social and economic conditions could not be more hostile to genuine Communist ideas. They had no social base and no political force that could, for instance, see through the land reform that they attempted in the countryside. Unable to raise a popular movement, the new 'Communist' regime relied on the old police and became increasingly threatened by the old elites. A Civil War began and the Government had to rely on the Russians for help.

Eventually, the Russian's invaded in order to stop their client regime being defeated in the Civil War. The invasion began in December 1979 and by February of the following year an estimated 70,000 Russian troops were in Afghanistan. The invasion instantly became a Cold War crisis as US President Jimmy Carter condemned Russia's actions. And Afghans began to resist the Russian invaders just as they had resisted the British almost exactly 100 years earlier. At first, they fought with captured Russian weapons, but as a directive signed by Carter began to take effect, the ten-year war was increasingly fought on the Afghan side with US arms. Under President Ronald Reagan, a massive arms and funding operation mushroomed in support of Islamic Mujahidden Guerrillas. In the four years between 1981 and 1985, CIA-orchestrated US aid to the Mujahidden rose from $30 million to $280 million a year.

This whole generation of fighters was trained with Saudi Arabian assistance and the expertise of the Pakistani Secret Service, the ISI. This was how the Taliban and Al Qaeda were created by the Western powers. But for the US it was all worthwhile if it meant defeating the Russians. As Jimmy Carter's National Security Advisor, Zbigniew Brzezinski, once put it: 'What is more important in the view of world history? The Taliban or the fall of the Soviet Empire? A few stirred up Muslims or the liberation of Central Europe and the end of the Cold War?' Eventually, the Russians withdrew and the last troops were out of Afghanistan by 1989. But it was the Afghan people who were the real losers. In this small, poor country an estimated 1.5 million people had lost their lives over ten years. But more bloodshed was to follow. Civil War came hard on the heels of Russian withdrawal. Again, Afghanistan was the object of outside intervention. The Saudi's favoured the Wahhabi groups and Pakistan favoured the Sunni groups and sympathetic warlords. Hundreds of thousands more lost their lives. Some 5,000 are said to have perished in the Siege of Jalalabad alone. Eventually, by the mid-1990s, the Taliban formed a government. Far from being made into a pariah by Western Governments, they were wooed by both Pakistan and the US, especially after it became clear that Afghanistan might be an important route for a pipeline carrying oil south from the former Soviet Central Asian Republics. Taliban leaders were to be seen being feted by US oil executives as they struck a deal for a new pipeline, even though Afghanistan was already a base for Al Qaeda. As a *Daily Telegraph* headline announced on 17 December 1997, 'Oil Barons Court Taliban in Texas'.

All this changed on 11 September 2001 when the twin towers of the World Trade Center in New York were attacked. None of the 9/11 bombers were Afghans. And Al Qaeda – the creation of the CIA with its bases long-known of and tolerated by the US – were already well dispersed by the time that the US and its NATO allies invaded Afghanistan later that year. Both indirectly and directly, the initial NATO onslaught took 20,000 lives, according to the estimate of *The Guardian*'s Jonathan Steele. The Taliban Government soon fell to be replaced with a government presided over by Ahmed Karzai. It included warlord figures guilty of atrocities during the Civil War.

General Dostum of the Northern Alliance claimed that his country was free of the Taliban in 2002. It was a premature assertion. The Government was in fact completely dependent on US military and economic support. Nothing so clearly demonstrates this fact than the biographies of the two US Ambassadors to post-invasion Afghanistan. The first, Zalmay Khalilzad, had previously been the Chief Negotiator for the oil giant UNOCAL in the Afghan oil pipeline deal. In 2005 he was moved to Iraq, replacing John Negroponte as the US Ambassador in Baghdad. The second, Ronald Neumann, was, literally, following in the footsteps of his father who had been US Ambassador in Afghanistan over 30 years before. After just over a year in office, Neumann told the *New York Times* that the US could only avoid defeat in Afghanistan by spending 'multiple billions' over 'multiple years'.

After seven years of war, the United Nations Development Report revealed what seven years of war and NATO occupation have done to Afghanistan. Only three countries in the world rank lower on the UN development index. Life expectancy has fallen since 2003 to just 43 years of age. Some 6.6 million Afghans, over a quarter of the population, do not meet their minimum daily food requirements. Another 69 percent have no access to clean water. Infant mortality has risen since 2001 and is one of the highest rates in the world. Neither has there been much political progress. In 2002, Karzai brought back the old king as a ceremonial Head of State, despite his previously favourable attitude toward Hitler and Mussolini right up to 1945. He returned from the Italian Rivera and was enthroned in the restored Presidential Palace, the very same palace that King Abdur Rahman had restored after the British destroyed it in 1878. The first election under the occupation took place in 2005 and was organized with the aid of two US PR firms. In that election, only a third of those eligible to vote actually did so. One thing that has increased is opium production, which rose 1,000 percent in the first year of occupation. President Karzai promised to reduce poppy production by 30 percent in 2005 and to eliminate it by 2011. But by 2007 Afghanistan still accounted for 92 percent of global heroin production. And now the local warlords are building heroin processing factories as well as selling the raw opium crop.

Foreign occupation has, as it always has done in Afghanistan, been met with fierce resistance. In 2003, the Rand Corporation estimated that a successful occupation requires one soldier for every 1,000 civilians. That would mean the occupation of Afghanistan would need 500,000 NATO troops. There was less than one-fifth of that number even when the surge of an extra soldiers ordered by President Obama was at its peak. The Taliban now once more control wide swathes of Afghanistan and many observers believe that the war is unwinnable. It is certainly unwinnable without more widespread killing and many of those who die will be civilians, especially as NATO has to rely on indiscriminate air attacks to compensate for a lack of troops on the ground. Worse still, the war has spread to Pakistan where many resistance bases exist. The US military now refer to the area of operations as 'AfPak', meaning Afghanistan and Pakistan and President Obama has ordered both air and ground attacks on Pakistani territory. So now the world's mightiest nuclear power is launching attacks on Pakistan, another nuclear power.

If the tragedy of Iraq is that it has been cursed by the attentions of the major powers because of what it has under its land, it is the tragedy of Afghanistan to be cursed with the attentions of the major powers because of where its land lies. For the British, it was the buffer State between the Russian Empire and India, the prize of the British Empire. For the Russians and the US in the Cold War, it was once again a border State that was unlucky enough to be caught between two great powers. Now, once more, Afghanistan is at the wrong place at the wrong time. Two of its neighbours are rivals of the US (Iran and China), one is an unstable State allied to the US (Pakistan), whilst others (Uzbekistan, Turkmenistan and Tajikistan) are Soviet successor states where Russian and Western influences rival each other.

In the minds of those who launched the war in Afghanistan, there are clear parallels with the past. Robert Cooper, a key advisor to Tony Blair, wrote at the time of the invasion: 'The opportunities, perhaps even the need for colonization is as great now as it ever was in the nineteenth century'. But such easy certainties are hard to maintain in a country where few things are certain. One former member of the Afghan parliament, Malalai Joya, sees things differently:

> Here there is no democracy, no security, no women's rights. When I speak in Parliament they threaten me... These men who are in power, never have they apologised for their crimes that they committed during the Wars, and now, with the support of the US, they continue their crimes in a different way.

There are two lessons from Afghanistan's past. The first is that ordinary Afghans have never profited from the interference of the great powers. Indeed, the dependence on foreign funds – from British subsidies in the nineteenth century to US aid in the twenty-first century – has made a small number of Afghans rich and kept most Afghans poor. The second is that Afghans have never tolerated the occupation of their country. Occupying powers have lost many lives and much money in Afghanistan, but they have never subdued its people.

Timeline: Afghanistan

1747: modern Kingdom of Afghanistan founded
1838: the first British invasion and defeat
1878: the second British invasion and defeat
1919: Afghan independence
1973: Mohammed Daoud's coup
1979: Russian invasion
1989: Russian withdrawal followed by Civil War
2001: US/NATO invasion
2008: war spreads to Pakistan

The Iranian Revolution

Iran is one of the storm-centres of international politics. Its nuclear programme, its influence in the Middle East, its controversial Government and the hostility directed towards it by the US have made sure of that. The turning-point of modern Iranian history is the revolution that deposed the Shah of Iran just over 30 years ago.

Iran was neutral in the First World War, but that did not stop the combatant powers from conducting heavy fighting in its territory. After the War, Military Commander Reza Khan took power and was crowned Reza Shah Pahlavi in April 1926. His son, Mohammed Reza, became Crown Prince. When the Second World War broke out, the Shah supported Nazi Germany and its allies. In response, Britain and Russia invaded Iran in 1941. The Shah was deposed and his son Mohammed Reza Pahlavi was enthroned in his place. In 1950, following the assassination of his predecessor, Nationalist politician Mohammad Mossadeq became Prime Minister. The following year, the Iranian parliament voted to nationalize the oil industry dominated by the Anglo-Iranian Oil Company, the forerunner of British Petroleum. The British Government was beside itself with rage. It imposed an economic embargo and a blockade upon Iran. The Iranian economy suffered serious damage and a power struggle ensued between Mossadeq and the Shah. In August 1953, the Shah fled Iran, but that was not the end of the matter. Fearful that their strategic and economic interests would suffer a lasting setback, the British and US Governments used their secret services to mount a coup against Mossadeq. The coup was a success and the Shah returned. To this day, the British role in the coup is remembered in Iran and has led to popular Iranian hostility to intervention by the major powers in their country.

The restored Shah embarked on a wholesale programme of land reform, industrialization and modernization. It was the Shah that established Iran's nuclear programme with the blessing of the Western powers. But while the State-led economic investment encouraged foreign investment, it continued to hold down the population with an iron hand. SAVAK, the Shah's secret police, was a brutal force that was internationally condemned for their repeated use of torture. This was combined with an international policy of close alliance with the US. During the Shah's reign, Iran accepted massive arms transfers from the US and became, with Israel, the key ally of the US in the Middle East. 'Iran, because of the great leadership of the Shah, is an island of stability in one of the more troubled areas of the world,' said US President Jimmy Carter on his New Year's Eve State Visit to Iran in 1977. In reality, the combined effect of the Shah's policies was to make the regime deeply unpopular with practically every section of Iranian society. From the small businesses, who suffered because of State-led industrialization, to workers in the factories, from the Left-Wing organizations persecuted by SAVAK to the Islamic clerics unhappy with the Shah's pro-Western stance; everyone seemed to have a good reason to detest the Government.

In November 1977, writers, artists and academics began a series of public poetry readings at Tehran University. The Shah's police attacked them. The following month, Ayatollah Khomeini called for the overthrow of the Shah. Khomeini's opposition to the regime had hardened during his long exile in Iraq, where he had been since 1964. The Shah's loyal press attacked Khomeini and, in response, religious leaders and students mounted demonstrations in the holy city of Qom. Scores of protestors were killed by the police, but the demonstrations, encouraged by Khomeini, continued into 1978. In the summer of 1978, a decisive new force emerged as workers began a strike-wave that swept through the economy. They demanded better pay, better working conditions and better welfare provision. But they also began to make political demands, and as the economic situation worsened, the strikes spread and workers began joining the opposition demonstrations. By September 1978, the lid was ready to blow off Iranian society. The Shah's authoritarian rule led to riots, strikes and mass demonstrations, as *The Washington Post* reported:

> The recent widespread waves of rioting across Iran are the work of little people lashing out against inflation, unequal distribution of wealth and corruption in high places. 'A year ago you wouldn't have found all these people to go rioting', a veteran economic analyst said 'they would all have been working in the construction boom'.

Money left the country at the rate of $50 million a day, much of it being exported by Government Ministers and the Iranian Capitalists. In response, the Shah attempted to impose martial law and persuaded Iraq to expel Khomeini, who was forced to move to France. But nothing could stem the tide of revolution now. The strike-wave continued to grow. On 11 December 1978, two million people protested in Tehran under the slogans 'hang the American puppet', 'Arms for the people' and 'the Shah must go'. Soldiers began to desert; the seemingly all-powerful State machine was falling to bits. The Shah appointed moderate opposition figure Shahpur Bakhtiar as Prime Minister, but it was too little, too late. Even the US was now convinced that the Shah was a liability. On the 16 January 1979, with strikes and demonstrations still shaking the country to its foundations, the Shah left for exile in Egypt. His departure hastened the decomposition of the State. Khomeini returned on 1 February, just as rebel military units joined by previously largely inactive Fedayeen and Mujahidin Guerrillas seized military bases and distributed arms across Tehran. The Shah's appointed Prime Minister fled and Khomeini endorsed new Prime Minster Bazargan.

The peak of the Revolution gave ordinary people the chance to take control of their society. Strike committees began to spread, then they began to link up across workplaces and then they began to co-ordinate their actions. The most general of these committees, the Shoras, began to exercise significant power over workplaces. In the community a similar development was taking place. Komitehs were being formed as bodies that could build and sustain protests, but they also began to regulate the society around them by distributing food, keeping order and adjudicating over local disputes. As the Shah's old State fell to bits, these bodies began to pick up the pieces of power. This was not at all what the new Prime Minister or Khomeini had in mind. A Committee for the Coordination and Investigation of Strikes was established within days of the Shah's departure. It was composed of business leaders and their supporters and within days they had persuaded some 118 workplaces to return to work. The Iranian Left proved completely incapable of responding to this offensive and were consistently caught off-balance by the new regime's radical and anti-Imperialist phraseology. It was this conservative strand in the Revolution, represented by the Bazargan Government and Khomeini, that was to gain the upper-hand during the course of 1979. Soon, the new Government began to establish its own coercive institutions: the Republican Guard and the Basij Militia. The Revolution had represented a riot of democracy. In addition to the workers' Shoras and the local Komitehs, there had been an upsurge of independent activity by the Left, national minorities, students and women's organizations. Now, the forces of the new Government moved to suppress this independent action and 'normalize' the situation. This was easier for Khomeini to achieve than it would have been for any

Empire and after **91**

mainstream pro-business figure, because Khomeini was a symbol of resistance to the Shah. His supporters had been part of the movement that had got rid of the Shah and, as so often the case in revolutionary situations, it took someone from within the revolutionary camp to end the Revolution and prevent its further development. This internal dynamic was closely connected, as modern Iranian history has always been, with relation s between Iran and the major powers.

On 4 November 1979, student radicals took over the US Embassy in Tehran, taking 53 Americans hostage. The following April, the US mounted operation Eagle Claw. This helicopter rescue mission collapsed ignominiously in a desert sandstorm that killed US servicemen and one Iranian. The whole affair was only ended with the signing of the Algiers Accords and the release of the hostage on 20 January 1981, just minutes after Ronald Reagan was sworn in as the new US President. The whole affair was a microcosm of what was to follow; revolutionary rhetoric met with hostility from the US that only served to strengthen the regime in Tehran. The struggle to stabilize the new regime went on throughout 1979 and into 1980. But the final smothering of the revolutionary energy only came with the outbreak of the Iran–Iraq War in September 1980. In Iraq, Saddam Hussein had only just come to power. His aim was to exploit the instability caused by the Revolution by invading Iran's oil rich Khuzestan Province. But, beside weakening its regional rival, Iraq also wanted to use the War to direct Iraqis away from opposition activity. Iran's new leaders also used the War for this purpose. The new regime in Tehran demanded discipline and sacrifice for the War effort. It used the War as an excuse for an even more draconian clampdown on the revolutionary currents opposed to it. And, as the War continued and the Western powers swung their support behind Saddam Hussein, Khomeini could articulate an anti-Imperialist rhetoric to mobilize support for the regime. As such, the Western powers' hostility to the Iranian regime only served to bolster support inside Iran for the Government. The War lasted until 1988 and cost over half a million Iraqi and Iranian lives. It was utterly futile. When the War ended there were no reparations, no change of borders and the same people were in power in Baghdad and Tehran.

Ayatollah Khomeini died in 1989, the year after the Iran–Iraq War ended. The regime's 'revolutionary' zeal abated in the years that followed. Internally, 'economic reform' has worked for the country's elite, but it has left too many Iranians excluded and embittered at what they

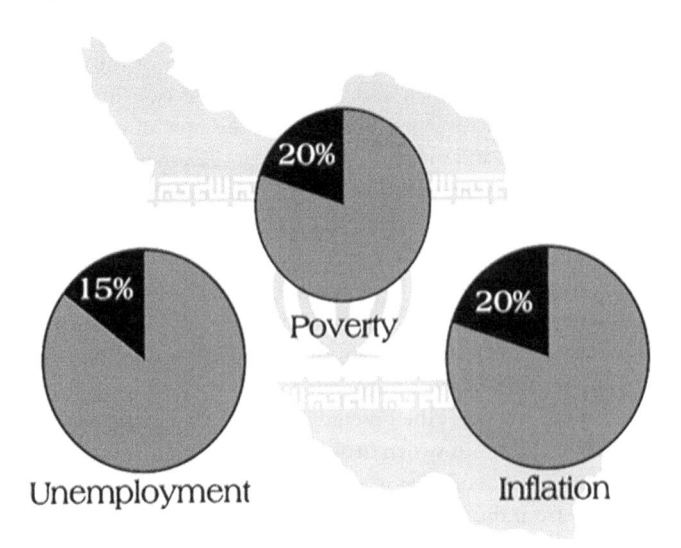

FIGURE 2.3 Iranian society, 2005

feel is an increasingly corrupt regime. These pressures were reflected in the 2005 Iranian election when Mahmoud Ahmadinejad was first elected. He campaigned on a populist platform, pledging to fight poverty and inequality. His message struck a chord with Iran's workers, the poor and the disaffected who were sick of the class divides and corruption in Iranian society. According to Iran's official statistics, in 2005 around 20 percent of the population lives under the poverty line, although private estimates put the number much higher. Official unemployment was around 15 percent – although in reality it was more than double that – and 20 percent inflation made life hard for the poor. Ahmadinejad's populist message was reinforced by his position as a relative outsider. He attacked corruption and talked about 'cutting the hands off the oil mafia'. Conversely, his opponent, Rafsanjani, seemed to be the embodiment of the corruption of the Iranian elite. He owned large parts of the South Korean car company Daewoo in Iran, and was also the sponsor of Iran's early 1990s privatization programme. Ahmadinejad's 'anti-Western' stance also seemed to fit the needs of the international situation in the wake of the US invasion of Iraq.

What the US wanted from the invasion of Iraq was a stable, pro-business, pro-Western base of operation in the Middle East. Partly they wanted this to compensate for the loss of Iran as such a base in 1979. But the occupation turned into a disaster and, rather than weaken Iran by creating Iraq as a Western ally, it accomplished exactly the reverse: it weakened Iraq and strengthened Iran. Now the US is intent on trying to diminish Iranian power. This is the main factor behind the constantly inflamed crisis over Iran's nuclear programme. Bombing Iranian nuclear sites – a tactic favoured by the Israeli Government – is difficult while the US is still bogged down in Afghanistan and Iraq, but it remains an option for the US Administration. By the 2009 election, many Iranians were questioning whether Ahmadinejad was delivering all that they had hoped he would. Whilst he retains a large constituency, his failure to fulfil his 2005 election promises of reducing inequality and tackling corruption, alienated many of his supporters. The Iranian regime's economic and political policies have made it increasingly unstable, as the mass protests following the 2009 election results show. At the same time, the hostility shown by the US and the Western powers to Iran means that the regime also finds itself opposed to their interests in the region. Both the Government and the opposition movement still see the 1979 Iranian Revolution as their starting point and there is a continuing struggle in Iran for the true legacy of this event. Ordinary Iranians must feel themselves doubly cursed: burdened with a government many of them do not want and threatened by US and Israeli Governments that they detest even more. Perhaps, some are now reflecting on the experience of the 1979 Revolution and wondering if it is possible to recreate a mass-movement that wants economic and political power in Iran and which is also is opposed to Imperialist intervention in the affairs of their country.

Timeline: the Iranian Revolution

1914–1918: neutral Iran sees heavy fighting during First
    World War
1921: military commander Reza Khan seizes power
1926: Reza Khan crowned Reza Shah Pahlavi
1941: Anglo-Russian occupation of Iran
1950: Mohammad Mossadeq becomes Prime Minister
1951: parliament votes to nationalize the oil industry; Britain imposes
    an embargo

1953: Shah flees the country; Mossadeq is overthrown in a coup; Shah returns
1963: the Shah launches the 'white Revolution'
1978: the Revolution begins
1979: Shah forced into exile
1979 (February): Ayatollah Khomeini returns from exile
1979 (November): militants take 52 Americans hostage in US Embassy in Tehran
1980: start of Iran–Iraq War
1981: American hostages are released
1988: Iran–Iraq War ends
1989: Ayatollah Khomeini dies; Rafsanjani is sworn in as the new President
2005: Mahmoud Ahmadinejad wins Presidential Elections
2009: Mahmoud Ahmadinejad is declared to have won Presidential Election; wave of protests follow

Palestine

In every decade of the last 100 years blood has been spilt on one tiny pocket of land in the Middle East: Palestine. Ottoman Turks, British, French, Arabs and Jews have lost their lives here; towns and villages have changed hands, been destroyed, rebuilt and destroyed again; guns and bombs from armaments factories in countries thousands of miles away have been used here; the atom has been split here; the only nuclear weapons in the Middle East are here; the President of Egypt, the Prime Minister of Israel and leaders of the Palestine Liberation Organization and of Hamas have been assassinated because of the events that took place here. Why?

The story begins with the great industrial powers locked in the 'Great War' of 1914 to 1918. Millions died in the trenches in Europe, but the consequences of the War were felt around the globe. The old, semi-feudal Ottoman Empire, already shaken by Nationalist Revolution in 1908, was, disastrously, allied to Germany and fell to pieces. The British and French were out to make the most of this collapse. The British were also out to protect the routes to the British Empire in India. They were willing to promise anything to anyone if they thought would help them win the War. In 1915 Sir Henry McMahon, the British High

Commissioner in Cairo, wanted to encourage an Arab revolt against the Ottoman Empire. He wrote to Sharif Hussein, one of the Arab leaders:

> As for the regions lying within the proposed frontiers, in which Great Britain is free to act without detriment to interests of her ally France, I am authorized to give you the following pledges on behalf of the Government of Great Britain, and to reply as follows to your note: ... Great Britain is prepared to recognize and uphold the independence of the Arabs in all the regions lying within the frontiers proposed by the Sharif of Mecca.

A year later, Lawrence of Arabia in an intelligence note to his British Commanders encouraged them to pursue this course of action, claiming it would be,

> Beneficial to us, because it marches with our immediate aims, the breakup of the Islamic 'bloc' and the defeat and disruption of the Ottoman Empire, and because the States [Sharif Hussein] would set up to succeed the Turks would be ... harmless to ourselves ... The Arabs are even less stable than the Turks. If properly handled they would remain in a state of political mosaic, a tissue of small jealous principalities incapable of cohesion.

Yet, a year after this, Lord Arthur Balfour, the British Foreign Secretary, made a contradictory promise to the Zionists, a small group within the international Jewish community. His Declaration of November 1917 claimed that, 'His Majesty's Government view with favour the establishment in Palestine of a national home for the Jewish people' with the understanding that 'nothing shall be done which may prejudice the civil and religious rights of existing non-Jewish communities in Palestine'. Thus two British promises were made about the same piece of territory: self-determination for the Arabs and a homeland for the Jews. Although, both promises could not be upheld, the Balfour Declaration was still written into the treaties that ended the War.

Nevertheless, treaties are just pieces of paper. Facts on the ground are a different thing. The British occupied Palestine in 1917 and still ran it after 1920 under a Mandate from the League of Nations. Neither the indigenous Arabs nor Jews, who had lived in the area of Palestine side by side for centuries, were granted any political rights. But the

Mandate did insist that the British must safeguard the interests of the Zionist settlers by 'placing the country under such political, administrative and economic conditions as will secure the establishment of a Jewish national home'. Under British rule, Zionist immigration into Palestine subsequently rose to unprecedented levels. In 1930, 4,000 Zionist settlers arrived into Palestine. By 1933, that figure had climbed to 30,000 and, in the peak year of 1935, 60,000 Zionist settlers arrived. Palestinian land was being bought up by the settlers, often from absentee landlords. Social upheaval was occurring in Palestine in a way that had never happened under generations of Ottoman rule.

Many Palestinians resisted. Revolts occurred in 1921, 1922, 1929, and, most notably of all, in the General Strike of 1936. The British struggled to keep control. Neither could they control the Zionists, led by future Israeli leaders David Ben-Gurion, Yitzhak Shamir and Menachem Begin who organized into militia and terrorist gangs like the Haganah, the Irgun and the Stern Gang. The Zionists aimed to drive the British out and take control of Palestine. The First World War gave the Zionist Project its start and the Second World War gave the Project its chance of victory. Britain was among the victors of the Second World War, but in 1945 Britain was an exhausted country no longer able to shoulder the demands of Empire. Labour was elected into power by a landslide victory, reflecting the massive popular reaction against the Empire. Britain began the long-retreat from Empire with India, Burma and Palestine the first to see the British depart. Palestine was in any case ungovernable for the British, a fact forcefully brought home to the Mandate Government when the Zionist Irgun blew up its headquarters at the King David Hotel in Jerusalem in July 1946. Less than two years later, the British were out and the newly formed United Nations were left in charge.

After the War, the UN enforced the partition of Palestine. Under its plan, the Zionists who, up until this point had purchased only six percent of Palestinian land, were granted control of 55 percent of Palestine. Towns, villages, factories and farms that had been Palestinian for generations were handed over to the settlers. The Zionists seized the moment and extended their gains by a campaign of terror against the Palestinian population. Armed militia and terror gangs swept through Palestinian towns and villages, shooting and bombing as they went. Hundreds of thousands of Palestinians were driven from their own homes. As the British left, the Zionists declared their own State: the State of Israel. The

■ Israeli land
▓ Palestinian land

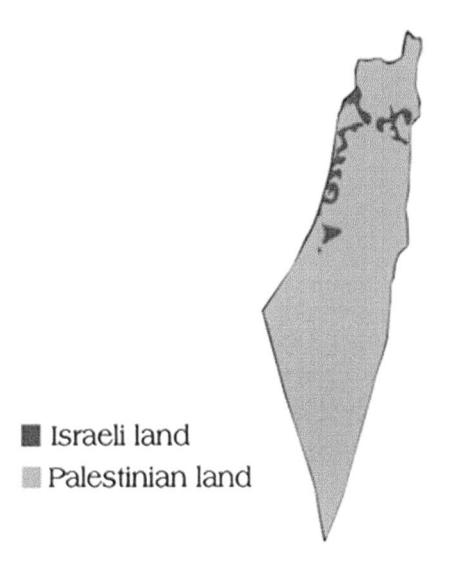

FIGURE 2.4 Palestinian and Israeli land, 1946

■ Israeli land
▓ Palestinian land

FIGURE 2.5 Palestinian and Israeli land, 1947

■ Israeli land
■ Palestinian land

FIGURE 2.6 Palestinian and Israeli land, 1949

Palestinians and their Arab neighbours rejected this unilateral breach of the UN plan. A short war ensued, but the disunited Arabs and the virtually unarmed Palestinians were now no match for the highly militarized settlers. By the end of the conflict in 1949, Israel had taken more land, and hundreds of thousands of Palestinians were exiled to places such as the Egyptian-controlled Gaza strip, to Jordanian-controlled East Jerusalem, to the West Bank, to Jordan, to Syria, to Egypt and to Lebanon. The State of Israel was born out of this terror, war, conquest and dispossession.

How could this ruthless expropriation of an entire people happen? Two things made the founding of the State of Israel possible. One was the support that the Zionists enjoyed from the major powers – first Britain, then the League of Nations acting through Britain, then the UN and, more recently, the US. Without this support the tiny band of Zionists, still a minority within their own community, could not possibly have established a foothold in Palestine. The second factor was the impact of the Holocaust. The industrial extermination of European Jewry by Hitler and the Nazis was only becoming fully known at the time that the Zionists were expropriating the Palestinians. The overwhelming horror of the Holocaust made many Jews more sympathetic to the Zionists, though most still wanted to go to America or Europe rather than to Israel. But the suffering of the Jews during the Holocaust also made non-Jews sympathetic to the Zionists, even if they did not always stop to reflect on whether the Zionists actually represented what most Jews thought. Yet, the truth is that the establishment of the State of Israel deepened the tragedy of the Jewish people. It has allowed the horror of the Holocaust to be used by the Zionists as an excuse for the dispossession of the Palestinians. Thus, one tragedy is used to justify a second; one great crime is used to hide another. The State born out of war in 1948 has been at war in every decade of its existence. In 1956, Israel assisted Britain in its ill-fated attempt to take back the Suez Canal when it was nationalized by Egyptian leader Gamal Abdel Nasser. In 1967, Israel massively expanded its territory after war with Jordan, Syria and Egypt. In 1973, another Arab–Israeli War partially reversed the Arab defeat of 1967. In 1982, Israel invaded and occupied Southern Lebanon, remaining in occupation throughout the 1990s and only withdrawing in 2000. In 2006, Israel invaded Lebanon again, but was forced to withdraw in the face of Lebanese resistance.

This remarkably conflict-ridden State is actually very small. In fact, Israel has a population slightly smaller than London. How does it survive? The truth is that it cannot survive simply from its own economic and military resources and it is wholly dependent on the aid that it receives from Western powers, especially the US. Consider the facts: Israel is the biggest recipient of US military aid in the world; it is the biggest recipient of US civilian aid in the world, receiving over half of the US aid budget whilst having only one-thousandth of the world's population; it is the only country in the world that can use US aid to buy non-US produce; it is the only country in the world that can buy non-US armaments with US military aid; it is the only country in the world that can buy weapons directly from US arms companies without the purchases having to be first vetted by the US Department of Defense; it, not Iran, is the only nuclear power in the Middle East; and it has broken more UN resolutions than any other country in the region. But what does the US get for its money and patronage? It does not do it simply to assist Israel in its conflict with the Palestinians. Nor does it do it because the economic resources of Palestine – the oranges and the olive oil – are economically vital. What the US needs from Israel is a strategic force that can police the whole Middle East, as this whole area is both strategically and economically essential to

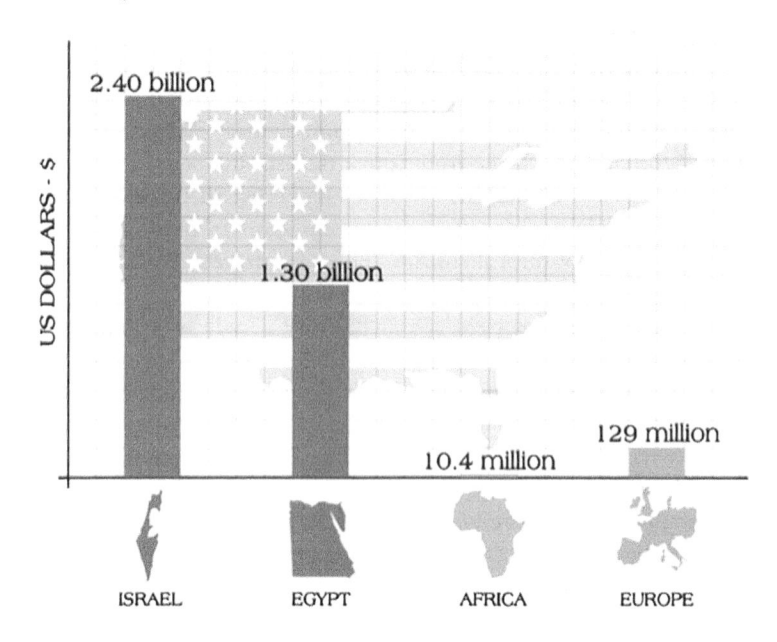

FIGURE 2.7 US military spending to foreign countries, 2008

US interests. But this task cannot be achieved only by supporting Israel alone. To exercise effective influence over the whole Middle East, the US and its allies must both support Israel and neutralize the Arab struggle for self-determination. Thus, although Israel is the biggest recipient of US military aid, Mubarak's Egypt was the second biggest recipient and Jordan the third biggest. In short, in the Imperial architecture of the Middle East, Israel is paid to hold the Arabs down and Egypt and Jordan are paid not to attack Israel.

It is this wider reality that has always given the Palestinian cause great resonance in the Middle East. And it is also why many Arab rulers find the Palestinians who live among them to be a disquieting presence, so disquieting that they have on occasion attacked the Palestinians themselves. This is what happened during the 'Black September' of 1970 when the Jordanian Army attacked the Palestinians. By contrast, when President Anwar Sadat of Egypt came to a separate peace with Israel in 1981 he was assassinated by a Military Officer who shouted 'death to the Pharaoh' as he shot Sadat during a military parade in Cairo. The same policy was being pursued by Egypt's President Hosni Mubarak when he was overthrown in the revolution of 2011. Only after the fall of Mubarak was the Rafah Crossing between Gaza and Egypt opened, providing a lifeline to the embattled Palestinians trapped in Gaza. The logic of incorporation has served the US well with the Arab Governments and they have now adopted the same approach with the Palestinian leadership themselves, creating a Palestinian Authority. But the Arab Governments are at least in charge of their own State machines and are secure behind their own borders. The Palestinians are not. And so the artificial State of the Palestinian Authority can neither defend the Palestinians from the Israelis nor contain the anger of the Palestinian intifada. This leaves the Palestinians and those who want economic justice and democracy in the Middle East as natural allies. It is why the common struggle for economic equality and democracy tends to draw together the ordinary people of the Middle East even when their rulers do not represent their aspirations. Yet, it is only in the realization of these aspirations that real and lasting peace in the Middle East can be found.

Israel was established as a State through Colonial settlement at a time when the major powers were carving States out of the modern Middle East from the remnants of the Ottoman Empire. As a result, the indigenous people of the area were displaced and dispersed by the settlers. The regime that the Zionist settlers established has been sustained by the support of the major powers, especially the US, ever since. Israel enjoys this unprecedented support because it is the defender of US's strategic interests in the Middle East. And just as the survival of Israel is linked to the wider politics of the Middle East, so too are the hopes and aspirations of the Palestinians. Parallels are often drawn today between the Israeli State and Apartheid South Africa. And it is indeed true that Israel treats the Palestinians as the white supremacists once treated the black population of South Africa. But there is also a vital difference. The mainspring of black liberation was the enormously powerful black working class of South Africa itself. The Palestinians do not have the same weight inside Israel as the black working class had in South Africa. However, the Arab masses of the Middle East together do wield even greater power than did the black masses of South Africa, a fact made visible during the Arab Spring of 2011. It will be this wider conflict – between Israel, the US and its allies on the one side and the Palestinians and the masses of the wider Middle East on the other – that will finally decide whether peace and justice can triumph in Palestine and the Middle East.

Timeline: Palestine

1915: McMahon promises Arab independence; the Arab revolt
1917: Balfour Declaration promises a national homeland to the Zionists
1920: British control Palestine under a League of Nations Mandateez
1920–1945: Zionist settlers battle with Palestinians for control of Palestine
1946: British Mandate crumbles; British prepare to leave
1948: UN plan to partition Palestine; State of Israel declared
1956: Israel fights alongside Britain and France to take back the Suez Canal
1987–1993: first Palestinian Intifada or uprising
2000: the second Intifada begins
2006: election of Hamas in Gaza
2006: Israel invades Lebanon
2009: Israel invades Gaza
2011: the Arab Revolutions

The Vietnam War

No modern Imperial power has suffered a defeat like the defeat that the US suffered in Vietnam. Decades later, US policy, politics and culture remain permanently marked by this struggle between the Vietnamese people and the greatest military power on earth. But why did the US fight a war in a small, poor country in South East Asia? And how did the Vietnamese topple their mighty enemy?

First, it should be noted that the Vietnamese struggle for national independence long pre-dated US involvement in their country. The French had colonized Vietnam and neighbouring Cambodia from 1850. They were still there 90 years later. French Indochina, which also came to include Laos, bred many opposition Nationalist Movements. In Vietnam, the most successful of these was the Viet Minh, which was founded in 1941. Vietnam was occupied by the Japanese during the Second World War and so the Viet Minh were funded by two of Japan's opponents, the US and the Chinese Nationalists. But they also enjoyed

FIGURE 2.8 French Indochina

support from the Vietnamese peasants, who had long been oppressed by a landlord class that took 40 to 60 percent of their output whilst charging interest at rates of 50 to 70 percent.

When the Japanese surrendered at the end of the Second World War there was a power vacuum in Vietnam. On 2 September 1945, Nationalist Leader Ho Chi Minh declared Vietnam to be independent in front of a crowd of 500,000 in Hanoi. But the main victors of the Second World War – Britain, the US and Russia – all agreed that Vietnam should be given back to the French. The French did not have the ships or troops to retake the country themselves, so the British, from the south, and the Nationalist Chinese, from the North, did it for them. As the British landed, they freed from internment and rearmed the French forces. Even more remarkably, they freed enemy Japanese prisoners in a bid to help them retake Vietnam. Ho Chi Minh, under instructions from Russia, tried to negotiate with the French. In January 1946, the Viet Minh won elections across Central and Northern Vietnam. In

March, the French landed in Hanoi and forced the Viet Minh from power. Soon after, the Viet Minh began a Guerrilla War against the French, which quickly spread to Laos and Cambodia. When the Chinese Communists came to power in 1949 they began to send arms to the Vietnamese Resistance. When the Korean War broke out in 1950, many US policy makers began to worry about 'Communist expansionism' in South East Asia. As early as 1954, the US was paying some 80 percent of the costs of the French War effort in Vietnam and was supplying them with 300,000 small arms. The US even considered the use of nuclear weapons against the Vietnamese. But none of it was enough to save the French. In May 1954 the Viet Minh crushed the French in the Battle of Dien Bien Phu. At a peace conference in Geneva, the French negotiated the partition of Vietnam at the 17th Parallel, promising independence for Vietnam, Cambodia and Laos. The following year (1955) the French were gone.

President Diem of the newly created South Vietnam had been a Colonial Administrator under the French. He refused to hold the elections as he was required to do by the Geneva Peace Treaty. The US supported him, with US President Dwight Eisenhower explaining that, '80 percent of the population would have voted for the Communist Ho Chi Minh'. Instead of elections, President Diem organized a referendum overseen by his brother. He supposedly won 98 percent of the vote. In the capital of the South, Saigon, he achieved the remarkable mathematical feat of getting 133 percent of the vote, despite the fact that his US advisors had advised him that '60 to 70 percent' of the vote would be more credible. In October 1955, Diem declared himself the President of the new Republic of Vietnam and began a 'denounce the Communists' campaign. His opponents were called the Viet Cong, which is short for 'Vietnamese Communist'. In 1956 the death penalty was introduced for any activity said to be Communist. The same year, North Vietnam began a Guerrilla War to unify the county. US Military Advisors in Vietnam now numbered 900. The National Front for the Liberation of Vietnam (NLF) was formed in 1960. This organization enjoyed much broader support than its forerunner, the Viet Minh. Only the widespread use of chemical defoliants like the infamous Agent Orange throughout the 1960s disrupted the NLF's link with the peasantry by literally destroying their villages and agriculture and forcing the population into the cities or into refugee camps. The US used defoliants for nine years, spraying 20 percent of all the South's jungles and 36 percent of its mangrove forests. The birth defects caused by Agent Orange continue to this day.

President Diem's regime relied upon the support of a narrow social base. Diem promoted fellow Catholics in a predominantly Buddhist country. More importantly, the levels of inequality and exploitation in the countryside remained as serious as ever under Diem. This did not stop the then US Vice President Lyndon Johnson describing Diem as the 'Winston Churchill of Asia'. Asked why he made this remark, Johnson replied that 'Diem's the only boy we've got out there'. President Kennedy received a more accurate prediction from economist John Kenneth Galbraith, who warned of the 'danger that we will replace the French as a colonial force and bleed to death as the French did'. But before they blamed themselves, the US blamed their South Vietnamese puppet government, just as today they blame President Karzai in Afghanistan. In mid-1963, US Officials began to talk of regime change in Saigon and the CIA was in contact with Army Generals planning to remove Diem. They were assured that such action would not be opposed by the US and there would be no restriction placed on US aid. President Diem and his brother were overthrown and executed in November 1963. President Kennedy had not been told in advance. Nevertheless, the coup leaders were feted at the US Embassy in Saigon.

When, following the assassination of Kennedy, Lyndon Johnson became President he reversed the policy of cautious withdrawal and began an aggressive expansion of the War. Johnson needed an excuse to escalate the conflict. The event which gave him that excuse was the Gulf of Tonkin Incident. The Incident occurred on 2 August 1964 as the *USS Maddox* was out on an intelligence mission along the North Vietnamese coast. It fired on, and damaged, several North Vietnamese torpedo boats that had been shadowing it. Two days later, the US Government claimed that the *USS Turner* and the *USS Maddox* were attacked in the same area. Retaliatory air-strikes were ordered and the US Congress passed the Gulf of Tonkin Resolution, which permitted the President to conduct military operations in South East Asia without declaring war. There was only one problem. The attack on the 4 August never took place; it was a pure invention, as National Security Agency documents declassified in 2005 proved beyond doubt. Yet, in 1965 the US poured more men and weapons into Vietnam. Air bombardments of the North reached a new peak. Curtis LeMay, Chief of Staff of the

US Air Force and a long-time advocate of saturation bombing, wrote of the Vietnamese Communists that his intention was 'to bomb them back into the Stone Age'. 1965 saw the beginning of the three-year-long 'Rolling Thunder' air campaign against North Vietnam in which millions of tons of bombs, missiles and rockets were dropped, mostly on civilians. On the 8 March 1965, 3,500 US Marines were deployed in Vietnam. Most Americans approved. By December, the numbers of US troops had risen to 200,000. US involvement in the War expanded throughout 1966. South Vietnamese Forces were defeated in pitched battles with guerrillas who had previously only used hit and run tactics. US General Westmoreland concluded that US forces would have to take on the battles that their South Vietnamese allies were failing to win. US allies were required to commit troops. Australia, New Zealand, South Korea and others did, but Britain's Labour Government refused. Westmoreland predicted victory by the end of 1967.

However, public support for the War among Americans began to ebb. Draft cards were burnt for the first time as the compulsory military service system met its first opposition. But this did not stop Johnson sending even more troops. By 1967, US troops in Vietnam numbered 389,000. They were accompanied by a vast bureaucratic machine, with 13 different intelligence agencies producing 1,400 pounds of reports every day. No such bureaucracy came with the regular North Vietnamese Army that was sent to assist the Viet Cong guerrillas the same year.

1968 was a year of global rebellion. Russian troops crushed the Prague Spring in Czechoslovakia, the international student revolt was in full swing, riots swept through US cities (most notably at the Democratic Party Convention in Chicago) and opposition to the Vietnam War reached new levels. And in the midst of all this, the puny forces of the North Vietnamese inflicted an almost inconceivable defeat on the US military giant.

Tet is the name for the Lunar New Year in Vietnam. In previous years there had been a ceasefire on this date. In 1968, however, the North Vietnamese and the NLF broke the ceasefire and went on the offensive in at least 36 Southern cities and towns. The so-called Tet Offensive took the US by surprise. In the end, over 100 cities were attacked. General Westmoreland's Headquarters were attacked, as was the US Embassy in Saigon. It was also during fighting in 1968 that the massacre in the village of My Lai took place. Here, US soldiers killed between 300 and 500 villagers, mostly women, children and elderly. Others were tortured and gang-raped. Lieutenant William Calley subsequently stood trial for this atrocity, but no other US Officer was found guilty. Calley served a three year sentence under house arrest.

The Vietnam War also wrecked Lyndon Johnson's Presidency. Domestically, civil rights legislation had made Johnson one of the most liberal Presidents in US post-War history. But the Vietnam War overshadowed it all. Johnson announced an end to the bombing of North Vietnam in October 1968, but it was too little too late. Support for the War in America had been declining before the Tet Offensive to the point where the polls were divided 50:50 for and against the conflict. After Tet, support dropped sharply and continued to fall until 1973 when only a third of Americans supported the War. But in 1968 the anti-war movement had already done enough to force Johnson to announce he would not stand for re-election.

Richard Nixon became President of the US in 1969. Johnson's policy of taking on the fight on behalf of a supposedly incompetent South Vietnamese Army had been destroyed by the Tet Offensive. And the mostly poor, often black and Hispanic, US Army was showing serious signs of strain. Between 1969 and 1972, there were a minimum of 788 confirmed cases of 'fragging' – the use of fragmentation grenades by rank and file US soldiers to try and kill their own officers. Nixon's policy was to throw Johnson's approach into reverse. Now 'Vietnamization' was the order of the day. US troops were to get out of the firing line and let the South Vietnamese Army do the fighting, just as today US politicians and Army Generals talk of the 'Afghanisation' of the war in that country. The Tet Offensive had been a political victory for the Viet Cong and the North, but it had come at a heavy cost in terms of casualties. This gave Nixon the room to reduce troop numbers, though in October 1969 he still sent 18 nuclear armed B-52s to the edge of Russian airspace to convince them of the US's continuing military capacity. But, just as in Afghanistan today, the policy of handing over to the South Vietnamese Army – whose Officer Corps had been chosen more for their political loyalty than their fighting skills – did not work.

In 1970, Nixon began the covert bombing of supposedly neutral Cambodia. The bombing was accompanied by a land invasion. However, US public opinion was now moving sharply against the War, a trend accelerated by the revelation of the My Lai Massacre and the attack on Cambodia that brought renewed anti-war protests in which

FIGURE 2.9 Ho Chi Minh trail

four students from Kent State University were shot dead by the National Guard. But it was not just Cambodia where a secret war had been taking place. The same was true in Laos, as South Vietnamese troops tried to smash up the Ho Chi Minh trail that had functioned as a supply line to the Viet Cong. In 1971, as US troop numbers fell to 160,000, South Vietnamese forces in Laos were roundly defeated and retreated in panic, abandoning vehicles and armour and clinging to the skids of evacuation helicopters. US planes had to bomb the abandoned equipment to prevent it falling into enemy hands. Overall, half of the South Vietnamese Army in Laos were killed or captured. Clearly, the War was unravelling for the US and its allies. North Vietnamese troops swept through the demilitarized zone in Easter 1972, quickly capturing Northern provinces. Only the massive airpower deployed by the US in Operation Linebacker stopped the advance. The last US ground troops were now leaving Vietnam and Nixon demanded that South Vietnamese President Thieu accept a peace deal.

When, in 1973, Secretary of Defence James Schlesinger said he would recommend renewed bombing of North Vietnam if the offensive against the South Congress immediately passed the Case-Church Amendment to make any such action illegal. In 1974, Congress voted to end all US military aid to South Vietnam within two years. In December, North Vietnam attacked areas 60 miles north of Saigon. In 1975, North Vietnam began an offensive in the Central Highlands. They were massively outgunned by their Southern enemies. The South had twice the number of armoured cars and tanks, 1,400 aircraft and a two-to-one superiority in combat troops. Much of the hardware, however, could not be used because of the oil crisis that was then affecting the world economy. As the Northern forces and the Viet Cong gained ground, President Thieu ordered a retreat to stop Southern forces being cut off in the North. The retreat quickly turned to a rout as panic set in and Officers abandoned their soldiers. By April, the so-called 'column of tears' had been all but annihilated. Thieu ordered that a stand must be made at Vietnam's third largest city, Hue. But panic seized Southern forces again. They fired on civilians to make way for their own retreat. Some 100,000 leaderless Southern troops surrendered. By the end of March Hue had fallen.

As April opened, the Northern forces and the Viet Cong were 40 miles from Saigon. President Thieu fled to Taiwan. In late April, 100,000 North Vietnamese troops surrounded 30,000 South Vietnamese troops in Saigon. The Southern Government surrendered. Tanks crashed through the gates of the Presidential Palace and at 11:30am on 30 April 1975 the NLF flag was raised. US Diplomatic Staff were lifted by helicopter from the roof of their own Embassy as it was overrun by Viet Cong. The images stand as reminder of the moment when a superpower was humbled. The cost of the unification and independence of Vietnam was high. At the moment they finally achieved liberation, the Vietnamese had been fighting foreign involvement in their country (by French, Chinese, Japanese, British and Americans) for 116 years. In the War with the US, one-in-ten Vietnamese had been casualties, with nearly a million and a half dead and another three million wounded. By contrast, 60,000 US troops had lost their lives. Yet, the Vietnamese had achieved much more than their own independence. They had shown the world that even the greatest power on earth can be beaten. It is a lesson that is still remembered every time people protest against war or fight against Imperial domination.

Timeline: the Vietnam War

1941: Viet Minh founded
1945: Ho Chi Minh declares Vietnam independent
1954: French defeated at Dien Bien Phu; Vietnam partitioned
1955: partition becomes permanent
1960: NLF formed
1963: President Diem assassinated
1964: Gulf of Tonkin Incident
1965: US bombs North Vietnam; 180,000 US troops enter Vietnam
1966: War intensifies; in US draft cards are burnt
1968: Tet Offensive
1969: US force numbers reach 540,000
1970: US and South Vietnamese troops invade Cambodia
1972: North Vietnam invades South
1974–1975: Fall of Vietnam
1976: unified Vietnam becomes the Socialist Republic of Vietnam

The Iraq War and the Iraq Inquiry

The British Government's Chilcot Inquiry into the Iraq War was not the first inquiry into the War, but it was the most far-reaching. Three previous inquiries had already been held into various aspects of the War, although none were full public inquires. Neither is the Chilcot Inquiry. Its inquiry panel was composed of a Baroness and four Knights. They were ITV Non-Executive Director Baroness Usha Prashar, former British Ambassador to Moscow Sir Roderic Lyne, War Studies Professor at King's College London Sir Lawrence Freedman (a key advisor to Tony Blair who described Barak Obama's plan to give a timetable for the withdrawal of US troops from Iraq as 'catastrophic') and historian Sir Martin Gilbert, who had already expressed the view that one day George Bush and Tony Blair would be seen in the same light as Franklin Roosevelt and Winston Churchill. The Chair of the Inquiry, Sir John Chilcot, has already served on a previous Iraq inquiry, the Butler Inquiry, into the intelligence that led to the Iraq War. The Chilcot Inquiry has no power to punish those in whom it finds fault, even though hundreds of thousands of Iraqis were killed in the War and over 4,000 British and American soldiers have lost their lives. In Britain, the cost of the Iraq and Afghan Wars is £4.5 billion a year. So what are the questions that should be answered by the Inquiry? To answer this we need to know a little of Iraq's history.

The very origin of Iraq as a nation was bound to the decisions of the great powers. Like Palestine, Iraq was a British Protectorate carved out of the defeated Ottoman Empire after the First World War. Unlike Palestine, however, Iraq had a commodity, oil, which attracted the great powers to its borders. In 1920, Iraq was placed under a British Mandate and the following year, 1921, Faisal, the son of the Sharif of Mecca, was crowned Iraq's first king. Seven years later, in 1928, the discoverer of Iraq's oil wealth and the creator of the Turkish Petroleum Company, Calouste Gulbenkian, created an oil cartel with rights to exploit Arab oil. The cartel eventually came to embrace Anglo Persian oil (the forerunner of BP), Shell, Standard Oil of New Jersey (later to be Exxon) and the corporation later known as Mobil. The British Government had also taken a major share in Anglo Persian oil, just at the time when Winston Churchill, as First Lord of the Admiralty, had converted British battleships from coal to oil before the First World War. No one quite knew where Ottoman lands began and ended, so Gulbenkian took a red pencil and drew a line on the map that included Iraq, Saudi Arabia, Turkey, Syria and much else besides. This was called, somewhat unimaginatively, 'The Red Line Agreement'. All this happened before Iraq even became an independent nation in 1932.

In 1958 the Monarchy was overthrown in a military coup led by Brigadier Karim Qasim and Colonel Abdul Salam Arif. Iraq was declared a republic and Qasim became Prime Minister. In 1963, Qasim was ousted in another coup led by the Baath Party. Arif became President. Western firms were restricted in 1961 and oil production was fully nationalized in 1972. Seven years later the then Vice President, Saddam Hussein, succeeded to the Presidency. Perhaps the one question that the Iraq inquiry should ask is this: did any British politician or civil servant really consider Britain's history in Iraq before taking the decision to go to war?

Saddam Hussein's Iraq, brutal dictatorship that it was, was not always an enemy of the West. The critical turning point came during the long and bloody Iran–Iraq War of 1980–1988. Initially, the US and Britain remained in a relative state of detachment for the early period of the War, happy to see two regional powers for which they had little sympathy damage each other. But as the War went on, the West began to worry about Iranian interference with oil tanker traffic and about what

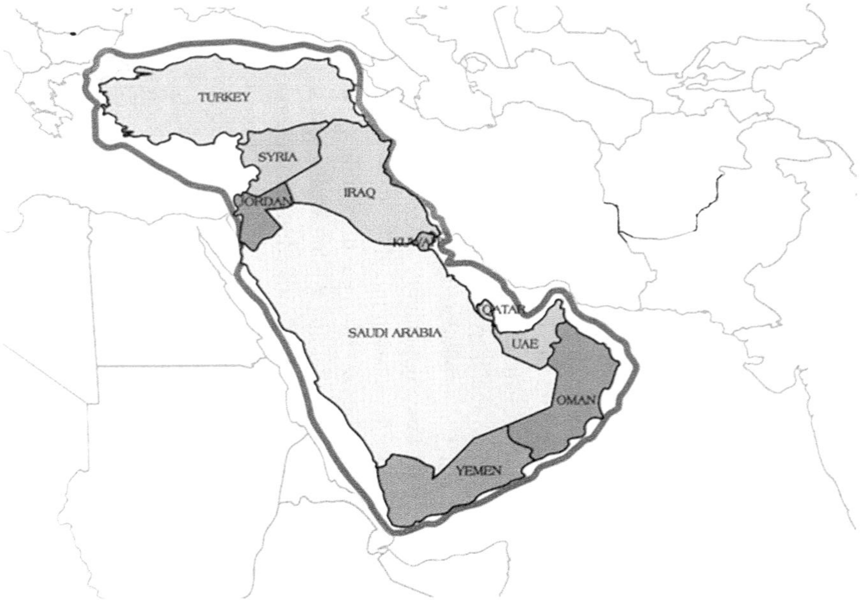

FIGURE 2.10 The 'Red Line Agreement', 1923

it would mean if the Iranian regime born out of the 1979 Revolution became dominant in the area. These concerns were the origin of the policy 'tilt' in favour of Saddam Hussein. From this moment on, the US and its allies armed and financed the Saddam Hussein regime. One incident in this war illustrates the West's attitude towards Iraq at this time and it is important because it later became a key piece of propaganda in mobilizing public opinion behind the invasion of Iraq in 2003. The incident in question is the use of chemical weapons by Saddam Hussein in Halabja in 1988. Some 5,000 were killed in this brutal assault, which was a bloody revenge by Saddam on the Kurds of this area who had favoured invading Iranian forces. But, at the time, the US said virtually nothing about Halabja because Saddam was its ally. In 1988, the year that the Halabja massacre happened, the LexisNexis news database shows the event was mentioned in 188 news stories in the US. That number is from over 1,400 daily newspapers plus magazines and other publications. The average number of mentions per-year in the whole of the 1990s was just 16. But in the invasion of 2003, during February and March alone, Halabja was mentioned more than 200 times in the US media. As the Human Rights Watch remarked:

> By any measure, the American record on Halabja is shameful... The US State Department even instructed its diplomats to say that Iran was partly to blame. The result of this stunning act of sophistry was that the international community failed to muster the will to condemn Iraq.

This transformation from friend to foe happened very quickly for Saddam Hussein. Given his friendly treatment during the Iran–Iraq War, he could have been forgiven for thinking that the US would turn a blind eye to his 1990 invasion of Kuwait. But it was not to be. The US was coming fresh from the ideological triumph handed to it by the fall of the Berlin Wall and it relished the prospect of being the only remaining superpower. Also, it was losing purchase in the vital oil rich Middle East and Iran had passed out of its sphere of influence, with the revolution of 1979 depriving it of an ally only slightly less important than Israel. The attack on Iraq was a way of humbling a regional power and gaining new bases in the region. Globally, it also showed friends and enemies alike who was to be the boss in the post-Cold War world. The conflict was as short as it was brutal. Saddam was expelled from Kuwait and his armed forces broken. Bur, still the US kept Saddam in power by refusing to support revolts in the south and north of Iraq. George Bush Snr. preferred stability under the devil he knew to instability created by forces he did not control and Iraq was kept under 'semi-occupation' after the War. No-fly zones covered much of the country, arms inspectors toured the area and sanctions were imposed that cost a million Iraqis their lives. As Colin Powell, Chief of Staff under George Bush Snr. and Secretary of State under George W. Bush, said, Iraq was no threat to its neighbours at the end of the 1990s. Perhaps the key question, then, for the Iraq inquiry should be, why if Iraq was a broken country as the millennium dawned was a second war and an invasion necessary?

The truth is that the US elite were moving towards an attack on Iraq long before the World Trade Center was attacked in 2001. One member of the Chilcot Inquiry, Sir Roderic Lyne, is uniquely capable of giving evidence on this issue, recalling in an interview in 2006 how during his time as a Downing Street advisor in the period 1993–1996:

> Iraq...was only a small issue in the period 1993–96 when I was in No 10 because he'd had the Gulf War...there were continuing skirmishes around Saddam Hussein, but we had the air exclusion zone and occasionally he tested it out, and occasionally there would be a response; no really big problem.

But Sir Roderick also said that there was pressure from the US for further action:

> What I do remember that is relevant to subsequent history...is that on one or two occasions in this period we had quiet approaches from the American Government to the effect, 'What are we going to do about Saddam? The guy's continuing to be a menace and we need to go back and deal with him...' That was happening even in those days...At the stage that I'm talking about, the Americans did not have a totally convincing answer...our line was: when you have better answers to these questions, come back and talk to us again. In the meantime, we can continue a policy of containment, air exclusion zones and so on. That was essentially what happened.

The US elite did go away and come back with stronger demands for action. In 1998, 18 foreign policy experts wrote to President Bill Clinton encouraging him to attack Iraq and to remove Saddam Hussein; 11 of the authors would soon be members of George W. Bush's first Administration. They included Donald Rumsfeld, Paul Wolfowitz, John Bolton, and the so-called 'Prince of Darkness' Richard Pearle. Their letter stressed that if Saddam were allowed to stay in power 'a significant portion of the world's supply of oil will be put at hazard'. It went on to encourage a US unilateral attack on Iraq because 'we can no longer rely on our partners in the Gulf War coalition'. This last point was, in part, a reference to Saudi Arabia, where US bases had been established before the first war with Iraq and were now unwelcome.

For the US elite, losing Iran in 1979 and losing purchase in Saudi Arabia after the first war with Iraq was too dangerous a situation to allow to continue. Containing Saddam might have been the best option in 1991, but if a stable base for US operations in the Middle East and access to oil were to be secured a decade later it looked as if war was the only way to get it. However, the Neo-Conservatives lacked two things at this time. First, they lacked governmental power; this they got when George W. Bush was elected in 2000. Second, they lacked a motive; 9/11 gave them that. However, to start a war unilaterally requires ordinary people to be convinced that they are threatened in some way. Many millions protested to show that they remained unconvinced and in opinion polls there was always a majority opposed to war with Iraq. The Government launched a propaganda offensive to try and persuade the majority of its citizens that they were wrong. One central argument put forwards by Tony Blair's Government was that Saddam Hussein possessed Weapons of Mass Destruction. A so-called 'dodgy dossier' was produced by the Government to bolster this claim and Tony Blair even declared that such weapons could be ready for use within 45 minutes. Hans Blix and the UN Weapons Inspectors insisted right up until the last moment that there was no definitive proof that Saddam possessed such weapons. Consequently, there was no UN resolution authorizing the use of force, as there had been in the first war with Iraq. It is this fact which underpins the argument that the Iraq War was illegal. The British Attorney General Peter Goldsmith seemed to concur but, late in the day, changed his legal advice to support the pro-war position. Elizabeth Wilmshurst, the Deputy Legal Advisor at the Foreign Office who had written the original advice insisting that the War was illegal, resigned when her boss reversed her decision days before the War was due to begin.

Actually, it was almost a year earlier in April 2002 that Bush and Blair met at the presidential ranch in Crawford Texas. It is probable that this meeting was the decisive meeting where the two leaders decided to go to war with Iraq. Interviewed by ITV, Bush said, 'I made up my mind that Saddam needs to go. The policy of my government is that he goes'. It is in relation to these crucial months and days before the War that any really effective inquiry will have to ask some of its most searching questions. It must insist on seeing all public and private communications between Tony Blair and George Bush's Governments so that we can know the real reasons we were taken to war, it must demand to see all the preparatory material for the 'dodgy dossier' so that we can see how it was constructed and it must publically examine the Government's Press Officers so that we can know how the propaganda campaign was orchestrated. The first piece of advice arguing that the War was illegal must be made public for the first time and Peter (now Baron) Goldsmith must be publically examined so that we can know why he changed his advice. The UN Weapons Inspectors must also be given a full public hearing so that their insistence that there was no final proof that Saddam possessed weapons of mass destruction can be vindicated.

Strangely, the disaster of the Iraq occupation was all foretold in those first jubilant images of Iraqis pulling down Saddam's statue in Baghdad. This much-repeated sequence, transmitted around the globe, contained in essence the whole disaster. At least it did for those with eyes to see. First, it raised the issue of who was liberating who. The soldier working to fix the chain around the neck of Saddam's statue was Private Ed Chin. He used an American flag to cover the statue's head. A ripple of discontent ran through the watching Iraqis before an Iraqi flag replaced the Stars and Stripes. And who and how many were in the square that day? US tanks and marines had sealed off the square before admitting any Iraqis. The whole affair had, the *Boston Globe* reported, 'a self conscious and forced quality'. 'Whenever the cameras pulled back', the *Globe* continued, 'they revealed a relatively small crowd at the statue'. Some estimates put the crowd numbers as low as 200. Certainly they were much fewer than the thousands who had protested nine days earlier against US forces entering the city. A *Los Angeles Times* reporter was a witness to the pulling down of the statue. He records the testimony of an Iraqi who was also in the square:

> A lot of people are angry at America. Look how many people they killed today. Today I saw some people breaking this monument, but there were people – men and women – who stood there and said in Arabic: Screw America. Screw Bush. So it is not such a simple situation.

Perhaps the final questions for the Iraq inquiry, therefore, are these: Why did no politician understand what this anonymous bystander knew six years ago and why have so many lives been lost and so much money been wasted before this was understood?

Timeline: the Iraq War and the Iraq Inquiry

1920: British Mandate over Iraq
1921: first king of Iraq crowned
1928: Red Line Agreement
1932: Iraq becomes independent
1958: Monarchy overthrown by military
1972: oil nationalized
1979: Saddam Hussein becomes President
1980–1988: Iran–Iraq War
1992: Iraq invades Kuwait; first Gulf War
2003: US invasion of Iraq

Ireland

Since the attacks on the World Trade Center in New York on the 11 September 2001, Britain has fought two wars, one in Iraq and one in Afghanistan, in the name of 'combating terrorism'. New legislation has been passed which curtails our civil liberties and the Muslim community has faced unprecedented levels of abuse, harassment and surveillance – all in the name of fighting terrorism. But this is not the first time that there has been terrorism in Britain. The so-called 'Irish troubles' of the 1960s, 70s, 80s and 90s produced terrorist activity on a far greater scale than anything we have witnessed in Britain recently. The 'troubles' were and are deeply rooted in Ireland's past.

118 Empire and after

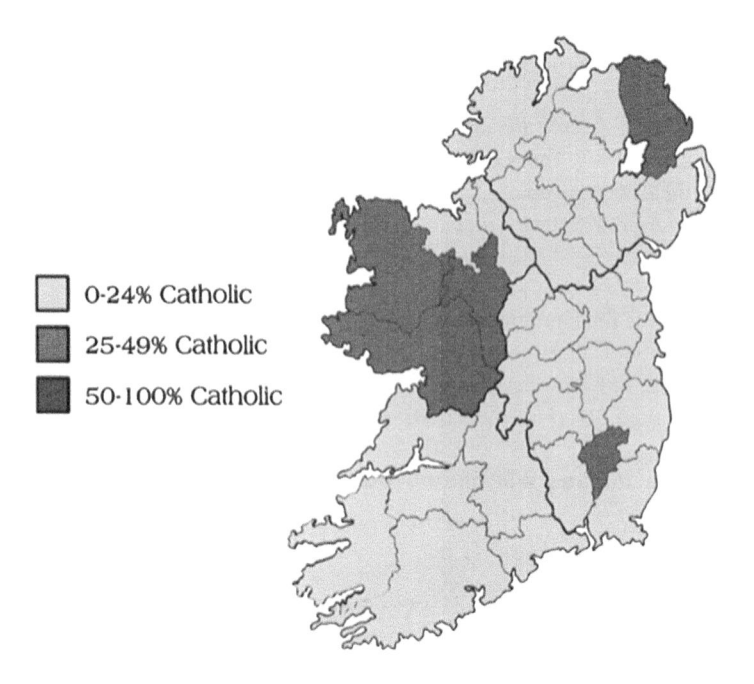

- [ ] 0-24% Catholic
- [ ] 25-49% Catholic
- [ ] 50-100% Catholic

FIGURE 2.11 Land ownership in Ireland, 1703

There is a very long history of British attempts to conquer and subdue the Irish. Oliver Cromwell invaded the island over 350 years ago, an event still celebrated by Unionist Protestants with wall murals in Belfast today. But even before Cromwell the English State had been handing Irish land to English settlers. By 1700 the Irish owned only 15 percent of the land in their own country even though they made up 75 percent of the population. The rest of the land was owned either by absentee landlords who lived in Britain or by a small number of Protestant settlers in this mostly Catholic country. In the 1800s the Nationalist Fenian Movement fought for Home Rule for Ireland. To guarantee her continued rule Britain installed thousands more Protestant settlers, particularly in the nine counties of Ulster in the north. They were given better jobs, houses and political rights than the native Irish. It was a policy of divide and rule. The growth of industry further widened the gap between Protestants and Catholics. Industrial growth was mostly in the Protestant North and the best jobs and the

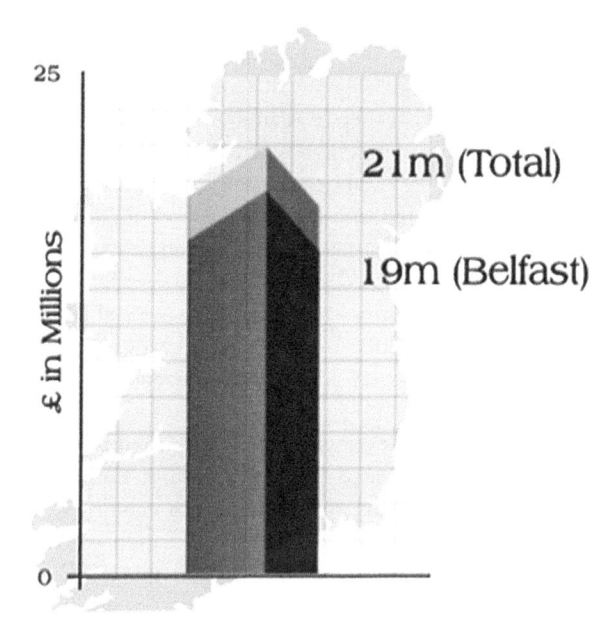

FIGURE 2.12 Ireland's exports, 1907

highest wages went to Protestants. Much of this discrimination was organized through the Orange Order, a Protestant secret society named after William of Orange (the seventeenth-century Protestant English king). Orange Order Marches, designed to intimidate Catholics, still take place to celebrate William of Orange's victory over the Catholic contender for the throne King James at the Battle of Boyne in 1690.

The modern history of Ireland begins with the hard-fought war against the British which ended in the creation of the Irish Republic in 1921. At the start of the twentieth century Britain was finding it impossible to hold down Ireland. The Easter Rising Rebellion took place in 1916 and in the 1918 election Sinn Fein and other Irish Republicans won 79 of the 105 seats. Led by men like Eamon de Valera, Sinn Fein and its armed wing, the Irish Republican Army (IRA), fought to get the British out. They did enough to drive them out of most of Ireland, but the British stayed on in the industrialized North. In 1907 Ireland's total exports were worth nearly £21 million; a staggering £19 million of that came from the northern city of Belfast. So when the British could fight on no longer, they partitioned Ireland, hanging on to the North. However, they did not keep the nine counties of Ulster, even though this was and is often the name given to the State in the North. Actually, they just kept six counties so that there was an inbuilt Protestant 'Loyalist' or 'Unionist' majority. Still, even this was not enough because there were some areas even in the North, like the city of Derry (or Londonderry as Loyalist Protestants preferred to call it), where Catholics were a majority. In Derry the electoral boundaries were rigged so that the majority Catholic population was rammed into two electoral wards electing eight councillors, whilst the minority Protestants were in the three remaining wards returning 12 councillors. Even with this corrupt setup the Irish Free State in the South was only granted full independence from Britain in 1948.

The Northern Ireland Government was dominated by the Unionist Party. Being a part of the United Kingdom, the anti-Catholic laws that had been passed in parliament in the nineteenth century were still in force. The Northern Ireland Civil Rights Association which arose in the late 1960s in response was largely based on the US Civil Rights Movement that fought for equality for black Americans. It wanted to see anti-Catholic measures abolished and equality given to Catholics in Northern Ireland. The first Civil Rights protest march took place in March 1968. The second took place in Derry in October, despite it being banned by the Minister for Home Affairs. The Royal Ulster Constabulary (RUC) were sent to break up the marches. The RUC were a wholly Protestant police force and they used excessive force. Much of this was televised and broadcast worldwide. A third march in January 1969 was broken up by Loyalist thugs who stoned and beat up the marchers. In April, police raids in Catholic areas resulted in the death of one Catholic man, Samuel Devenny.

The attacks on the peaceful Civil Rights Movement enraged Catholics. The British Government made some cosmetic reforms, but even these were unacceptable to the Unionist Protestants, whose emblematic leader was the Reverend Ian Paisley. Catholic demands were no nearer being met as the date of the two main Orange marches approached. Tension between Catholics and Protestants was high. As the Orangemen marched past the Catholic Bogside area of Derry there were clashes in which the RUC intervened. This provoked rioting and the police were stoned and petrol-bombed. The Civil Rights Movement called on Catholics in other cities to take the pressure off Catholics in Bogside by mounting demonstrations. The rioting spread to Belfast

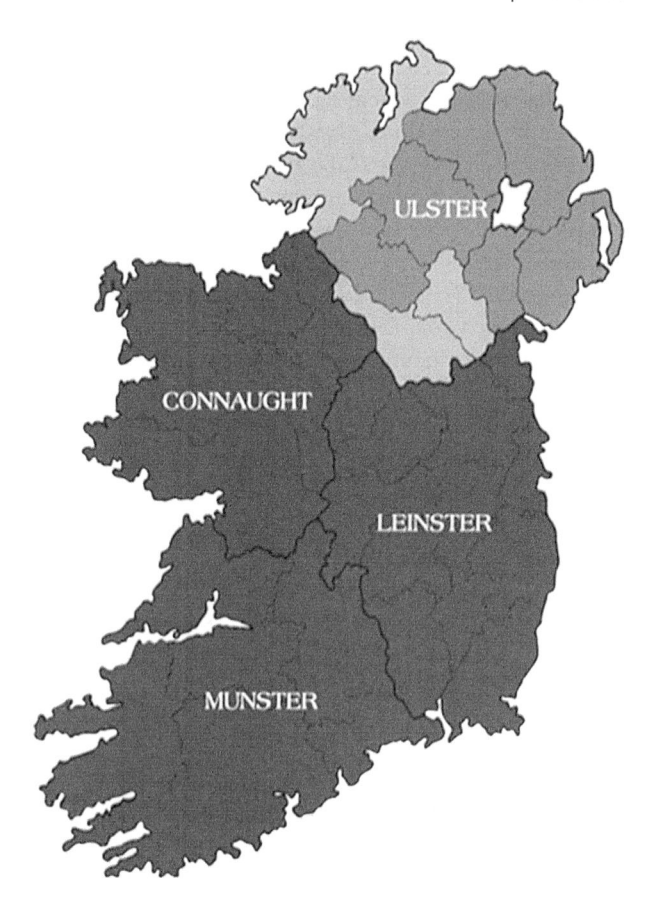

FIGURE 2.13 The North–South divide in Ireland

and the RUC were unable to cope. The Northern Ireland Government then called for British troops to be sent in to put down the riots. The first British troops arrived on the 15 August 1969. In Bogside, barricades were put up and neither the RUC nor British troops were permitted access to the Catholic area. The British troops allowed the 'no go' areas to stand. From within these areas, independent radio stations began broadcasting and newspapers were produced. The IRA had played little role in the Civil Rights Movement; it was mainly composed of old Republican volunteers who remembered the Civil War 50 years before. But as the British Army deployed more men and the violence against Catholics continued, tensions grew within the Official IRA. They began to recruit new, young and angry volunteers who wanted to defend their communities. In the last days of 1969, the militants broke away from the Official IRA and the Provisional IRA was born. The deployment of the British Army and the recreation of the IRA meant that the battle was not just about civil rights in Northern Ireland, but the unification of Ireland as a country independent of Britain.

In July 1970, the Orange parades were about to begin again. The British Army imposed a curfew on the Catholic Lower Falls Road in Belfast and did house-to-house searches, ransacking homes as they went. Up to this point no British troops had been killed by the IRA, but in their assault on the Lower Falls the British Army did shoot dead four innocent civilians. The National Council for Civil Liberties report on the killings concluded that:

> No proof has ever been offered that those killed were engaged in illegal activities of any kind. Their only 'crime' was to come within the sights of a British soldier who shot to kill without any attempt to ascertain the identity of his target...No criminal proceeding or disciplinary action of any kind was taken against the soldiers involved.

A war had begun and the IRA began to launch deadly attacks on British forces. The Civil Rights Movement continued to protest despite a ban being placed on all marches and the IRA continued to recruit. In response, the British Government introduced internment for IRA members in August 1971. Some 350 people were immediately arrested and interned. The following 48 hours saw violence and protests against internment that left 17 dead, including 10 civilians. Throughout the remainder of the year protests against internment continued. The protests included violence, withholding of council rents, strikes and resignations by officials. Even British sources admitted that internment had acted as a recruiting sergeant for the IRA.

A march organized by the Civil Rights Movement against internment and the ban on marches took place in Derry on the 30 January 1972. In order to ensure that the march was peaceful, the IRA had promised to stay away. British soldiers had put up barricades to prevent the marchers entering the city centre. A section of the marchers

Empire and after **123**

and some observers confronted soldiers manning the barricade. British paratroopers opened fire, killing 14 and injuring 13 others. Outrage at the events of 'Bloody Sunday' swept through the Catholic community and there was a further rise in support for the Provisional IRA. The British Government suspended the Government of Northern Ireland in March 1972 and governed the province directly from Westminster. One of their first actions was to order the dismantling of the 'no-go' areas set up in 1969. British rule backed by the British Army brought a change in tactics from the IRA, who launched a new bombing campaign which targeted public areas both in Ireland and on the British mainland. Bombs exploded in Dublin, Monaghan and Woolwich. The October 1974 the Guildford Pub Bombing killed five and injured 44. In November 19 died and 182 were injured in the November Birmingham Pub Bombings. The anti-Irish hysteria that followed the bombings claimed its own victims. In 1975 three men and one woman were convicted of the Guildford Bombing and six Irishmen were convicted of the Birmingham Bombings. It would be decades until they proved their innocence.

After the Birmingham Pub Bombings, the Government introduced the Prevention of Terrorism Act which allowed suspects to be detained without charge for up to seven days. The IRA were banned. It even became an offence to show support for, to wear or display anything showing support for, or to hold a meeting in support of, the IRA. In the first five years the Act was in force, some 4,524 people were detained. However, of these only 49 were charged with an offence under the Act. Another 249 were charged under other legislation. Of the 299 charged, only 208 were actually found guilty of any offence at all; and most of those had nothing to do with terrorism. In addition, another 217 people were deported without ever having been convicted of any crime. Moreover, the Act was not used at all against unionist paramilitary groups like the Ulster Defence Force or the Ulster Volunteer Force. Even the Home Secretary, Roy Jenkins, had to admit that 'these powers are draconian and in combination they are unprecedented in times of peace'. The Prevention of Terrorism Act did not stop the IRA either. In August 1979, Lord Mountbatten, (the Queen's uncle) and three others were killed by a Provisional IRA bomb placed in his boat off the coast of County Sligo. The same day, 18 soldiers were killed in bomb attack at Warrenpoint, County Down. The same year, Airey Neave – Conservative MP and a close associate of Margaret Thatcher – was blown up by a bomb from a

Republican splinter group in his own car on the ramp of the House of Commons car park. In July 1982, two more bombs exploded in London's Hyde Park and Regent's Park, killing a total of eight soldiers. In December 1983 five people were killed and 80 wounded in a bombing at Harrods department store.

Then, in October 1984, a huge blast at the Grand Hotel Brighton during the Conservative Party Conference killed five. Among the injured were the Cabinet Minister Norman Tebbit and his wife. The media campaign against the 'terrorists' seemed to sweep all rational debate before it. Yet a British Army report leaked just after the Tories had come to power should have warned the Government that there was no military victory to be had over the IRA. It said:

> The Provisional IRA is essentially a working class organization based in the ghetto areas of the cities and poorer rural areas... the movement will retain sufficient popular support to maintain secure bases in Republican areas.

But the British Government was deaf to such arguments and continued to treat Republicans as common criminals rather than political activists. The Labour Government reversed the position of the Tory Government of 1970–1974 over IRA members being treated as political prisoners. In 1976 it removed the 'special prisoner status' for those imprisoned for political acts. Many of these prisoners had certainly ended up in prison in a 'special' way through special courts that had no juries and in which the Judge himself decided whether the defendant was guilty or innocent. The prisoners had campaigned for 'political prisoner status' after 1976 by using both the 'blanket protest' – refusing to wear prison clothes and donning a blanket instead – and the 'dirty protest' – where prisoners refused to clean their cells and smeared excrement on the walls. When these had failed prisoners began going on hunger strikes. Bobby Sands was the first hunger striker in 1981. He and nine others died in protest. They were considered martyrs and around 100,000 people attended Bobby Sands' funeral in 1981. Although no concessions were won from the British Government, support for Sinn Fein – the political wing of the IRA led by Gerry Adams and Martin McGuiness – increased considerably.

Eventually, the political elite had to look for solutions other than military repression. Leaders of Britain and Ireland met to discuss the situation. The resulting Anglo-Irish Agreement of 1985 gave Dublin some control over Northern Irish affairs. Unionists were outraged and the agreement was never fully implemented. But Unionist intransigence just meant that the conflict went on longer than it need have done. In November 1989 a blast at the Remembrance Day parade in Enniskillen, County Fermanagh, killed 11 people. In July 1990 Ian Gow, Conservative MP for Eastbourne and former Northern Ireland Minister, was killed by bomb at his Sussex home. In February 1991 three mortar bombs were launched from across Whitehall at Downing Street while the Cabinet was in session. One exploded in the garden, but no-one was injured. In 1993 a bomb hit Saturday shoppers in Warrington, Cheshire, and a month later a bomb in Bishopsgate in the City of London caused £350 million worth of damage. It was now becoming clear that the British did not have the same economic reasons for defending Northern Ireland as they had 30 years before. It was also clear that the Unionists were declining in strength and that the cost of the War was too great to sustain. Even the propaganda war was running against the British. In 1990 the conviction of the Guildford Four was declared unsafe and. And a year later the Birmingham Six walked free from the Old Bailey as their convictions were quashed. It was British justice that was in the dock now.

Following talks between Britain and Ireland, a declaration was issued stating that the people of Northern Ireland should be free to decide their own future and that representatives of various groups should meet to discuss a solution. Sinn Fein was offered a seat provided that IRA violence was ended. As a result, the IRA declared a ceasefire in August 1994. This was followed a month later by a ceasefire declaration from Loyalist groups. But there was to be no quick solution to a deal. In February 1995, a massive bomb at Canary Wharf in East London ended the IRA ceasefire. Two years later talks were revived, but then brokedown again. In 1997 the British Government proposed a resumption of peace talks. Once again Sinn Fein was invited on the condition that a six-week ceasefire had to be observed. In July 1997 the IRA announced the cease fire. After months of discussion a settlement was reached on Good Friday 1998. It was agreed that Ireland should not be one united country without the consent of a majority in Northern Ireland, but that the people of Northern Ireland have the right to call themselves either Irish or British; that all people should have basic human rights, civil rights and equality; that linguistic diversity should be recognized; that paramilitary groups were to be disbanded within two years; and that there would be gradual reduction in the number of security forces deployed in Northern Ireland. A referendum held on 23 May 1998 showed an overwhelming majority of the people of Ireland supported the Good Friday Agreement.

The Irish War was long and bloody. The 'terrorists' of the IRA had bombed with greater ferocity and effectiveness than any protest group had managed before or since on the mainland of Britain. The violence and the killing of leading politicians were on a far greater scale than anything we have seen so far in the War on Terror. But the restriction of civil liberties and the imprisoning of innocent 'terrorist suspects' affected the Irish in Britain much as it does Muslims today. In the end, it was not the brutal revision of civil liberties or the military campaigns of the British Army, MI5 and the police that ended the War. Instead, it was talking to the IRA that paved the way to the uneasy peace that now prevails. Still, policing remains a flashpoint and the peace is fragile. It will not last if the continuing discrimination against the Nationalist community is not removed. Ultimately, peace will not be permanent unless Ireland becomes politically what it once was: a united country.

Timeline: Ireland

1921: the Irish Republic formed
1967: Northern Ireland Civil Rights Association formed
1968–1969: Civil Rights protests
1969: Battle of Bogside
1969 (August): British troops deployed
1971: internment introduced
1972: Bloody Sunday
1974: the Prevention of Terrorism Act
1980s: hunger strikes
1985: Anglo-Irish Agreement
1993: Downing Street Declaration
1998: Good Friday Agreement

A short history of immigration in Britain

Immigration is one of the most contentious and divisive subjects in British politics. Even the very facts on which arguments about immigration are based are hotly contested. Inescapably linked to the debate about immigration is the question of racism in British society. Of course, the truth is that human beings have always travelled and settled and all modern Nation States have been made by people from different places coming together and forming societies. Britain is not an exception to this rule. Indeed, it is a nation of settlers, a nation of migrants. Sometimes these settlers came in peace, sometimes they arrived through war. But throughout Britain's history there have always been new people arriving on its shores. These included the Romans, the Angles, the Saxons and the Vikings. Then, in 1066, the Normans invaded Britain and became our rulers. They laid the foundations of the Britain we live in today and their castles still punctuate the British landscape, now preserved by the 'English Heritage' and cherished by the 'National Trust'.

In 1560, Dutch Protestants fleeing religious persecution at home made their way to Britain. Similarly, in 1685 religious persecution forced 100,000 French Protestant Huguenots to leave for Britain. Huguenot houses – subsequently inhabited by Irish migrants, Jewish settlers and Bangladeshi immigrants – can still be seen off London's Brick Lane. In the 1840s, meanwhile, widespread famine forced thousands of people to leave Ireland, many for America and many for Britain. When they arrived many became, among other things, the navigators, or 'navvies', who built the canals and railways of the Industrial Revolution. More refugees came to Britain from mainland Europe following the failures of the revolutions of 1848. In the 1880s anti-Semitism and oppression in Russia and Eastern Europe drove hundreds of thousands of Jews to seek sanctuary in Britain. Likewise, during the First World War huge numbers of refugees chose to escape mainland Europe and come to Britain. Again, with the outbreak of the Second World War, refugees seeking to escape either Nazi rule or the fighting on the Continent came to Britain. These migrants always had to fight for their place in British society in the face of prejudice, discrimination and violence. Many of the views expressed about them may seem ridiculous today, until we look around us and realize that equally biased, but harder to recognize, prejudices still exist about migrants today.

The modern debate about immigration begins in earnest after the Second World War, which brought massive changes to Britain. Britain had long been an Imperial and Colonial power and at its height ruled over more than 400 million people and covered nearly a quarter of the globe. In the immediate post-War period, the British Empire disappeared. India, the West Indies and a host of other Colonies gained their independence. In order to maintain political and economic links with these former colonies, Britain encouraged them to remain part of the British Commonwealth. These 'New Commonwealth' countries had had their economic development distorted by decade after decade of Colonial rule. Some West Indians, Indians, Pakistanis and other citizens of these countries wished to exercise their rights as British passport holders and travel to Britain, mostly in search of work and a higher standard of living. Some of the first of these immigrants entered Britain aboard the *Empire Windrush*, which arrived at the Tilbury Docks in London on the 22 June 1948 carrying 492 Jamaican passengers. These passengers faced no immigration controls since at that time any citizen of the British Empire could travel freely to any other part of the Empire. Jamaica was only to attain full independence till 1962. At the time, the arrival of the *Windrush* did not excite much interest. A few Labour MPs asked sympathetic questions about whether the immigrants would be assisted in finding jobs and houses. The arrivals were originally housed in Clapham Deep Shelter near the Coldharbour Lane Employment Office in Brixton where many looked for work.

British industry was short of labour as the post-War economic expansion took hold. British employers advertised in the former colonies for workers and the British Government was happy to see this vital resource tapped for the benefit of the economy. A committee reporting to the Cabinet in 1951 considered that any question of immigration controls would be dependent on 'an apparent or concealed colour test' and therefore 'so invidious as to make it impossible of adoption' because the 'adoption of any powers taken to restrict the free entry of British subjects to this country would ... be more or less confined to coloured persons'. However, in the following years voices were raised against immigration. It was possible to see the direction in which events were moving when Conservative MP Cyril Osborne asked this question of the Prime Minister:

> What is Her Majesty's government's policy regarding the ... increase in immigration into this country of coloured people without tests of either health, technical skill or criminal record; in view of the recent increase in unemployment, what action [does] the government proposes to take.

In four short lines Osborne managed to compress many of the prejudices that were to haunt the 'immigration debate' in the coming years. First, Osborne referred only to coloured immigrants; second, he suggested that these migrants were carriers of disease; third, he supposed that these migrants were likely to be unskilled; fourth, he claimed that they were likely to be criminals; fifth, he assumed that they were responsible for unemployment; and finally, he implied that the Government had to restrict immigration to deal with this problem. At the time, Osborne spoke there were very few black or Asian people in Britain and unemployment was at a historically low level. But the construction of the anti-immigrant argument relied on prejudice not fact and it began to have an impact on the political mainstream. In 1955 the Cabinet discussed immigration controls. The meeting was headed by Prime Minister Harold Macmillan and contained the man he had replaced as Tory leader, Winston Churchill. Even Churchill was unhappy at the thought of introducing immigration controls as Macmillan records in his memoirs, 'I remember that Churchill rather maliciously observed that perhaps the cry of "Keep Britain white" might be a good slogan for the election'. As it turned out, there was no further Cabinet discussions of immigration controls before 1958 when the trouble flared up again.

In August and September 1958, there were riots in Nottingham and London. In Nottingham a fight between West Indians and British-born residents turned into two successive Saturday nights of attacks by a large mob on local West Indian people and their property. In the Notting Hill area of London between the 23 August and the 2 September there were a series of attacks on West Indian people and property by mobs chanting 'down with the niggers'. Some 177 people were arrested, a majority of whom were British-born. It might be expected that the response of the press and politicians to these events would be to condemn the racism, but it was not. *The Times* was the first to respond on 27 August with the headline 'Nottingham MPs Urge Curb on Immigration'. The following day the headline read 'Renewed Call for Changes in Immigration Law'. The press and the politicians were moving to redefine the problem. The issue became not of the racism directed against the immigrants, but the immigrants themselves. In this framework, the victims became the authors of their own misfortune. The clamour against immigrants continued to grow and in 1962 the Tory Government withdrew the right of Commonwealth citizens to freely enter the UK. Under the new

Commonwealth Immigration Act it was now only possible to enter the country by getting a Ministry of Labour employment voucher, if you were a dependent of a person already resident in Britain or if you were a student. It was said that the Act would only be temporary, but in reality it was the start of ever more restrictive immigration legislation. It was also said that the Act was not directed specifically at black and Asian people, yet it did not cover the citizens of the Irish Republic, 60,000 to 70,000 of whom were coming into the country every year, as the Home Secretary admitted in the Commons.

However, the Act turned out to be counter-productive even in its own discriminatory terms. Migrants who came to work and who intended to return home after a period of time were now faced with choice of staying for good or being unable to return to Britain once they left. Many decided to settle and bring their dependents to live with them so the number of dependents coming to Britain soon exceeded the number of new immigrants. And, of course, once there were immigration controls there were also people who tried to evade them. So the whole 'illegal immigration' issue now became part of the argument. This then led to further racist and anti-immigration campaigns. When the Act came up for renewal in 1964 a Labour Government was in power. It promptly renewed the Tory legislation, but in order to mitigate the effects of the racist atmosphere generated by the immigration debate, Labour also introduced the 1965 Race Relations Act. Well meant by some in the Labour Party and opportunistically supported by others, the Act did not mark a shift by the Labour Party away from its new commitment to immigration controls.

The Tory Shadow Minister Enoch Powell had been carving out a name for himself as an anti-immigrant rabble rouser long before 1968. But in that year he made a speech in Birmingham that raised the rhetoric of the anti-migrant debate to a wholly new level. Powell painted a picture of mass immigration destroying the foundations of British society. He attacked the Race Relations Act for giving 'the stranger, the disgruntled and the agent provocateur the power to pillory' the indigenous population 'for their private actions'. The classically educated Powell claimed that, 'as I look ahead, I am filled with foreboding. Like the Roman, I seem to see "the River Tiber foaming with much blood"'. Powell predicted that by the year 2000 immigrants would make up 10 percent of the population. In actual fact, statistics show that, at about the time Powell was speaking, 6.5 percent of the population (including

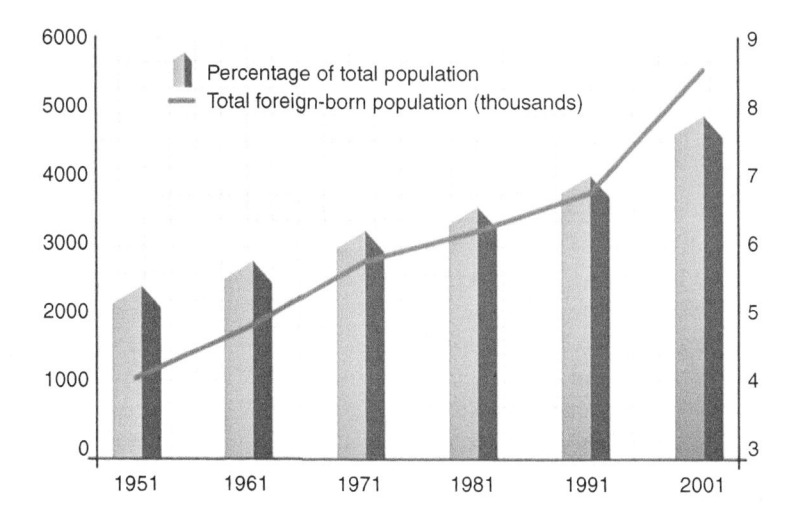

FIGURE 2.14 Immigration in Britain, 1951 to 2001

white people) had been born abroad. By the year 2000 this figure was still significantly below 8 percent. But in 1968 the inaccuracy of Powell's predictions were irrelevant, the effects of the highly publicized speech were immediate. Powell was sacked from the Tory front bench, but the racist tide unleashed by his speech continued unabated. London dockers went on strike in his support and 1,000 of them marched to Westminster from the East End. More dockers, Smithfield meat porters and some local factories also went on strike in the days that followed. There was a counter-protest 1,500 strong that marched to Downing Street under the banner 'Arrest Enoch Powell', but overall it was a shameful episode in working class history.

The Labour Government erected further barriers to migrants by passing the Immigration Appeals Bill a year later. The Tories won the 1970 election and one of their early tasks was to address what were now called 'legitimate fears' about the country 'bursting at the seams' with 'coloured immigrants'. The Government replaced all previous legislation with the Immigration Act of 1971. This new law did away with any special status for Commonwealth citizens and gave the Home Secretary and Immigration Officers wide discretionary powers to deport and refuse entry to migrants. In one respect, however, the Act significantly increased the number of people who could come to Britain. It gave the right of immigration to the future children of the two generations of people who had left Britain to live in Australia, Canada, New Zealand, India and parts of Africa at the end of the War. In other words, it significantly increased the rights of mainly white children born to Britons abroad, whilst further restricting black and Asian immigration. There was no outcry against the millions of people who had just been given the right to come to Britain; they were, after all, white. This legislation set the pattern for all that was to follow. The nine years between the Commonwealth Immigration Act of 1962 and the Immigration Act of 1971 had set the terms of debate about immigration in a fundamentally discriminatory pattern. It was pattern from which the political Right in both its Tory and Fascist forms would benefit and under Margaret Thatcher the British Nationalities Act was passed in 1981. Previously, any person born in Britain (with limited exceptions, such as children of diplomats and enemy aliens) was entitled to British Citizenship. After this Act came into force, however, it was no longer good enough to be born here; it was also necessary to have at least one parent who was a British citizen or who had been granted permanent resident status.

There has been a progressive clampdown on immigration over the last 50 years. Since 1993 there have been five major pieces of legislation

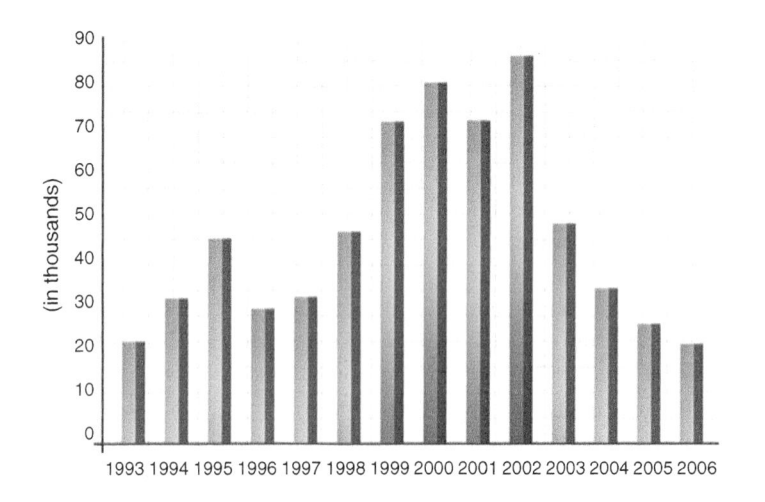

FIGURE 2.15 Asylum applications in Britain, 1993 to 2006

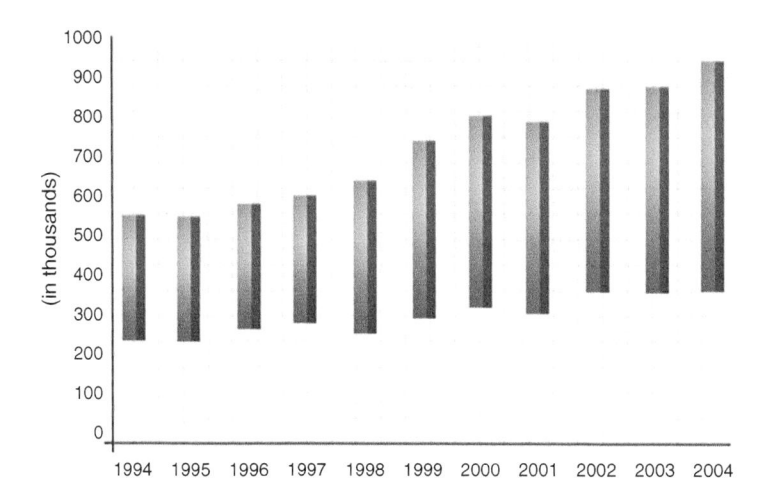

FIGURE 2.16 Migration to Britain, 1994 to 2004

relating to immigration. This has meant that the anti-immigration lobby has had to select new targets. The opening of EU borders in 2004 and the subsequent arrival of migrants from Eastern Europe has given rise to discrimination against white immigrants on a wide scale. But the main focus of the popular antipathy whipped up by the press and the anti-immigrant lobby has been asylum seekers and refugees. With ever-stricter controls imposed upon immigration it is these most vulnerable migrants, often victims of the wars that Britain has fought in Iraq and Afghanistan, who have been singled out. Indeed, asylum applications rose sharply at the time of the Balkan War in 1999 and at the start of the conflicts in Afghanistan and Iraq in 2002 and 2003 respectively.

The decades-long illusion that there is a threat to British society from immigration is one of the most sustained but least factually supported arguments in modern politics. Just look at this graph which shows both people coming into and those leaving the country. The difference between the two – constituting the number of new people – actually living here, hardly justifies the scare-mongering of the anti-immigration lobby. Immigration has not produced the 'rivers of blood' that Enoch Powell predicted. In fact, society has often changed for the better because migrants have arrived in these shores. Most studies show migrants to be better qualified than the native population and to add net wealth to the economy. What threatens our society is a lack of jobs, poverty, poor housing, poor healthcare and poor education. What disfigures the society is not immigration but racism. If a quarter of the time spent discussing immigration in the press and in parliament were spent on these issues we might begin to find our way to a more secure, more democratic and less divided society.

Timeline: a short history of immigration in Britain

1066: Normans invaded Britain
1685: 100,000 Huguenot refugees come to Britain
1840s: Irish immigration
1945: Commonwealth immigration begins
1948: the *Empire Windrush* lands in Britain
1958: 'race riots'
1962: Commonwealth Immigration Act
1968: Enoch Powell and 'Rivers of blood'
1971: the Immigration Act
1981: the British Nationality Act

3
THE RULERS AND THE RULED

Recessions and resistance

The recession that began in 2008 has been described as the deepest for a generation and the deepest since the depression of the 1930s. It is the issue of the hour, one that bankers, politicians, economic pundits and workers in offices and factories around the globe are all debating. Everyone knows that this is a very serious economic crisis indeed. Unlike the 1997 meltdown in South East Asia, it is a truly global crash. In the first year, Japan, the second biggest economy in the world, sank into a depression (when the economy shrinks by 10 percent or more). A string of countries in Eastern Europe were already in the same condition. But this is hardly the first great crash in history. Two others stand out: the South Sea Bubble Crash in the 1720s and the Great Depression of the 1930s.

The free-market system that today encompasses the globe first took root in the northern regions of Europe in the seventeenth century. Soon, its tentacles spread to other parts of the globe, drawing them into a world market. This system has always seen booms and busts, economic expansion, stagnation and contraction. It was well established by the eighteenth century in England when one of the most notorious stock market failures of all time occurred in 1720. The South Sea Company was a slave trading company which had been granted a monopoly on trade with South America by the Government. But the real emphasis of the company's trade was not slaves, but banking. Founded in 1711 by the Lord Treasurer Robert Harley, the Company took on the national debt of Great Britain after the War of the Spanish Succession in 1713 in return for exclusive trading rights. The Government and the Company

FIGURE 3.1 Value of South Sea Company shares (log scale)

convinced the holders of around £10 million worth of Government debt to exchange their credit for a new issue of stock in the South Sea Company. In return, the Government granted the Company's new equity owners a steady stream of earnings, funding the interest payments by placing a tariff on the goods brought from South America. This early private finance initiative would produce, the Government thought, a win–win situation. In 1717 and 1719 the South Sea Company bought out even more Government debt.

The South Sea Company became all the rage among the political and economic elite. Shares in the Company were 'sold' to politicians at the current market price. But, rather than paying for the shares out of their own money, they just held on to them and 'sold' them back to the company when they chose; and received as 'profit' the increase in market price of the shares. Ultimately, they parted with no money and just took the profit. Politicians, Ministers and the King's mistress all bought shares and found themselves bound to the fate of the Company. In order to secure their own profits they had to help drive up the share price. Meanwhile, by publicizing the names of their elite stockholders, the Company managed to clothe itself in an aura of legitimacy, which attracted other buyers. The Bubble had begun. The price of South Sea Company shares rocketed from £100 each to £1,000 each in a year. And the frenzy spread from the South Sea Company to others trading in the Americas and then to all stocks. Among the companies advertising their stock in 1720 were ones that declared their purpose to be: 'To Make Salt Water Fresh', 'For a Wheel of Perpetual Motion', 'For importing a Large Number of Jack Asses from Spain' and, most famously, 'A Company for Carrying out an Undertaking of Great Advantage, but Nobody to Know What it is'.

But, as with every Bubble, it had to burst. As the price hit £1,000 per-share people rushed to sell. The price crashed back to £100 per-share before the end of the year. Short-selling – selling borrowed shares in the hope of buying them back more cheaply as the price falls – was blamed for the Crash in 1720, just as it was in 2008. As always, people were caught as the shares that they had bought at a high price became worth less than they had paid for them. Bankruptcies followed. Broken investors were outraged. Parliament was recalled and an investigation was announced. When it reported back in 1721 it revealed fraud at the highest levels among company directors and the Cabinet. The Chancellor of the Exchequer, the Postmaster General, the Southern Secretary, Lord Stanhope and Lord Sunderland were all implicated. Ministers were impeached and the Lord Chancellor imprisoned. There was also an international dimension to the South Sea Bubble Crash and there were crises in Amsterdam and Paris as well as London.

However, the Crash of the early 1720s pales into insignificance compared to the stock market crash of 1929 and the slump of the 1930s. By the twentieth century the Capitalist system dwarfed its previous incarnation. Firms and banks were bigger than before and they were international. The world market was also incomparably greater. When the crash came in 1929, therefore, it heralded not just a governmental crisis, but a crisis of the whole global system. Revolution and the rise of Fascism in Europe and, eventually, worldwide war all came in its wake. There had been no inkling of this in the minds of the corporate leaders and politicians of the US in 1928. Everything had looked set fair to

FIGURE 3.2 The stock market crash of 1929

them. On 4 December 1928 President Coolidge announced in his State of the Union message that:

> No Congress of the United States ever assembled . . . has met with a more pleasing prospect than that which appears at the present time. In the domestic field there is tranquillity and contentment . . . and the highest record of years of prosperity. In the foreign field there is peace, the goodwill which comes from mutual understanding.

This blind optimism, only since matched by Prime Minister Gordon Brown's recent prediction that there would be 'no return to boom and bust' just ahead of the current recession, was soon to receive the most brutal of reverses. Less than a year after Coolidge's State of the Union speech, the New York Stock Exchange was in free-fall. 'Black Thursday' (24 October 1929) saw over 12 million shares change hands. The price of many of them was dropping vertically. Selling was so fast that the 'ticker' (the paper tape that transmitted share prices to banks and boardrooms around America) fell behind the deals transacted on the floor of the exchange. Companies and investors, large and small, were ruined and they did not even know it. This uncertainty led to more panic and more selling. But towards the end of the day there was some recovery. People hoped the worst was over; it was not. On the following Monday, the market collapsed even further. The next day, Tuesday 29 October, some 16 million shares were sold. The ticker was two and a half hours behind the sales at the end of the day. There were better days after this, but not many. The die was cast and the crisis rolled on into the banking system and manufacturing industry. In America alone, millions lost their jobs, their homes and their farms in the early 1930s. Globally, the victims of the recession numbered many millions more. The 1929 Crash was blamed on short-selling, just as the crash of 1720 had been and just as the crash of 2008 has been. Likewise, the Crash of 1929 saw a great deal of anger directed at bankers and politicians. Speculators were condemned and corruption in banks and businesses was revealed on a massive scale, just as it is being revealed today. But the real reason why the 1929 stock market crash turned into a recession is more fundamental than the greed of bankers or the negligence of politicians.

Economic crises have two fundamental causes: the first is that the free-market is a blind system. Individual firms produce, buy and sell with no real idea of who else is producing, buying and selling. When demand is high firms rush into the market and produce more. But since no one controls when the market is saturated there always comes a point where too much is produced. Goods then go unsold, profits are cut and production is cut back. The system goes from boom to bust. The second factor is that in order to make a profit each firm tries to pay its workers as little as possible and charge its customers as much as possible. This might be fine if one were looking at the system from the point of view of an individual firm, as that firm can kid itself that even if it pays its workers low wages it can still sell its products to the workers of other firms who might be getting more money. However, if every firm is doing the same thing then all workers are having their wages pushed down, even though these are the very people that are supposed to have enough money to buy the products they produce when they reappear on the market. Thus, downward pressure on wages cuts the market for what is produced. This happened in the 1920s as wages were pushed down. So when the stock market crash turned to recession the mass of ordinary Americans did not have the income to sustain growth in the economy.

There is no question that the crisis we face today is one of the greatest. In the worst year of the depression of the 1930s, US manufacturing

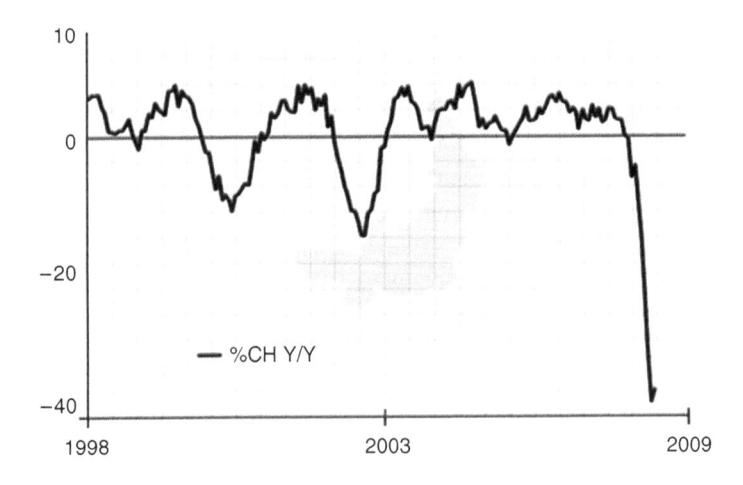

FIGURE 3.3 Japanese industrial production, 1998 to 2009
Source: GFC Economics.

slumped by 21 percent. In the three years from the peak of the boom to the bottom of the slump it fell by nearly 48 percent. In the first year of this crisis Japan's manufacturing has fallen by almost as much. In the US there are seven million people who have dropped out of the unemployed statistics because they have simply given up looking for work. If these people are included in the figures, unemployment in the US is already at nearly 15 percent. In the UK, meanwhile, the number of unemployed is already 2.5 million. The crisis has also already effectively bankrupted entire nations: Ireland, Portugal, Greece. Even the US has narrowly avoided default on its debts. Even before the full extent of the recession took hold, there were 11 countries from the Balkans and the former Soviet Central Asian Republics who were in more trouble than Thailand was at the pit of the South East Asian collapse of 1997.

How did this happen? Deregulation of the market, low wages and debt are at the heart of this crisis. When Margaret Thatcher and Ronald Reagan came to power in 1979 and 1980, respectively, they began the privatizations, cuts in welfare spending and attacks on living standards that have been with us ever since. The rich got richer and the gap between them and the poor grew wider. Today in the US it takes two wages to secure the same standard of living that one wage could secure in the late 1960s. And when people are not earning enough to live

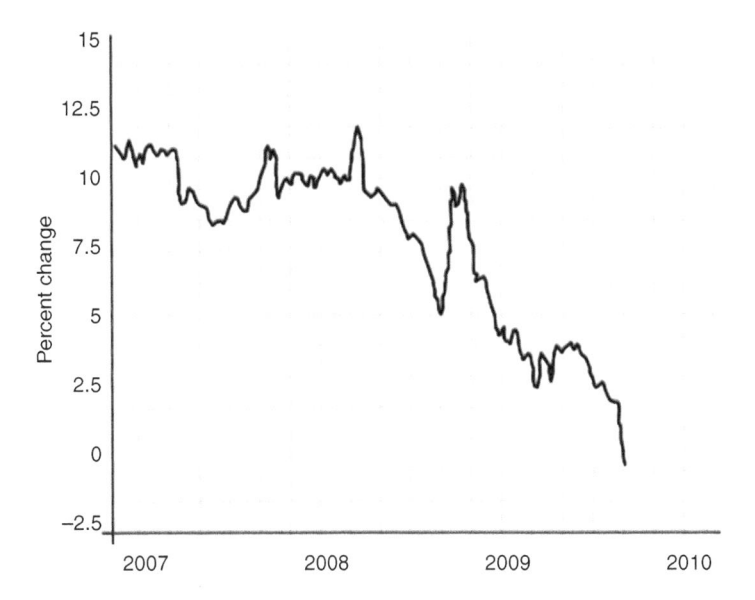

FIGURE 3.4 Bank losses of all commercial banks between 2007 and 2010
Source: Boards of Governors of the Federal Reserve System.

on, they borrow. Debt has ballooned. Look, for example, at the way these factors came together in the housing market in the US when this crisis began. Poor people could not afford to borrow to buy homes, but banks and mortgage companies were so desperate to find extra customers and make more profit than their competitors that they leant to 'sub-prime' borrowers who did not really have the wages to repay the loans. The banks didn't care because, just like the owners of shares in the South Sea Company, they thought the value of houses would keep on going up. The banks and mortgage companies were so certain of this that they even borrowed more money from banks than they had themselves. This allowed them to give out even more loans to 'sub-prime' poor borrowers. Even worse, though, the banks resold the loans to other banks and mortgage companies around the globe, meaning that bad debt has now been spread far beyond the banking system in the US. All this has meant that people who could not afford to repay loans were being leant to by banks that did not have the money themselves and were instead selling the debt on to other firms. You do not have to be an economist to see that this is not going to work for long.

142 The rulers and the ruled

In Britain, it was Thatcherite deregulation, sustained by New Labour when the Tories fell from power, which allowed the banks to borrow and lend in this way. And it was the global offensive against wages that has made it impossible to sustain economic growth, forcing people into

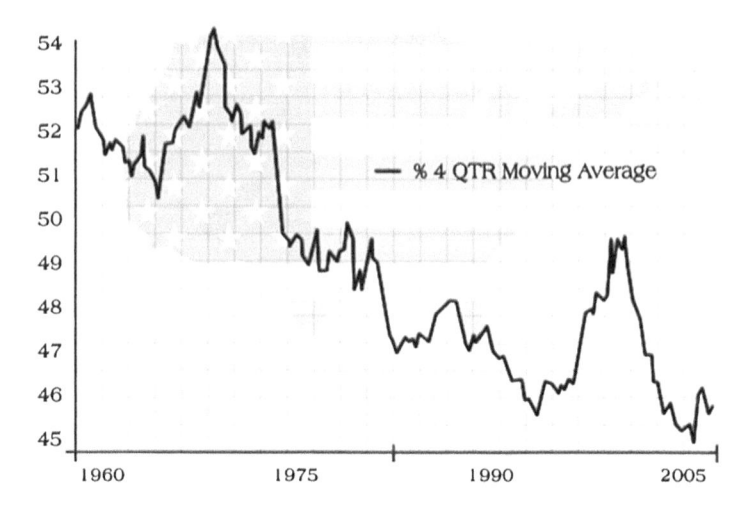

FIGURE 3.5 US Wages/GDP between 1960 and 2005
Source: Bureau of Economic Analysis.

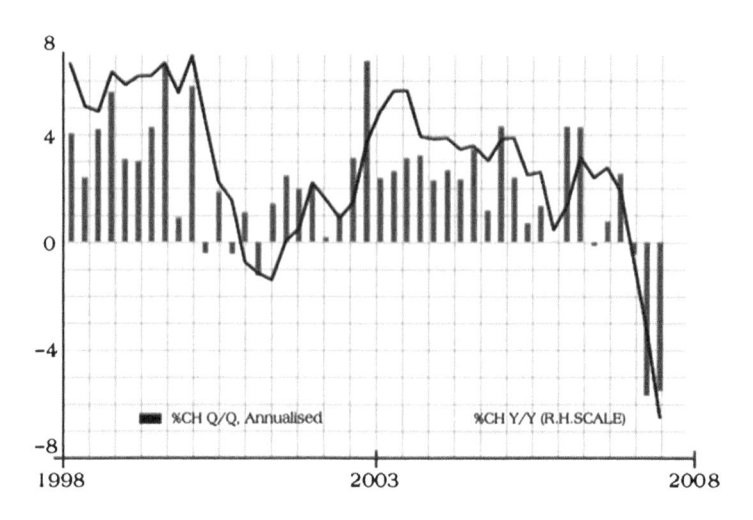

FIGURE 3.6 US Real GDP

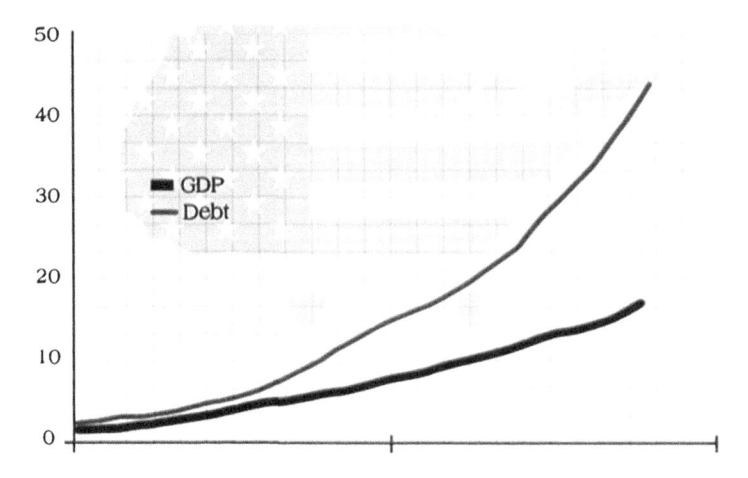

FIGURE 3.7 US GDP and total debt
Source: Economic Report of President, 2006.

debt. Government attempts to end the crisis have failed because they do not address this fundamental problem at the heart to the slump.

Recessions are moments of political danger as well as economic hardship. Desperate people seek desperate remedies. Some will try and lash out at those nearest to them because they cannot reach their oppressors or do not understand that the cause of their difficulties lie further afield. Racism and Fascism were the outcome of the 1930s depression. The potential for this exists in Britain and Europe again today. Far-Right parties everywhere from Scandinavia to Italy are enjoying more support than at any time since the 1930s. But there are other responses too. In the 1930s, workers rebuilt their Trade Unions to protect themselves. The great 'sit down' strikes in the US extended Union membership to greater numbers than ever before. In Britain the Unemployment Marches highlighted the condition of the unemployed and in the recessions of the 1970s and 1980s the Right to Work marches and the People's March for Jobs gave workers the hope and solidarity they needed to overcome the temptation to scape-goat their neighbours. Today, similar choices will be faced by everyone in Britain and by everyone who faces the impact of the recession in any corner of the world. Economic crises have been part of the system we live in since its very beginnings. Until a new and better economic model replaces the free-market it will always threaten us with collapse and the political dangers that come along with it. The policies that are pursued by governments can make a difference to how long the crises last and to how much ordinary people must suffer. But governments tend to listen more to the rich and powerful than to the poor and weak. So such policies have, more often than not, to be urged on governments by ordinary people who organize themselves to make their voices heard.

Timeline: recessions and resistance

1711: South Sea Company founded
1720: South Sea Bubble Crash
1929: Wall Street Crash
1998: South East Asian Crash
2008: global economic crisis begins

The Civil Rights Movement

America was the wealthiest and most powerful nation on earth in the 1950s and 1960s and the living standards of working people rose faster than they have ever done, before or since. Nevertheless, the great stain of systemic racism marked America in a way that it did no other Western democracy meaning that black Americans were outlawed from the American Dream. Inspired by figures like Martin Luther King and Malcolm X, black Americans fought and died on American soil to end discrimination. This is the story of their struggle.

Racial discrimination has a long history in America. Many of the first colonies established in the 'New World' of the seventeenth century were based on slave ownership. By the nineteenth century, the slave-owning plantations of the Southern States of America formed a distinct economy within the US. But by 1860 the States of America were anything but united. A central issue of the American Civil War (1860 to 1865) was whether the slave economy of the South or the more industrialized economy of the North would set the course of American Capitalism. Ultimately, the North won, but only after President Abraham Lincoln had freed the slaves in the Emancipation Proclamation of 1863. Yet, after the Civil War, the white Supremacists of the South, organized in the Democratic Party, returned to power and introduced a series of discriminatory laws which sought to retain as much of the old slavery inspired racism as they could. In every walk of life to be black was to be excluded from mainstream society. Systematic violence by the police, armed forces of the State, organized lynch mobs and the Klu Klux Klan preserved this white dominance.

The US in the 1950s was, however, a different place from the US of the Civil War years. The Second World War had transformed the US economy, which was bigger than ever and still expanding. As a result, the US needed more labour and it needed it fast. Blacks had fought in the army and they had worked in industry on an unprecedented scale during the War. The Jim Crow discriminatory laws (so-called after the comic African American figure played by white actor Thomas D. Rice in blackface) were primed to be challenged and throughout the early 1950s a series of legal decisions began to undermine the so-called 'separate but equal' policy by which blacks were excluded from white institutions. In education and public transport the courts began to rule in favour of integration. On 17 May 1954, the US Supreme Court ruled against 'separate but equal' education and in favour of integrated schooling in the landmark case of Brown vs. The Board of Education of Topeka, Kansas. In November 1955 the Inter-State Commerce Commission extended the logic of Brown vs. The Board of Education by banning segregation on inter-State buses. The following month a black woman called Rosa Parks refused to give up her seat on a bus. Her actions started the Montgomery Bus Boycott. But Rosa Parks was not the first to refuse to give up her seat under the segregation laws. Nine months earlier, even before segregation on buses had been made illegal, 15-year-old school girl Claudette Colvin refused to give up her seat. It was Colvin's legal case which eventually ended the practice in Montgomery.

Changes in the law, however, were never going to be enough. Segregation continued to be an issue. In 1956 a black woman called Autherine Lucy was admitted to the University of Alabama. Riots followed and she was suspended. When she challenged the suspension, she was expelled. In March 1956 the Southern Manifesto opposing integrated education was issued. It was signed by 19 Senators and 81 members of the House of Representatives, including the entire delegations of the States of Alabama, Arkansas, Georgia, Mississippi, South Carolina and Virginia. In April, singer Nat King Cole was assaulted at a segregated performance. Likewise, his TV show stopped running after a year because no national sponsor could be found. In May of the same year, a legal ban was imposed on the civil rights organization, the National Association for the Advancement of Coloured

People (NAACP) preventing them from operating in Alabama. In the same State the parsonage of civil rights leader Fred Shuttlesworth was bombed in December. In the same year the head of the FBI, J. Edgar Hoover, began a programme to investigate and disrupt 'dissident' groups in America. This was all part of a pattern of State and private harassment and terror specifically directed at civil rights activists and, more generally, at blacks. In 1951 NAACP activists Harry and Harriette Moore were killed when the Klu Klux Klan bombed their home. In 1955 NAACP activist Rev. George W. Lee was killed in Belzoni, Mississippi. In August of the same year a black teenager Emmett Till was killed for whistling at a white woman in Money, Mississippi. In 1958, the Bethal Baptist Church in Birmingham, Alabama was bombed by the Ku Klux Klan. And a year after that Mack Charles Parker, a black man accused of raping a white woman, was kidnapped from jail by a mob and lynched three days before his trial.

Amidst this darkness, 1957 opened on a hopeful note. In January an organization called the Southern Christian Leadership Conference was formed. Its chairman was Dr. Martin Luther King Jr., a 28-year-old Baptist Minister who had already been involved in the Montgomery Bus Boycott Campaign. In May 1957, the largest civil rights demonstration ever held – the Prayer Pilgrimage of Freedom – took place in Washington. But the next flash point was in the South, when Arkansas Governor Orval Faubus, called out the National Guard to prevent the integration of nine black students at Little Rock Central High School. Elizabeth Eckford and the rest of the 'Little Rock Nine' were turned back at the school entrance. But President Eisenhower placed the National Guard under federal control and instructed the regular Army to escort the Little Rock Nine into school. They were taken up the school steps by soldiers from the 101st Airborne. By the end of September, Eisenhower had signed the 1957 Civil Rights Act. However, this was still not enough. In 1960 the struggle rose again when, in February, four black students began a sit-in at the segregated Woolworth's lunch counter in Greensboro, North Carolina. The tactic spread. In October, Martin Luther King was part of the sit-in at an Atlanta Department store. King was arrested and the President's brother, Attorney General Robert Kennedy, had to intervene to set him free. Students were also joining the Civil Rights Movement in increasing numbers. In 1960 the Student Non-violent Coordinating Committee (SNCC) was formed and became one of the key mobilizing forces in the new

FIGURE 3.8 Mississippi freedom rides

phase of the struggle. Late in 1960, the US Supreme Court ruled in the case of Boynton vs. Virginia that waiting rooms had to be desegregated for inter-State buses, a logical extension of the earlier desegregation of the buses themselves. This set the scene for the Freedom Rides of the following year.

In May 1961 the Freedom Rides, organized by the Congress of Racial Equality and designed to test the implementation of desegregation on the buses, began. The first bus left from Washington and was attacked when it reached Anniston, Alabama. Then a mob beat the Freedom Riders on their arrival in Birmingham, Alabama. But it was the Freedom Riders not the mob who the police arrested. They were jailed for between 40 and 60 days. In the same year, a meeting of Freedom Riders with Martin Luther King was besieged by a mob at Reverend Ralph Abernathy's First Baptist Church. The following year, 1962, the US Supreme Court ruled segregation illegal on both State and inter-State transportation. Yet, racism was still alive and well. In 1963 George Wallace, the Governor of Alabama, proclaimed

'Segregation now, segregation tomorrow, segregation forever'. Later in the year he would personally block the door of the University of Alabama to deny entry to two black students, Vivian Malone and James Hood. The so-called 'Stand in the School House Door' only came to an end when Wallace was confronted by the Federal Marshall. In September 1963, four young girls died in the bombing of the 16th Street Baptist Church in Birmingham. At the very same moment the Great March on Washington for Jobs and Freedom was taking place. It was the occasion of Martin Luther King's famous 'I have a dream' speech. It *was* inspiring, but the dream must have seemed a long way off to the parents of those girls killed in the bombing of the church in Birmingham. The dream must have seemed more distant still when two months later President John F. Kennedy, widely seen as a friend of the Civil Rights Movement, was shot dead in Dallas. In the Mississippi Freedom Summer of 1964, the SNCC turned to another front in the fight for civil liberties: voter registration. Electorally, blacks faced legal hurdles and intimidation and many were effectively disenfranchised. Voter registration was about challenging all that. It was a tough battle. Voter registration campaigns dominated Alabama and Mississippi in 1964. In June three civil rights workers in Mississippi disappeared; later they were found murdered.

For radical black leader Malcolm X, who founded the Afro-American Unity Organization in 1964, voter registration missed the point. For him, the power system would never change for blacks as a result of voting reform. Many blacks seemed to agree. Martin Luther King might have received the Nobel Peace Prize and another Civil Rights Act might have got signed into law in 1964, but the conditions under which many blacks still remained deplorable. If we want to know what caused the new militancy of the Civil Rights Movement, we need look no further than the early life of Malcolm X. Born Malcolm Little in 1925 in Omaha, Nebraska, he was raised by Earl and Louise Little, who were followers of Marcus Garvey, the leader of what was, until the Civil Rights Movement, the largest black movement in America. In 1929 the Little family were living in Lansing, Michigan when their home was set ablaze by racists. Malcolm later wrote in his autobiography that, 'the white police and firemen came and stood around watching as the house burned to the ground'. The police then arrested Malcolm's father on suspicion of arson and for carrying a revolver without a permit. Two years later Malcolm's father was found dead, his head bashed in on the town's trolley tracks. Perhaps if the Little family had lived in the Southern States of America the racism and violence they suffered might have been even greater. After the death of Earl Little the family fell into poverty and Louise Little was committed to an asylum. In 1946, at the age of 21, Malcolm was sentenced to eight to ten years for armed robbery. He served six and a half years in Massachusetts State Prison. While in prison he converted to the Nation of Islam.

It was intense awareness of the slave past of American blacks which brought Malcolm Little to change his name to 'Malcolm X' in 1953. Millions of slaves had been brought to America from the seventeenth century on. They laboured, especially on the plantations in the South, right up until the emancipation of the slaves during the American Civil War of the 1860s. They had no surnames other than those given to them by their masters; their original African names were lost. Members of the Nation of Islam replaced their slave names with the letter 'X'. Malcolm became Minister in the Nation of Islam's Detroit Temple in 1953 and then, the following year, in the Nation's New York Temple. Under its leader Elijah Mohammed, the Nation of Islam's message was openly radical and separatist. Elijah Mohammed taught that the 6,000 year rule of whites was coming to an end and that the only hope for blacks lay in a complete separation from white society. At about the same time as Malcolm became a Minister, the Civil Rights Movement was taking off. But as the Civil Rights Movement grew, so too did the Nation of Islam. In 1952 Elijah Mohammed's entire Detroit congregation could fit in ten cars; by the early 1960s the Nation of Islam claimed 100,000 members across the country. It was the militancy as much as the message which attracted newly radicalized blacks to the Nation of Islam. And Malcolm X was becoming the best known militant. In 1959 Louis Lomax made a documentary called *The Hate that Hate Produced*. It revealed Malcolm X's unswerving opposition to racism and, as Lomax describes, had a big impact on the US public: 'Within a fortnight every major magazine and news media was carrying long stories about black Muslims and particularly about Malcolm.'

Malcolm's message at this time was one of black pride and black self-reliance. His emphasis on separatism was actually at variance with the Civil Rights Movement's demand for integration and equal rights, but it struck a chord which the peaceful, non-violent tactics of the mainstream Civil Rights Movement did not. Malcolm's famous distinction between the 'house negro' and the 'field negro' – one loyal to 'the Master', the other detesting him – struck right at the heart of the message offered by the more conservative leaders of the Civil Rights Movement. When Malcolm X talked of fighting 'by any means necessary' and refused to uncritically endorse 'non-violent tactics', he was directly going against the views of Martin Luther King. Malcolm's message was also becoming different to that of the Nation of Islam. He was not becoming any less militant in his fight against racism, but he was beginning to question whether black separatism was the right strategy. This conflict was brought to a head by the assassination of President John F. Kennedy in 1963. Many in the Civil Rights Movement had looked on Kennedy and his brother, the Attorney General Robert Kennedy, as allies. Malcolm X saw things differently and when President Kennedy was shot Malcolm described the assassination as 'the chickens coming home to roost'. The US establishment was outraged and the Nation of Islam quickly moved to disassociate themselves from Malcolm. He was ordered not to speak to the press and suspended for 90 days. When the 90 days were up, Malcolm spoke out in his own defence. It was a parting of the ways for the Nation of Islam and Malcolm X.

In March 1964, Malcolm X left the Nation of Islam and began to publically reevaluate their separatist strategy. His earlier travels in Africa and in Islamic countries, including his pilgrimage to Mecca, had convinced him that whites could be part of the fight for equal rights and justice. Malcolm was also influenced by the Socialist experiments that were going on in the 1960s in post-Colonial Africa, stating that:

> It's impossible for a white person to believe in Capitalism and not believe in racism. You can't have Capitalism without racism. And if you find one and you happen to get that person into conversation and have a philosophy that makes you sure they don't have this racism in their outlook, usually they are socialists or their political philosophy is socialism.

In May 1964, he started a new secular political organization called the Organization of Afro-American Unity. He continued to speak out against racism, perhaps even more eloquently than before. But now he had two enemies. One was the old enemy: the racist power structure of the US. The second enemy was the separatist Nation of Islam, of whom Malcolm was newly critical. In retaliation, Malcolm X's house was firebombed on 14 February 1965. One week later he was shot dead as he began a speech at the Audubon Ballroom in New York. The US establishment heaved a sigh of relief, claiming that Malcolm had been responsible for creating the hate that took his life. The truth is different: Malcolm X was the most charismatic, articulate and uncompromising spokesman that the Civil Rights Movement produced. But he had also shown that he was capable of responding to new challenges and was flexible enough to review his own deeply held views. His assassination deprived the Movement of these gifts.

The US political elite is one of the most violent in any parliamentary democracy. And it tolerates violence from the political Right to a degree unusual in the West. Both these qualities were evident aspect of society were on display during a peaceful protest march in Selma, Alabama, in February 1965 when State trooper James Bonard Fowler shot and killed Jimmie Lee Jackson (Fowler was convicted for the murder 47 years later). The following month protesters in Selma began a march to Montgomery. A massive police blockade confronted them at the Edmund Pettus Bridge. A conflict broke out and many were injured and one marcher was killed. Just 18 days later, on 25 March, white civil rights volunteer Viola Liuzzo, was shot and killed by Ku Klux Klan members, one of whom was an FBI informant. Again, legislation was enacted after the violence. On 6 August 1965, President Lyndon Johnson signed the Voting Rights Act into law. Again, it was not enough. Five days after the Act was signed, the Watts Riots shook the city of Los Angeles to its foundations. The riots lasted six days, inflamed by LAPD Chief William Parker describing the rioters as 'monkeys in a zoo'. By the time the riot subsided, 34 people had been killed, 2,032 injured, and 3,952 arrested. But no amount of violence could stop the Movement now. When James Meredith began his lone March Against Fear on 6 June 1966 from Memphis to Jackson he was shot and injured. But the Movement rallied and the March continued. Stokely Carmichael, soon to be a leader of the newly formed Black Panther Party for Self Defense, used the occasion to make a speech in which the militant slogan of 'Black Power' was used for the first time. The Movement was becoming radicalized. Many still followed Martin Luther King's path of non-violent resistance, but many were also looking for liberation 'by any means necessary', to use the phrase that Malcolm X had made famous. The new mood of radicalism burnt on through the Detroit riots of 1967. They had been sparked by a police raid on the Blind Pig After-Hours Bar and lasted five days. The National Guard were sent in and then President Johnson sent in the regular army. When it was over 43 were dead, 467 injured, and 7,200 arrested. More than 2000 buildings were destroyed and parts of the centre of Detroit remained unreconstructed for decades.

Malcolm X was an exceptional exponent of the radical mood sweeping the Civil Rights Movement, but he was not alone. Opposition to the Vietnam War also radicalized the Movement. Malcolm X had long opposed the War and Martin Luther King soon joined him. The relentless physical violence used against the Civil Rights Movement (the killings, the lynchings, the bombing and the beatings) were another main source of the new mood of radicalism. It was this context that brought Malcolm X to issue his call for black self-defence. Others, like James Forman of the SNCC, were reevaluating their pacifist tactics as a result of the extreme violence that beset the Movement. SNCC Leader Stokley Carmichael had, in fact, already used the phrase 'Black Power'. He told Martin Luther King that he had deliberately used it in order to force King to take a stance on the issue. But after Malcolm X's death, his call was taken up most vociferously by the Black Panther Party for Self Defense, formed in Oakland, California by Huey P. Newton and Bobby Seale in 1966. Stokely Carmichael also became a Black Panther. Their newspaper was edited by Eldridge Cleaver and reached a circulation of 250,000. Most of the Party's leaders were Socialists or Marxists, influenced by the then fashionable Maoist ideology. Their programme was a straightforward series of economic and social demands; their radicalism lay in how they organized themselves. Citing the US Constitution's provision that every citizen has the right to bear arms, the Panthers confronted the armed power of the State and the racists directly by carrying shotguns and other small arms in their 'patrol the pigs' campaign. Their armed patrols followed police cars around the black areas of Oakland with the intention of preventing the police from harassing the local population. The tactic was initially successful and the number of cases of police harassment declined in Oakland in 1967. However, the State soon responded. Huey P. Newton was framed for murder in October 1967. The resulting Free Huey Campaign was huge and he was out of prison by 1970. But while he was in jail, the full weight of the State came down on the Panthers. The police killed 28 Panthers in just two years and Panthers and other black radicals like Angela Davis were hounded from their jobs.

In so many ways 1968 was a year of change. But in 1968 the Civil Rights Movement trod a thin line between hope and despair. The reasons for despair were obvious. In February, 200 students gathered to protest at segregation in the All Star Bowling Alley in Orangeburg, South Carolina. Trouble flared with the local police and the police opened fire, killing three and injuring 27. All the police officers were acquitted, but SNCC activist Cleveland Sellers was convicted of inciting a riot (25 years later he was pardoned). Despair reached new depths the following month when Martin Luther King was assassinated in the Lorraine Motel, Memphis by petty criminal James Earl Ray. Two months later Robert Kennedy was assassinated after winning the California Primary in his bid to follow his brother to the White House. But there was also hope in 1968. Civil Rights legislation continued to be passed and a new Civil Rights Act, The Fair Housing Act and the extension of the Civil Rights legislation to private colleges all made the statute books in 1968. On top of this, anti-racism and Black Power references began to register in surprising ways in mainstream culture.

Indeed, after a history so steeped in sacrifice and struggle, 1968 ended with a touch, a kiss and a salute. The touch came on a US primetime TV special for British singer Petula Clark. In a duet with Harry Belafonte, Clark touched Belafonte's arm. The show's producer and the shows sponsors, the Chrysler Corporation, insisted the scene be cut. Clark refused and the scene, touch included, was broadcast on 8 April 1968. The kiss was the first interracial kiss to be broadcast on US television. Nichelle Nichols had thought twice before agreeing to play Lieutenant Uhura in Star Trek. She was encouraged to do so by Martin Luther King. The episode she was filming contained two possible plot lines: one with a kiss between Nichols and William Shatner and one without the kiss. Nichols and Shatner kept acting the plot variant without the kiss so badly that only the takes with the kiss could be used. The salute, meanwhile, was by athletes Tommie Smith and John Carlos at the 1968 Summer Olympic Games in Mexico. As they took the podium to collect their medals for the 200 metre race they both raised black-gloved clenched fists in the Black Power salute. White silver medalist Peter Norman also wore the badge of the Olympic Project for Human Rights, of which Carlos was a founder, as an act of solidarity. The struggle for civil rights was long, dangerous and bloody and such success as there was in 1968 had only been bought at the price of great sacrifice.

Not everyone benefited equally from the gains that the Civil Rights Movement had won though. As the first black Mayors and Representatives began to take their positions many of those who had elected them remained detached from the American Dream. Malcolm X and the Black Panthers had warned about the co-option of the black middle class. The Panthers did not have a stable strategy of trying to build stable working class and middle class support (both black and white) from their bases in the poor black neighbourhoods. Black Socialists in the Detroit Revolutionary Union Movement did try to build such a base in the Dodge Main Chrysler plant, but they could not make their model work on national scale. In fact, although the political position of all US blacks was improved, it was actually the black middle class and not the black poor and working class that gained most from the Civil Rights Movement. They were now becoming Representatives in Congress and the Senate, Mayors of major cities and successful managers and business people, or at least a minority of them were. However, most blacks remained poor and working class, and to be poor and working class was to experience racism in its worst forms. And the next time the inner cities rioted it would be black Mayors who ordered the police to arrest the rioters. Black Power had always contained two meanings. Did it mean power for some blacks inside the system or did it mean the overthrow of the system that oppressed blacks? That question is still being asked today.

Timeline: the Civil Rights Movement

1955: Montgomery Bus Boycott
1957: the year of Little Rock
1961: the Freedom Rides
1963: Martin Luther King's 'I have a dream' speech
1964: Mississippi Freedom Summer
1965: Malcolm X assassinated
1966: the Black Panthers formed
1968 Chicago Riots

1968: the year that changed the world

1968 was one of those years when the accumulated pressures of previous decades suddenly explode. Afterwards nothing is ever quite the same. It was the year that the full disaster of the Vietnam War became obvious. Martin Luther King was shot dead. So was Robert Kennedy. Russia invaded Czechoslovakia. In Europe, French students and workers created the biggest crisis a Western democracy had faced since the Second World War as hundreds of thousands took to the streets to protest.

Politicians of the Centre and Right have detested the memory of 1968 ever since. On the eve of becoming President of France, Nicolas Sarkozy declared it was his aim to rid France of the harm done by 1968. The Deputy Editor of *The Wall Street Journal* also recently blamed the current recession on the effects of the 1960s. Tony Blair too blamed the 1960s for many of society's ills. What follows here, however, is the real story of 1968. I have chosen to tell the story of 1968 chronologically, month by month as the year unfolded. This ruptures the continuity of the various strands of historical development, but it has the advantage of showing how crisis after crisis confronted the consciousness of those who were living through these events. In many ways it was this interaction of historic events which produced the unique radicalism of 1968.

January proved not to be a good start to the year for US President Lyndon Johnson. On 10 January, a week before he had to deliver his State of the Union Address, the US lost its 10,000th plane over Vietnam. Worse, much worse, was to follow. On the last day of the month at half-past midnight the North Vietnamese launch the Tet Offensive. Nearly 70,000 North Vietnamese troops took part in this broad action, taking the battle from the jungles to the cities. At 2:45am that morning the US Embassy in Saigon was invaded and held until 9:15am. Whatever the reality, the US looked as if it was losing the War. But it was not just that the War looked as if it was being lost, it also looked wrong. On 1 February, the first day of the Tet Offensive, a South Vietnamese General was captured on film by American photographer Eddie Adams executing a Viet Cong prisoner. The Pulitzer Prize-winning photograph galvanized anti-war protestors as it seemed to call into question everything claimed by the US about its South Vietnamese allies. Seven days later international reporters arrived at the embattled city of Ben Tre in South Vietnam. Peter Arnett, then of the Associated Press, wrote a dispatch quoting an unnamed US Major as saying, 'it became necessary to destroy the town to save it'. The quote ran nationwide the next day. By the middle of February, the US State Department announced the highest US casualty toll of the Vietnam War with 543 killed in action and 2,547 wounded.

For many, the Vietnam War seemed to epitomize everything that was wrong with American society. Perhaps the most important of these wrongs was racial discrimination, which was still endemic in America 100 years after the abolition of slavery. Martin Luther King was at the heart of the Civil Rights Movement. On 4 February 1968 he delivered a sermon at his Ebenezer Baptist Church in Atlanta, Georgia, saying that if he should die he would,

> Like somebody to mention that day that Martin Luther King Jr. tried to give his life serving others. I'd like for somebody to say that day that Martin Luther King Jr. tried to love somebody... that I tried to love and serve humanity. Yes, if you want to, say that I was a drum major for peace... for righteousness.

The Vietnam War was even polarizing US establishment politics and 1968 was a Presidential Election year. On 12 March, the New Hampshire Primary Election brought a shock result. Senator Eugene McCarthy's campaign had benefited from the work of 2,000 full-time student volunteers who had cut their hair, dressed respectably and become 'clean for Gene' in order to win over conservative voters in the State. McCarthy came just 230 votes short of defeating sitting President Lyndon Johnson. Four days later Senator Robert Kennedy, former Attorney General and brother of former President John F. Kennedy, announced that he would enter the 1968 Presidential race. Coincidently, on the same day (16 March) an horrific event took place in Vietnam as US ground troops rampaged through the hamlet of My Lai, killing more than 500 Vietnamese civilians, including babies and the elderly. The massacre went on for three hours until three American pilots positioned their helicopters between the troops and the fleeing Vietnamese, eventually carrying a handful of wounded to safety. The incident was only reported in the press more than a year later and so it was unknown to the thousands who fought the police outside the US Embassy in Grosvenor Square, London, on the 17 March. But had the world known about My Lai, the protesters' chants of 'Hey, hey LBJ... how many kids have you killed today?' would not have seemed so extreme. On 22 March, there was the clearest signal yet that 1968 would not only be a year of crisis for the West as Antonin Novotny resigned the Czech Presidency. The very next day leaders of five Warsaw Pact countries met in Dresden, East Germany, to discuss the crisis as the Prague Spring began, openly challenging the Stalinist apparatus in both the Eastern bloc and Russia.

Martin Luther King spent the 4 April at the Lorraine Motel in Memphis working on plans for his Poor People's March in Washington later that same month. At 6:00pm, as he greeted friends in the motel courtyard, King was shot by James Earl Ray. Rioting broke out in Baltimore, Boston, Chicago, Detroit, Kansas City, Newark, Washington D.C. and many other US cities, causing 46 deaths across the country. One consequence of King's assassination was that many black activists turned away from his civil rights agenda towards more militant forms of activism like that offered by the Black Panther Party. Meanwhile, just a week after the assassination of Martin Luther King, there was an eruption of anger across Germany after the failed attempt on the life of student leader Rudi Dutschke. The attempt on his life followed weeks of a hate campaigning by the Right-Wing Springer Media Empire.

However, May was *the* month of 1968 and Europe was the focus. Italian students had already been protesting in a series of demonstrations about the stifling conformity of the education system. But the most decisive chapter was written in Paris, France, on the 6 May. 'Bloody Monday', as it became known, marked one of the most violent days of the student revolt as 5,000 students marched through the Latin Quarter. Fighting with the police became intense. The students set up barricades and the police attacked with gas grenades. Overnight the battle subsided, but only after the students had engaged the solidarity of millions of French Trade Unionists. On 13 May strikes broke out across France. By the 22 May, some nine million workers were on strike. President de Gaulle took action to shore up governmental power, making strident radio addresses and authorizing large movements of military troops within the country. The French General Strike was, and remains to this day, the largest general strike in European history.

On the night of the 4 June, the day of the California Primary in the US, Robert Kennedy addressed a large crowd of supporters at the Ambassador Hotel in San Francisco. He left the stage at 12:13am on the morning of the 5 June and was shot by Sirhan Sirhan, a 24-year-old Jordanian living in Los Angeles who was apparently angered at several pro-Israeli speeches that Kennedy had made during his campaign. On the 24 June, Ralph Abernathy, Martin Luther King's designated successor, and over 2,500 supporters were cleared from their Resurrection City Camp in Washington by a police raid. In July, a cultural event that seemed to capture the huge change in consciousness, especially among the young, took place at the Newport Folk Festival when singer

Arlo Guthrie performed his 20 minute ballad *Alice's Restaurant* to rave reviews.

In a portent of things to come, Richard Nixon became the Republican Presidential candidate at the Party's Convention in August. Later the same month the Democratic National Convention opened in Chicago. The City's police attempt to enforce an 11:00pm curfew. Demonstrations were widespread and the next two days brought increasing tension and violence to the situation. On the 28 August the police, without provocation, took action against crowds of demonstrators. They beat some marchers unconscious and sent at least 100 to hospital. Chicago's Mayor Daley famously tried to explain that, 'the policeman isn't there to create disorder, the policeman is there to preserve disorder'. 28 years later, when the Democrats next held a Convention in Chicago, some police officers still on the force wore t-shirts proclaiming, 'We kicked their father's butt in '68 and now it's your turn'.

But while this was going on in Chicago, repression on an even greater scale was taking place in Czechoslovakia as, on the 20 August, over 200,000 Warsaw Pact troops invaded Czechoslovakia, putting an end to the 'Prague Spring' in the face of massive protests. It was the beginning a period of enforced and oppressive 'normalization'. The example of the anti-war movement, the student struggles and the fight for black civil rights was now spreading to all sections of society. On the 7 September, Women's Liberation groups targeted the Miss America Beauty Contest in Atlantic City. Nothing was actually set on fire, but one organizer's comment, quoted in the *New York Times* the next day, that the protesters 'wouldn't do anything dangerous, just a symbolic bra-burning,' lives on to this day.

October 1968 saw the start of the so-called 'troubles' in Northern Ireland. A peaceful demonstration demanding civil rights by Catholics in Derry's Bogside Ghetto was viciously attacked by police. It was the start of the greatest revolt against British rule since the sectarian Northern Ireland State had been created by the partition of Ireland in 1921. But October was also the month in which the focus turned from the Northern hemisphere to the Southern when on the 2 October police and military troops in Mexico City, host to the 1968 Olympics, reacted violently to a student protest. Hundreds of the demonstrators were killed or injured, but the police forbade the press to report what had happened. On the 12 October the Summer Olympic Games opened in Mexico City, although they were boycotted by 32 African Nations in protest at South Africa's participation. On the 18 October, Tommie Smith and John Carlos, US athletes and medallists in the 200 metres disrupted the games by performing the Black Power salute during the 'Star-Spangled Banner' at their medal ceremony. They were banned from the sport. US troop numbers in Vietnam had peaked at some 541,000 in August 1968, but by 31 October President Johnson, who had already pulled out of the Presidential Race, had to announce a total halt to US bombings in North Vietnam. Election day in the US was 5 November. Richard Nixon was returned with 43 percent of the vote. Nine days later, national 'Turn in Your Draft Card Day' was observed with rallies and protests on college campuses throughout the country.

The conformity and orthodoxy of the post-War world died in 1968. It became harder to believe in the moral superiority of the West when people could see what was happening in Vietnam. More difficult also to believe in free-market 'democracy' at home as the police battened, shot and bludgeoned protestors in Chicago, London, Derry, Paris, Rome and Mexico City. It was also more difficult to believe that peaceful reform was possible after the assassinations of Martin Luther King and Robert Kennedy and the attempted assassination of Rudi Dutschke. But it was equally impossible to believe that Stalinist Russia offered a possible solution to the crisis in the West after the crushing of the Prague Spring. The New Left that subsequently emerged in 1968 did have some important strengths. First among these was that it was self-reliant; students, blacks, those facing Imperialism, women and (after the French May) workers had a renewed faith in their own self-activity and a renewed faith that such activity could change society. 'We shall fight, we shall win, Paris, London, Rome, Berlin' was the slogan of the hour. It took the international ruling elite years to regain full control as the movement broadened and deepened in the early- and mid-1970s, increasingly involving working class action as in the Italian 'May in slow motion' and the industrial struggles in Britain. Only the humiliating scurry out of Vietnam in the early 1970s could end the damage the US ruling class had inflicted on itself at home and abroad by the debacle in South East Asia. Over 40 years later it is still this message from 1968 that the rich and powerful fear: 'if you don't like it, you can change it!'

Timeline: 1968: the year that changed the world

January: Tet Offensive
February: US records highest casualties of Vietnam War

March: New Hampshire Primary; My Lai Massacre; Novotny resigns
    the Czech Presidency
April: Martin Luther King assassinated
May: 'Bloody Monday' student revolt, Paris; General Strike in
    France
June: Robert Kennedy assassinated
August: Democratic Convention Chicago; Russia invades
    Czechoslovakia
September: Women's Liberation protest, Atlantic City
October: Mexico Olympics; Civil Rights protest Northern Ireland
November: Richard Nixon elected President

South Africa's struggle for freedom

When Western leaders are called on to justify military intervention in other countries they often deploy the argument that such action is necessary to overcome tyranny and to spread democracy. Odd then that the argument was never deployed in the case of Apartheid South Africa, one of the most brutal and barbarous regimes in the world. It was, of course, eventually overthrown, not by foreign armies but by a mass rising of its own population. The struggle had been long and bloody, but ultimately it was victorious. It broke the racist Apartheid State and won black majority rule. It was the culmination of decades of struggle, but it resulted in one of the greatest democratic revolutions in the post-War world. What, then, can this great movement tell us about the potential and the limits of revolution in the modern age?

The Union of South Africa, to give the country its full name, was created in 1910. The union was between the British colonists in South Africa and the Afrikaans-speaking Boer settlers of Dutch extraction whom the British had fought twice in the previous decades. Two years later the organization that would become the African National Congress, the Native National Congress, was founded. In 1913 a Land Act was passed that prevented blacks from owning land outside the reserves, except in the Cape Province. As a result, Africans made up 73 percent of the population, but were entitled to only 13 percent of the land. A year after that, in 1914, the National Party, the mainstay of the future Apartheid State was founded. South Africa was built on racial segregation from the beginning. Every black person had to carry a passbook showing that they had the right to be in a 'white area'. Some

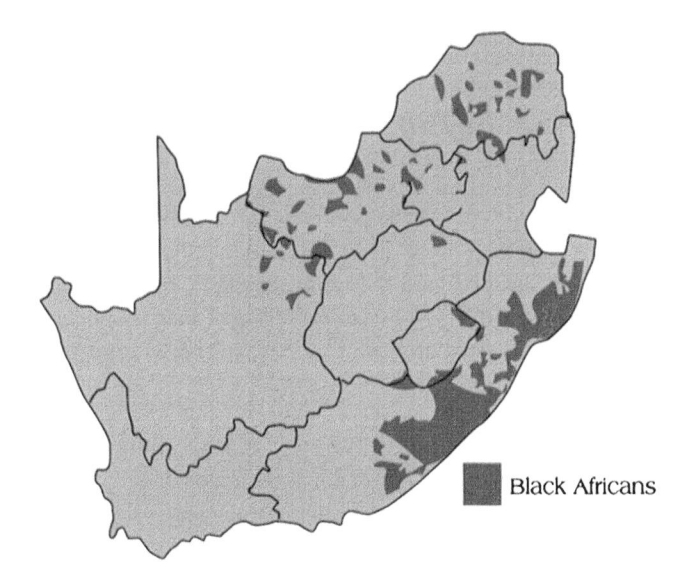

FIGURE 3.9 South African Land Act, 1913

18 million Africans were arrested under the Pass Laws between 1916 and the mid-1980s.

Apartheid took on an even more extreme form when the National Party took power after the Second World War. The fully Apartheid system they introduced was the most systemic and institutionalized form of State racism seen since Nazi Germany. The black majority were discriminated against in the most brutal manner and the Pass Laws were rigidly enforced. Blacks lived corralled in Townships and Bantustans. At the heart of the profitability of the gold mines and the rest of South African industry lay the system of migrant labour which kept black workers imprisoned in the poverty stricken Townships. Blacks were brutalized by police and employers alike, prevented from lying on the same beaches or sitting on the same public benches as whites. And, of course, only whites got to vote. In 1950 the whole of the South African population were classified by law into distinct racial groups. From the very beginning, Apartheid was fiercely resisted by its victims. Again and again, black South Africans demonstrated, protested, rebelled, rioted, boycotted and struck against the racial discrimination at the heart of their society. And again and again, the South African State responded with the most extreme violence.

162   The rulers and the ruled

In March 1960 in the Sharpeville Township a relatively small demonstration assembled to protest at the Pass Laws. The police opened fire on them and some 69 unarmed protesters lost their lives. At least another 180 were injured. It all happened in 40 seconds, during which time 705 rounds were fired from police revolvers and machine guns, but only 30 shots entered the wounded or killed from the front of their bodies. No less than 155 bullets entered the bodies of the injured and killed from their backs. A huge 'stay away' strike followed the Sharpeville Massacre, but this was also crushed with the utmost savagery. In the wake of the Sharpeville Massacre the ANC were banned and, four years later, Nelson Mandela was arrested and tried for treason. He did not deny the charge, telling the court:

> I do not deny that I planned sabotage. I did not plan it in a spirit of recklessness nor because I have any love of violence. I planned it as a result of a calm and sober assessment of the political situation that had arisen after many years of tyranny, exploitation and oppression of my people by the whites.

It would be 27 years until he was free again. The banning of the South African Communist Party, which was a mainstay of the ANC, and the jailing of Mandela and other black leaders drove resistance underground or into exile. Apartheid seemed triumphant. But in the diamond and gold mines, in the Townships and factories and in the schools and colleges, blacks continued to dream of overthrowing the system. Among them there was very little talk of democratic change without a wider social transformation, even though this was the official policy of the ANC and few thought that Apartheid could be dismantled without a revolutionary overthrow of the Government.

A new phase of the struggle reached its peak with the uprising in the South Western Township of Johannesburg, Soweto, in 1976. The spark for the uprising was the Government's decision to enforce the use of Afrikaans, the language of the Boer oppressors, in black schools. School students took over the streets of Soweto and the police reacted as they had done in Sharpeville and shot them down. That turned the uprising into a year-long revolt that spread throughout South Africa and included three 'stay-aways'. The State eventually regained control by the use of massive repression. Some 700 deaths were recorded; it is probable that there were more. The Soweto Uprising was inspired by a new current in the struggle against Apartheid: the Black Consciousness Movement.

Drawing from the Black Power Movement in the US, Black Consciousness was a militant assertion of black demands for equality. It was in many ways a reproach to the seeming lack of progress being made by the traditional ANC leadership. Student leader Steve Biko was one of the Black Consciousness Movement's most potent symbols. Arrested under the Terrorism Act, he was killed in police custody in 1977. Over 10,000 people came to the funeral, including US and Western diplomats. Even the South African Justice Minister said the killing 'left me cold'.

In 1978, two years after Soweto, P. W. Botha became Prime Minister. He began a cautious process of trying to adapt Apartheid to the pressures that were building up within the system. A limited reform of the franchise was adopted for 'coloureds', those of mixed race, and Indians, (just three percent of the population). But, more importantly, in 1979 African Trade Unions were legalized. Black workers, many more of them now skilled, were increasingly central to the economy and by 1970 there were over four million black workers living in 'white areas'. This led to more fundamental changes as became evident as the next and even more powerful movement of opposition hit the Apartheid State. The

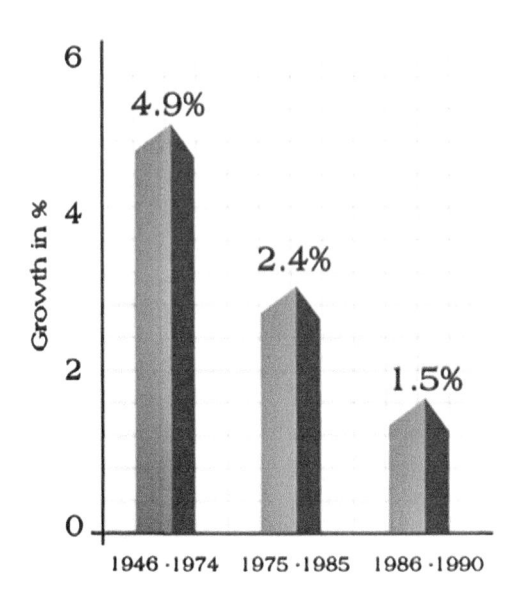

FIGURE 3.10 South African economy, 1946 to 1990

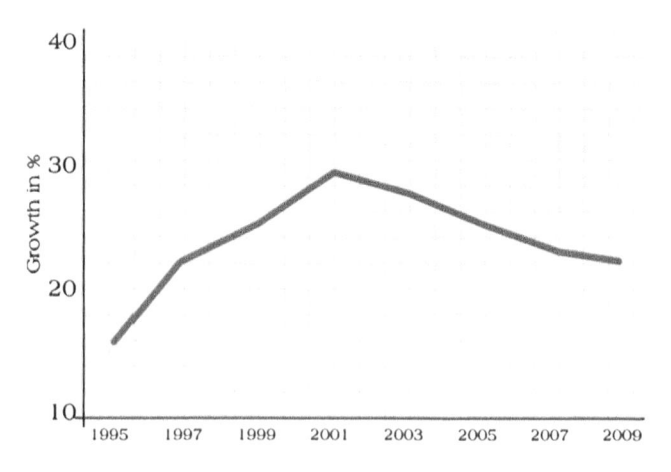

FIGURE 3.11 Unemployment rate in South Africa, 1995 to 2009
Source: www.personal.umich.edu; www.quantec.co.za.

Township Revolt of the mid- to late-1980s was a sustained campaign of opposition and it was strengthened in a way that no previous movement had been when new labour federations began to organize black workers in more radical ways than ever before. In the three years running up to the start of the Township Revolt in 1984 the number of Africans in the Trade Unions trebled. Rank and file organization drove the new unions, centred on the power of the National Union of Mineworkers and the National Union of Metalworkers of South Africa. There was, on average, a strike every day in South Africa, with the *Economist* magazine describing it as, 'the biggest political strike in the country's history'.

The militancy of the workers broke up Botha's attempts to incorporate the black middle classes. As the *Financial Times* recorded, 'a black proletariat is turning against a black establishment' creating 'the danger of polarization on a class rather than a racial basis'. The new federation of unions, the Congress of South African Trade Unions (COSATU) was a direct threat to the stability of Apartheid and it made it clear that the final crisis of the system was at hand. The Minister for Law and Order deployed 7,000 troops in the Transvaal Townships, telling them to search out 'revolutionary . . . criminal and intimidatory elements'. It was the language of an Apartheid State that was now isolated internationally and embattled internally. The international campaign of protest and boycott organized by the international Anti-Apartheid Movement was helping to make South Africa a pariah State. In South Africa itself, the economy was stagnating. It had averaged 4.9 percent growth between 1946 and 1974, but in the next decade it slumped to less than half that figure. Then, in the second half of the 1980s, it fell still further to a mere 1.5 percent. Even some sections of big business were beginning to ask themselves if racial discrimination was really necessary for the future of South African Capitalism: was the Civil War being created by Apartheid more dangerous than granting some kind of equality to black workers? As early as 1985, ANC President Oliver Tambo was meeting with Gavin Relly, Chairman of the massive Anglo-American Corporation, to see what a negotiated settlement might look like.

The possibility of a new strategy by the elite became reality when F. W. De Klerk became President in 1989. De Klerk realized that the only way of preventing a full-scale revolutionary upheaval by the organized working class was to come to a serious settlement with the ANC. He moved swiftly to dismantle the laws that underpinned Apartheid, starting with the Land Act of 1913. He lifted the ban on the ANC and freed the ANC leadership from prison. Finally, in 1990, Mandela himself walked free. South African workers and the wider mass-movement held the fate of the country in their hands at this moment. There were still great dangers to be overcome. White supremacists like the Fascist AWB Party, led by Eugene Terreblanche, were quite prepared to use violence to stop Apartheid being overthrown. And the Government was also quite willing to promote the conservative nationalism of the Zulu Inkatha Movement as a way of weakening and dividing the African forces. It took great persistence and discipline for ANC supporters to force through a genuine democratic settlement. But was this all that could have been won?

Many ANC supporters and many radicals in the new Unions wanted more; they wanted a Socialist transformation that would give them power over the economy as well as the right to vote. Perhaps one anecdote captures the masses' power at this time. The Mercedes Benz South African Plant had been a base of labour militancy for years. The line supervisors used to clock-on and hide in their office, according to the company's Chairman Christoph Kopke, as workers on the line wore replica AK47s over their shoulders. When Mandela was freed the workers worked overtime to build him a special car. The Mercedes Benz Chairman complained that:

> That car came off the line with 9 faults. In this company cars don't come off the line with less than 68 faults. In Germany, about 13 faults. Normally it takes about 14 days to build that car ... Mandela's car was built in four days!

But this unique combination of political mobilization and economic power at the point of production was not used to transform the whole of South African society in both its political and economic aspects. The ANC's long struggle was limited to a transformation of the Apartheid political system only and to the achievement of black-majority rule. So the most ambitious hopes were not to be realized as the ANC and the Government managed the transition away from Apartheid. This has left a bitter-sweet legacy in the new South Africa. The abolition of Apartheid was sweet, but the privatization and continuing poverty are the bitter fruits of liberation. Many of the corporate interests who profited from Apartheid still profit under black-majority rule. More than ten years after Mandela walked free some 57 percent of South Africans were still in poverty. Unemployment has averaged a quarter of the workforce ever since the end of Apartheid. It is this circumstance that gave rise in 2007 to the largest public sector strikes since the end of Apartheid. The achievement of the South African struggle should inspire all those who want to see a more just and democratic world, but the continued economic domination of the majority of South Africans should serve as a warning to all those still fighting for a democratic revolution that liberation can only be complete when economic power as well as political power lies in the hands of the majority.

Timeline: South Africa's struggle for freedom

1910: formation of South Africa
1912: Native National Congress founded
1913: Land Act passed
1914: National Party formed
1948: the National Party comes to power

1950: population classified by race
1950: CP banned; Nelson Mandela leads civil disobedience
1960: Sharpeville Massacre; ANC banned
1964: Nelson Mandela jailed
1966: Prime Minister Verwoerd assassinated
1976: Soweto Uprising
1978: P. W. Botha becomes Prime Minister
1979: legalization of African Trade Unions
1984–1989: Township revolts
1989: F. W. De Klerk becomes President
1990: ANC ban lifted; Mandela freed
1991: last race laws revoked; Inkatha battles ANC
1994: ANC wins elections; Mandela becomes President
2007: public sector strikes

Thatcherism

David Cameron became the first Tory Prime Minister for 13 years after the General Election of 2010. Many of those who voted in that election had no real memory of living under a Conservative Administration. For many more, Margaret Thatcher's first election victory in 1979 is the stuff of history books. So what is the real story of Britain's longest-serving Tory Prime Minister?

Thatcherism was a Conservative reaction to what came before it. In the late 1960s the long post-War period of economic expansion began to ebb. By the early 1970s Britain was in its most serious economic crisis since the 1940s. Inflation and unemployment were rising. Working people had become used to the idea that there was not going to be a return to the economic hardship and deprivation they had known in the 1930s. They reacted with a series of industrial disputes aimed at defending their living standards. Dockers and miners struck in 1972 and the miners struck again in 1974. Tory Prime Minister Edward Heath put the country on a three day working week, hoping that voters would blame the strikers. The plan backfired. Heath called an election in 1974 demanding that he be given a new mandate to confront the unions. He was thrown out of office by the electorate.

There was real fear among Britain's traditional rulers at this time. The Left was strong (still riding a wave of radicalism that had begun in the late 1960s), the Unions had just broken a Tory Government and the economy was weak. The immediate solution was to let a Labour Government do the work a Tory Government had been too unpopular to achieve. And this is indeed what happened. Labour's long-serving leader Harold Wilson became Prime Minister in 1974, but resigned a year later to be succeeded by Jim Callaghan. But the Tories also began to reorganize and in 1975 a surprise result gave Margaret Thatcher the Tory leadership. By the time Jim Callaghan became Prime Minister in 1976, the old Welfare State consensus of the 1950s and 1960s was falling apart in both the Labour and Tory Parties. If there is a moment when this idea disappeared from British politics to be replaced with a monetarist, free-market, anti-welfare State consensus among the political elite, then it was in 1976, three years before Margaret Thatcher won the election of 1979. It was then that Jim Callaghan's Chancellor of the Exchequer, Denis Healy, had to run to the IMF to get a loan that could bail out the economy. The IMF terms for the loan meant that the Government had to impose wage controls and cuts in public services, and that meant that Labour had to attack its own supporters in the Trade Unions. This it did in a way that no Tory Government could have done.

The public sector strikes of 1979, the so-called 'Winter of Discontent', marked the breach between the Labour Government and its traditional supporters. The press and the Tories blamed the strikers and Margaret Thatcher won the General Election the same year. From the beginning, Thatcher and her supporters realized that if their free-market policies were to triumph then they would have to break the Unions. They formulated a plan to smash the weaker Unions first, but chose not to confront the most powerful Unions (like the Miners' Union) until they could choose their own ground. The steel industry was the first to be attacked. The steelworkers' union struck in 1980 but its Right-Wing leaders were no match for Thatcher and they were defeated. But the Unions were not the only ones to react to Thatcher's economic diet of mass unemployment. Riots by black and white youth hit Liverpool, Manchester and London in the summer of 1981. Thatcher dealt with the critics from the more moderate wing of the Tory Party and she and the hawks in her Cabinet, Keith Joseph and Norman Tebbit, prepared more assaults on working people.

The Falklands War in 1982 gave them the chance to partially revive a kind of 'Little Englander' patriotism that had not been seen in Britain since the 1950s. Thatcher's project only really reached its fullest expression, though, after the Tories won the 1983 General Election. Her strength, and continued electoral success, was to an important degree due to the fact that her opponents were divided. Labour's Left Wing had reacted angrily to the self-inflicted defeat of 1979. The Left, grouped around Tony Benn, tried to ensure that no future Labour Government could disappoint and demoralize its own supporters in the way that the Callaghan Government had done. But the rise of the Left was unacceptable to the Labour Right-Wing. Some senior figures – like David Owen, Shirley Williams, Bill Rogers and Roy Jenkins – split from the Labour Party to form the Social Democratic Party in 1981. They eventually joined the Liberals, but they split the Labour vote keeping the Tories in power even though Thatcher never gained more than 43 percent of the vote at any time during her term of office.

Thatcher's offensive was not just domestic; the 'Iron Lady', as the Russian press dubbed her, was also the perfect Cold War Warrior to compliment Ronald Reagan as President of the US. Their most controversial joint venture was the agreement to station the new generation of nuclear-armed cruise, trident and pershing missiles in Britain. Starting from 1980, there was a public outcry in this country and in other European States where the missiles were also based. In huge marches organized by the CND and at the Missile Base at Greenham Common, where the largest protest was in 1983, hundreds of thousands took to the streets. But the decisive trial of strength between the Government and its opponents was the year-long miners' strike of 1984–1985, which was the longest mass strike in European history.

Thatcher had bided her time until she felt confident in her second term. Then she, the hawks in the Tory Party and the management of the National Coal Board drew up a plan to decimate the coal industry through a programme of pit closures. There was no economic logic to this closure programme, as the miners' leader Arthur Scargill repeatedly pointed out. Instead, the attack on the miners was political from the start. The NUM was the most powerful section of the Trade Union Movement. If it could be defeated then Union opposition could be broken and demoralization would sweep through the wider working class. The path would also be open for the full-Thatcherite, Neo-Liberal programme of privatization, anti-Union laws and welfare cuts to be implemented. The miners and their supporters fought with incredible tenacity. The courts seized NUM funds, the Government sent in the police and the army, pit villages were put under curfew and hundreds of miners were arrested. The decisive confrontation was at the Orgreave Coke Plant in the summer of 1984. Mass picketing had been decisive in the miners' victories in the 1970s. The Tories knew they had to break the mass pickets and the pitched battle at Orgreave was where the police acted on this plan. So important was this battle that on the evening news the BBC even altered the film sequence to show the miners attacking the police, even though it had actually been the police who had first attacked the miners' pickets. In the end, the long war against the miners wore them down and a year after they began the strike they voted to return to work. But it was not just the military operation against the miners that had defeated them, it was the fact that the Trade Union and Labour Party leaders had left them to fight on their own. Neil Kinnock, the then leader of the Labour Party, began a process which eventually led to Tony Blair and New Labour, when he refused to effectively support the miners or to encourage other Trade Unionists to take action in solidarity with them.

Resistance continued after the miners were defeated. The police brought the tactics they had been encouraged to use in the miners' strike to the policing of the inner cities. Cynthia Jarrett died during a police raid on her North London home in 1985. Tottenham exploded in a riot. Another black woman, Cherry Groce, was shot by police in a raid on her home in Brixton. The South London centre of the black community also rioted. And there was resistance to Thatcher's abolition of the Greater London Council (GLC). On the industrial scene, more defeats followed as the dockers and printers, two of the strongest sections of the Trade Union Movement, were defeated. Neil Kinnock and the leaders of the Unions were no more supportive of these workers than they had been of the miners. Perhaps the Kinnock strategy of distancing the Labour Party from the Left and the strikers might have been forgiven if it had worked. Some certainly would have seen it as worthwhile if it had got Thatcher out of 10 Downing Street, but Kinnock's strategy failed even in its own terms. He was beaten in the 1987 election and Thatcher returned for a third term. There was, however, another kind of revenge waiting for Margaret Thatcher. Partly as a result of the huge sums spent on defeating the miners, the Tories had to raise taxes.

The introduction of the poll tax to replace local council rates was to be Margaret Thatcher's downfall. The poll tax embodied the inequality and class discrimination that was the hallmark of Thatcherism. It was a flat rate tax; that is, you pay the same amount irrespective of how rich you are. As Tory Secretary of State for the Environment Nicholas Ridley boasted, 'A duke would pay the same as a dustman'. Introduced first in Scotland and then later in England and Wales, it provoked a

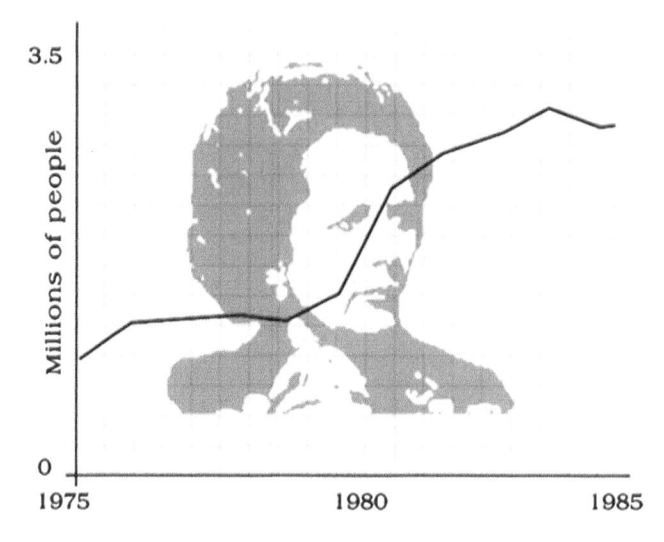

FIGURE 3.12 Unemployment in Britain, 1975 to 1985
Source: ONS Labour Force Survey.

massive non-payment campaign organized by the anti-poll tax groups that mushroomed in every town and city. By August of 1990, one in five of the entire population had refused to pay, with figures reaching up to 27 percent of people in London. Some 20 million people were issued with court summons for non-payment. Many Local Authorities were faced with a crisis, and councils faced a deficit of £1.7 billion for the next year. The anti-poll tax campaign culminated in a huge national demonstration in London in March 1990. As the march reached Trafalgar Square, the police attacked it. A huge battle ensued and a riot spread through central London. Cars were burnt outside the English National Opera in St. Martins Lane, jewellers' windows were broken in Regent Street and, back in Trafalgar Square, the crowd tried to set fire to the South African Embassy. When they failed another building on the south side of the Square was set ablaze. As the struggle with the police reached its peak a handmade banner reading 'Yorkshire Miners Against the Poll Tax' could be seen heading into the thick of the struggle. A few months later Thatcher was gone. The immediate cause was a struggle over Europe in the Tory Party, but the real reason was that Thatcher was massively unpopular and the poll tax had shown that she was presiding over a society where the Government was losing its authority. Even

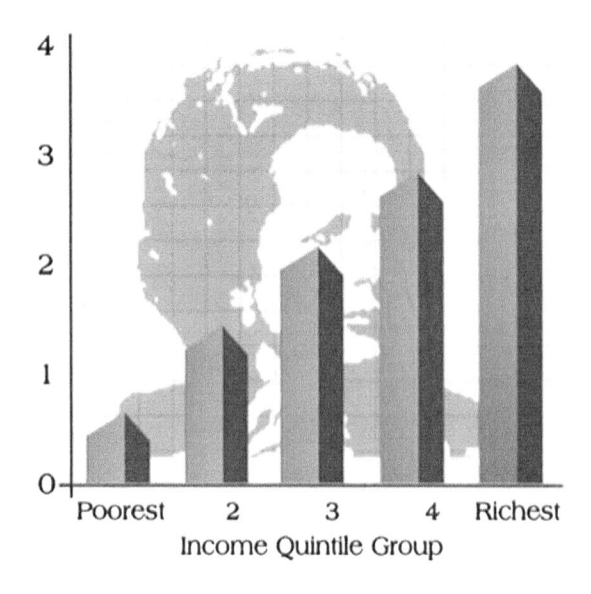

FIGURE 3.13 Average annual income gain in Britain, 1979 to 1990
Source: IFS; HMT.

after this popular revolt had got rid of Thatcher, Neil Kinnock's Labour Party was too weak to beat her successor, John Major, in the 1992 election. Five more years of accumulated discontent with the Tories, and another economic crisis, were necessary before the Tories were confined to political oblivion for more than a decade by the landslide victory that brought Tony Blair to power in 1997.

The 1980s was a low and dirty decade. Mass unemployment, poverty, privatization, and worsening health and education services corroded the lives of working people as they had not done since the 1930s. The basic dignity that working people had maintained by being able to organize themselves in Trade Unions to defend their wages and conditions at work was eroded. Their self-confidence was undermined and their political freedoms diminished. But for the rich and the corporations it was the 'loads o' money' decade, a 'Champagne decade' like the roaring 1920s. New Labour, which Margaret Thatcher herself has claimed as her greatest achievement, accepted that Thatcherism was here to stay. It mimicked and extended her policies, squandering its huge victories in three General Elections. Now the political wheel has turned full-circle and in 2010, as in 1979, an exhausted Labour Government that has

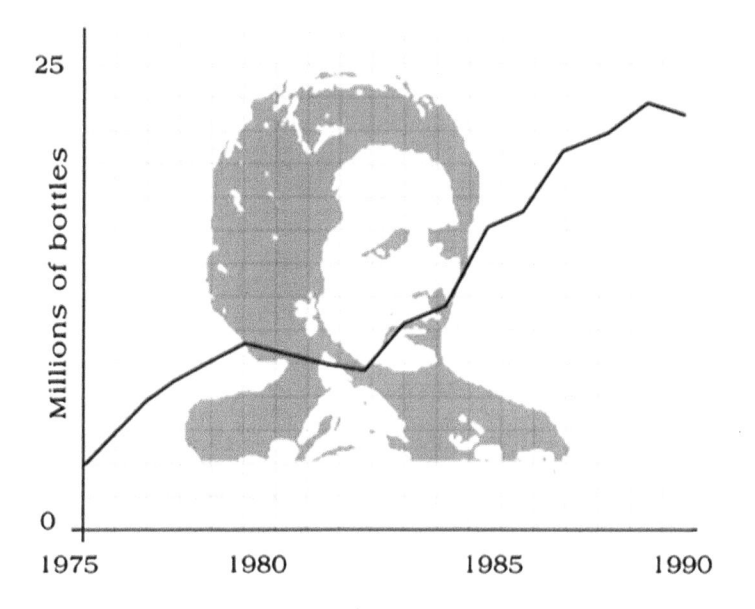

FIGURE 3.14 Champagne shipments to UK between 1975 and 1990
Source: Champagne Information Bureau.

disappointed its own supporters had to face an angry electorate. David Cameron has tried to distance himself from the Thatcher era in order to profit from this mood and the Tories have tried to reposition themselves by borrowing stylistically from Tony Blair just as he borrowed politically from them. But even this was not enough to give the Tories an outright victory and they had to depend upon a coalition with the Liberal Democrats to regain office. Moreover, the massive Government debts accumulated in the recession have meant that David Cameron has had to launch an even wider offensive on working class living standards and the Welfare State than Thatcher ever dared to mount.

Timeline: Thatcherism

1972: dockers and miners' strike against Heath Government
1974: miners' strike and General Election
1975: Margaret Thatcher becomes Tory Leader
1976: IMF austerity package
1979: Winter of Discontent; Thatcher wins election

1980: steelworkers' strike defeated
1981: inner-city riots
1982: Falklands War
1983: Thatcher's second election victory; cruise missile protests
1984–1985: Great Miners' Strike
1985: Tottenham and Brixton Riots
1986: abolition of the GLC
1990: poll tax riot; the fall of Thatcher
1992: Labour loses General Election to John Major
1997: Tony Blair's New Labour wins election landslide

The revolutions of 1989

In 1989 a series of revolutions in the so-called Communist States of Eastern Europe and then in Russia changed the history of the world. They tore down the Berlin Wall and with it the 'iron curtain' that had divided Europe since the 1940s and they ended the Cold War, the nuclear armed stand-off between Russia and the US. But what actually caused the revolutions of 1989? This is the focus of this next section.

The very last moments of the old Communist regime in East Germany seemed to turn on a slip of the tongue. There were, at that time, mass demonstrations in the streets and thousands of East Germans were trying to flee the country. Then on the 9 November 1989 Gunter Schabowski, the spokesman for the East German Communist Party, held a press conference. A reporter asked him about the new travel regulations issued by the Government which seemed to indicate the possibility of easier travel into West Berlin through the Berlin Wall. Schabowski had only recently received a copy of the new regulations and had not yet read them carefully. The reporter asked when, exactly, East German citizens could begin to take advantage of these new travel rules. Schabowski shrugged and responded, 'from now'. The result of this misstatement was a flood of East Germans heading into West Berlin. That evening *Reuters* reported (incorrectly) that East German citizens could cross into West Germany by any border crossing and West German television news programmes reported that the Berlin Wall was opening. Within minutes, thousands, then tens of thousands, then hundreds of thousands of Berliners, both East and West, began converging on the Berlin Wall. Without orders for how to handle the surging crowds, the East German border guards simply opened the gates. Crowds poured through in both directions and within minutes began tearing down the Berlin Wall.

The real causes of the fall of the Berlin Wall, however, reach further back and to another country. The most serious challenge to any Eastern bloc State came in 1980 with the creation of the Solidarity free Trade Union in Poland. Polish workers had a history of rebelling against their rulers. In 1970 protest demonstrations over food price rises had taken place in the northern cities and spread nationwide after troops shot and killed workers returning to their factories. The protests were so widespread that the Communist leadership resigned and their replacements agreed after face-to-face talks with the workers' leaders to rescind the prices rises and to increase wages. More strikes followed in 1976 and then, in 1980, the top blew off Polish society. The Lenin Shipyard in the port of Gdansk was occupied when activists excluded from the yards after the strikes of the 1970s built up support by distributing leaflets and eventually scaling the walls of the yard and addressing the workers. The occupations and strikes spread nationwide and Solidarity became a mass-movement of insurrectionary power. There had been revolts before in Eastern bloc States – in East Germany in 1953, in Hungary in 1956 and in Czechoslovakia in 1968 – but Solidarity was the greatest and most sustained revolt of all. However, Lech Walesa (the shipyard worker who came to head Solidarity) and the other leaders of the movement saw Solidarity as a 'self-limiting revolution'. Nervous of a Russian invasion and fearful of what a revolution might mean, they decided to negotiate a peace deal with the Government. It was a dangerous moment. The compromise gave the Government the chance to go on the offensive and institute a crackdown and in 1981 they instituted martial law. However, they could not really return to the old-style repression because they had been so weakened by the battle with the Union. By the late 1980s, the Government was having to negotiate with the Union again. These roundtable talks led to semi-free elections in 1989 and in those seats that Solidarity was allowed to contest it swept the board. It was the prelude to the amazing events of the rest of the year. But there was darkness before dawn.

In January 1989, the 77-year-old East German Leader Erich Honecker announced that the Berlin Wall 'will be standing in 50 and even in 100 years'. The following month (February), saw 20-year-old Chris Gueffroy shot dead as he tried to scale the Wall. What nobody knew then was that his would be the last death on the Berlin Wall. Many more, however, were about to lose their lives in China. On 15 April, the pro-market, pro-democracy and disgraced Communist Party Leader Hu Yaobang died. Mourners began gathering in Tiananmen Square in Beijing. On the 17 April – the day Solidarity won legal status in Poland – 3,000 students from Beijing University marched to join them. On the night of 21 April, 100,000 gathered in the Square. In early May the protests were still taking place in Beijing and now they were spreading to other major cities. By mid-May some 400 cities were aflame with protests. On the 3 June, the 27th Army shot its way into the centre of Beijing. By the following day the barricades had been smashed and Tiananmen Square was cleared. Pictures of one last, lone, anonymous figure confronting the tanks were flashed around the globe. Official Chinese Government figures say 241 people were killed; foreign correspondents say the figure was 3,000 dead. Tiananmen Square was a reminder that change was not inevitable in 1989. Indeed, by the middle of the year the thaw in Poland seemed more than outweighed by the continuing autocracy in the rest of Eastern Europe and the crackdown in China.

But there were signs that change was coming. The Russian State, led by Mikhail Gorbachev since 1985, had not intervened in Poland. No tanks had rolled West: that was new. Boris Yeltsin, a maverick from the elite, then took advantage of a tiny concession in the electoral law that allowed independent candidates (but not parties) to stand in elections. He won 84 percent of the vote in the race to become Deputy for Moscow. That had not happened before either. Moreover, the Hungarian CP Leadership condemned the massacre in Tiananmen Square as 'abject, uncivilised mass murder'. Likewise, a Politburo Member said that it was inconceivable that they would give the order to open fire on protestors. Nobody had heard that kind of talk before. Imre Nagy had been a martyr of the 1956 Hungarian Revolution; his body had lain in an unmarked grave since his death. On 16 June he was reburied as a hero. Then, just after events in Beijing had reached their climax, a seemingly innocuous event began the revolutionary process in Europe. Late in June, a pan-European picnic was held on the Austro-Hungarian border. It was a modest affair of beer, sausages and a bonfire held to celebrate the decommissioning of the alarm system on the border. A gate in the border, closed since 1948, was to be symbolically opened so that the small delegation could pass through to the small Austrian town of St. Margarethen. As the news of the planned picnic began to spread a great migration began. East Germans began heading across Czechoslovakia and into Hungary to join the picnic. Lieutenant Colonel Bella Arpad was commanding the local border guards. He was expecting a small delegation, but instead he saw:

> A large group appeared a hundred metres away. They didn't look like a delegation. They looked like East Germans...I approached them, it became clear that they wanted to go over to Austria. They didn't give me any time to ask questions. They pushed open the gates and rushed through like an express train.

Some 700 of them got through to be welcomed in local guesthouses and cafes. They were the first of many. In about six weeks in August and September the East German State lost 40,000 of its citizens.

In October, flight turned to fight. The first mass resistance inside East Germany came as thousands poured onto the streets of Leipzig. Gorbachev arrived in Berlin and made it clear that Russia would not intervene – the Sinatra doctrine (so-called after the song 'My Way', was here to stay). On the 7 October, Hungary voted to transform itself into a parliamentary democracy. On the same day there were violent clashes between protesters and riot police in Leipzig and Dresden in East Germany. The marches and protests continued and on the 16 October the Politburo got rid of Honecker in a last-ditch attempt to halt the Revolution. Now events piled on top of each other with dizzying speed. On the 23 October, Hungary declared an end to the Stalinist system. On the 3 November, Bulgarians began demonstrating in the capital Sofia. On 4 November, a million people demonstrated in Alexanderplatz in the heart of East Berlin. Before they had shouted 'we want out'; now they chanted 'we want to stay'. On 9 November, Gunter Schabowski held his press conference and his slip of the tongue was all that was needed to finally let the floods of people loose over the Berlin Wall. The momentum was now unstoppable. On the 10 November, the day that the Berlin Wall fell, so did the 78-year-old dictator of Bulgaria Todor Zhivkov. After another month had passed with demonstrations filling the streets of Prague, the 'Velvet Revolution' in Czechoslovakia got rid of its tyrant Gustav Husak.

There was, however, one more revolution to come. It started in the Romanian town of Timisoara, when a rebel local priest was about to be evicted from his flat by the authorities. Local people gathered to prevent the eviction. The protests grew and rioters broke into the local Party Offices of the brutal regime run by President Nicolai Ceausescu. The hated Securitate Secret Police could not deal with the emerging revolt so the army was called in and martial law was declared. It did not work. On the 20 December, 100,000 protestors defied martial law in Timisoara; the Christmas Revolution was under way. The next day, Ceausescu made a televised speech in which he denounced the Revolution in front of a large audience in Bucharest. It was a bad mistake. The crowd whistled, jeered and heckled and the live TV feed had to be cut off. Security forces and the army opened fire as the crowd took to the streets. The following day, Ceausescu tried to address the crowd again but had to be rescued from the building by helicopter as the angry masses rushed toward him. When he landed, Ceausescu was arrested, held and tried by a military tribunal and executed on Christmas Day.

The revolutions of 1989 were the greatest wave of rebellion to hit Europe since the revolutions in Russia and Germany at the end of the First World War. With the exception of Romania they were also remarkably peaceful. Why? The most fundamental explanation of the East European Revolutions is that they took place in societies where the old economic and political structure had been hollowed out long before the final revolutionary upheaval. They had been hollowed out economically by competition with the West, although they had initially grown faster than the Western economies after the Second World War. But they were much smaller to begin with and, as the world economy recovered, the State-dominated economies of the East were excluded from the international markets for materials, labour, capital and finished goods. By the 1980s they were lagging behind economically and in debt to Western banks. The military competition with the West was also a big part of the problem. The West was stronger and richer and by the time Ronald Reagan began a second arms race in the 1980s it was obvious that Russia and her allies could not match their rivals. Gorbachev's policy of 'Perestroika' and 'Glasnost' – reconstruction and openness – was an attempt to reform the system and come to an accommodation with the West. But this meant loosening both the bonds of Empire in Eastern Europe (the 'Sinatra Doctrine') and loosening the authoritarian structure of society. The first achievement of Solidarity had been to force this alternative onto the Russian agenda by creating a movement that would be too politically costly to repress. Solidarity's second achievement was to continue to struggle until the old regime gave way a decade after the Union first emerged onto the political scene. In Hungary and Czechoslovakia, the revolt from below did not need to be as strong or as sustained. The State bureaucrats in both these countries looked at Poland, noted the change in Russia and began an elite transition in which they got rid of the old 'Communist State' and turned themselves into private Capitalists. In East Germany, it was the role of the Russian Empire that mattered most. East Germany was an artificial nation, a third of a country created by Cold War partition. Once Russia had refused to intervene to prop up the East German Government the mass revolt from below were effectively pushing against a regime that had lost its reason for existence and its means of defence. Romania was different because it had remained much more isolated from Western economic loans and more independent of Russian military backing. It was, therefore, poor and isolationist and Romania's revolutionaries had to fight a brutal old order that had not been hollowed out in the same way as other States in Eastern Europe. More traditional revolutionary methods were therefore necessary.

For a moment, it looked as if the Winter of 1989 had opened a new phase of peace and prosperity in world history. But the hopes of those who made the revolutions were frustrated by the events that came after them. I reported on the demonstrations in East Germany for the three days before the Berlin Wall fell. I talked to the people who organized the demonstrations in their headquarters in Gesthemane Church in East Berlin. What they wanted was the economic security that they had in the East combined with the political freedom they thought existed in the West. What they got instead was the economic insecurity of free-market, globalized Capitalism and a political system in which the interests of the rich seemed as entrenched as the powers of the State bureaucrats against whom they had just fought. In Russia, Hungary and elsewhere many of the same old State bureaucrats turned themselves into the new rich. Demons frozen by the Cold War were set free when it ended. Globalization left most people in Eastern Europe poorer and new wars in Iraq in 1991, in the Balkans in 1999 and then again in Iraq and Afghanistan showed the real face of the post-Cold War world.

George Bush Snr. called it a 'New World Order', but many experienced it as a new world of disorder, violence and inequality. Now the very things that the revolutionaries of 1989 fought for are being fought for again by anti-war protesters, climate change campaigners, anti-poverty movements and Trade Unionists.

Timeline: the revolutions of 1989

January: Polish Government agrees to roundtable talks with Solidarity Movement
February: roundtable talks begin in Poland
April: protest begin in China
June: Tiananmen Square protests crushed; Imre Nagy reburied in Hungary
August: thousands of East Germans leave through Hungary
October: thousands demonstrate as Gorbachev visits East Berlin; end of 'Communist rule' in Hungary
November: Berlin Wall falls; Bulgarian Revolution; Velvet Revolution in Czechoslovakia
December: Romanian Revolution

Hugo Chavez's Revolution

Venezuelan President Hugo Chavez is one of the most controversial politicians in the world. His supporters argue that he has done more for the poor of his country than any previous Venezuelan leader. They also say that he has begun a revolutionary process that will define a new Socialism for the twenty-first century. Yet, his opponents say that this former military officer is an authoritarian figure whose economic policies are unworkable. So where does the truth lie?

In 1999 Hugo Chavez initiated a referendum that introduced a new Constitution for Venezuela. At the same time the country was given a new name. Since then, Venezuela has been known as 'The Bolivarian Republic of Venezuela'. The new name was chosen to honour Simon Bolivar, the early nineteenth-century hero who fought to liberate much of South America from the Spanish Empire. Bolivar came to London in 1810 to ask for British support. He did not get it, but he succeeded anyway in a series of dramatic political and military campaigns between 1810 and 1824, freeing an area that includes modern Peru, Ecuador, Colombia, Bolivia and Venezuela from European rule. Indeed, until

1830 Venezuela was part of Gran Colombia, the first post-Colonial State that Bolivar established. Gran Columbia also covered modern Ecuador and Colombia. Since that moment, Bolivar has remained a potent symbol of national independence and in modern day Venezuela Bolivar's name continues to have enormous resonance. His image still adorns the walls of the Venezuelan capital Caracas, his birthplace. Hugo Chavez has deliberately recalled the legend of Bolivar to underline his own radical and anti-Imperial policies.

For most its history, Venezuela has been ruled by military dictators; democratic government only replaced military rule in 1959. Even then, a pact between the two major pro-business mainstream parties meant that most ordinary Venezuelans still had little impact on how the elites governed the county. Venezuela's economy is dominated by oil, with revenues accounting for half the Government's budget. Venezuela is also a member of OPEC and its most valuable commodity shapes the country's economic welfare. But even with its oil earnings Venezuela has remained a deeply divided society. In Caracas, desperately poor shanty town dwellers live a world away from the rich. In the 1960s, it was said that there were more Cadillac owners in Caracas than in Chicago. The oligarchy treated the nationalized oil industry as their own personal fiefdom.

Hugo Chavez knew all about the inequalities in Venezuelan society from an early age. He was born in a mud hut, the second son in the impoverished family of two school teachers. At the age of 17 he joined the army. His first political organization was a political cell of army officers, although it sought alliances with Left-Wing groups outside the army. Founded in 1982, it was committed to overthrowing a political establishment that Chavez regarded as corrupt and unrepresentative. It was called the Bolivarian Revolutionary Movement, and became known as MBR200. The figure '200' was a reference to the 200th anniversary of Simon Bolivar's birth.

But it was not Chavez or his fellow officers that first revolted against the corrupt oligarchy that dominated Venezuelan life, it was the poor of the shanty-towns themselves as the Venezuelan elite adopted Neo-Liberal, free-market economic policies and poverty soared from 36 percent of the population in 1984 to 66 percent in 1995. Unemployment doubled, making Venezuela the country with the most unemployed in Latin America. The rich got richer and the poor got poorer. In February 1989, petrol prices rose and so too did the fares on public transport.

The students organized a bus boycott. Protests then spread throughout the country, although they were strongest in Caracas. The poor stormed on to the streets. President Perez sent in the army, and the army shot to kill. No one knows how many died but the toll is unlikely to be less than 2,000. The dead were mainly from the slums. The so-called 'Caracazo Uprising' was suppressed. But ever since demonstrations, protests and street actions have become part of Venezuelan life. The workers and the poor could be suppressed temporarily, but they were not willing to allow Venezuela's rulers to go back to their old ways. Following the defeat of the Caracazo, Hugo Chavez and his MBR200 Movement attempted to remove the Perez oligarchy in a coup just three years later. They attempted to seize the Presidential Palace and other key buildings, but the coup failed and Perez gave Chavez a single minute of TV time to announce his surrender. Chavez told viewers that the coup had failed 'for the moment'. The attempted coup earned Chavez national recognition and a two year prison sentence. A year later, President Perez was suspended from office after the High Court ruled that he had embezzled and misused public funds. Chavez emerged from jail in 1994 after a Presidential pardon and reformed the MBR200. He also created a new political party, the Fifth Republic Movement.

In December 1998, Venezuela's rulers were stunned when Hugo Chavez won the Presidency with 57 percent of the vote. It was not the last shock the old elites had to endure. Chavez took office in February 1999 and ordered a referendum asking Venezuelans if they wanted to elect an assembly to draw up a new constitution. Some 88 percent voted in favour of Chavez's proposals. Chavez supporters dominated the Constitutional Assembly and, in December 1999, 71 percent voted in favour of the new constitution. The following year, Chavez was elected for a six year term on 59 percent of the vote under the new constitution. The new constitution of the Bolivarian Republic was distributed throughout the country and even printed on packets of food. Within the year, Fedecamaras – Venezuela's leading business association – was working with the conservative forces of the CTV labour confederation to call a one-day general strike against Chavez's economic and land-reform policies. But this was just a prelude, the real struggle in Venezuela was still to come.

In February 2002, Chavez sacked General Lameda as Head of the State oil giant PDVSA and replaced him with a former Communist militant. Privileged oil workers slowed down vital oil production in response and, in April, Fedecamaras declared an indefinite general strike. The privately owned media mounted a huge campaign against Chavez and the opposition called a 150,000 march which headed for the Presidential Palace, clashing with Chavez supporters en-route. Snipers opened fire on the Chavez supporters and they returned fire. Ten were left dead and 110 injured. When the privately owned TV stations showed the footage of the shooting they reversed the order of the film, cutting out film from camera angles, so that it appeared that the Chavez supporters opened fire first on a peaceful demonstration.

High-ranking Military Officers demanded that Chavez resign. On the following day, the 11 April 2002, the military launched a coup, arrested Chavez and appointed Pedro Carmona – one of the strike organizers and head of Fedecamaras – as head of a transitional government. The poor surged back on to the streets. Massive protests by ordinary Venezuelans surrounded the Presidential Palace and demanded the return of Chavez. The demonstrations were so large and the crowd's anger so great that Carmona was forced to resign. Chavez was flown back to the Presidential Palace in a helicopter. Relief swept through the crowd and registered in the faces of Chavez's besieged Ministers and supporters within the Palace. Mass mobilization had saved the Chavez Government and the coup had been defeated. It was a turning point, but the old rulers had not finished trying to destroy Chavez's Government. Business leaders initiated another strike in the crucial oil industry, which did massive damage to the economy. But it also backfired as most Venezuelans blamed the Right rather than Chavez and the strike ended in February 2003. Three months later the opposition was ready to act again, but the previous defeats now forced them to work within the constitution. In May 2003, they began collecting signatures to trigger a new referendum on Chavez's rule. They finally got their way in 2004, but, much to the dismay of the business elite, Chavez went on to win the referendum. In 2006 he won another six year term as President.

So why is it that Hugo Chavez's Government is so bitterly opposed by the Venezuelan elite? Is it because of his radical economic policy? Well, it is certainly true that the business leaders do not like nationalization because it gives to the State revenues that previously came to them as private profit. But, in fact, the level of nationalization in Chavez's Venezuela is not that extraordinary. Some point to the fact that the most important industry (oil) is nationalized, but so too are the oil industries in Saudi Arabia, Kuwait and Iran. And, in any case,

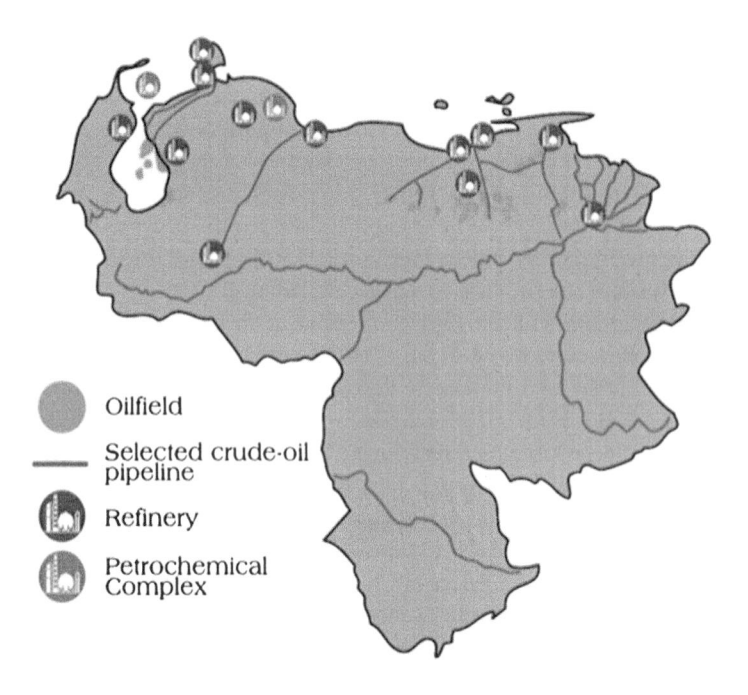

FIGURE 3.15 Petroleum production in Venezuela

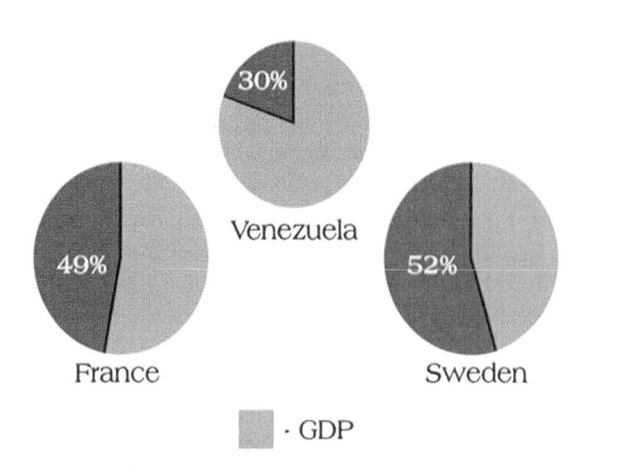

FIGURE 3.16 Overall spending of GDP in Venezuela, Sweden and France

oil was nationalized long before Chavez came to power, although he did move against the managers who were exploiting it for their own gain. In 2006 Chavez nationalized the telecommunications giant CANTV and some other electricity generation companies; but telecommunications had previously been nationalized and then privatized, so Chavez was just bringing it back into public ownership. And electricity generation was already 80 percent publicly owned. There has recently been some more nationalization, but these and the earlier nationalizations have all generously compensated the private owners. Plus, the Venezuelan State's overall spending is 30 percent of GDP, which is a figure well below the 49 percent spent in France and the 52 percent spent in Sweden.

So if Chavez's nationalization programme alone is not the cause of the disquiet for the political Right, what is? Chavez's social policy provides part of the answer. Venezuela's massive oil revenues have been used in ways that no previous government would even have considered. Central Government social spending has rocketed from 8.2 percent of GDP when Chavez was elected to 13.6 percent in 2006. That is an increase of 170 percent for every Venezuelan; and even that is an underestimate. If the social spending of the nationalized oil giant PDVSA is included, the increase is 314 percent per-head of the population! Access to education at all levels has risen by an average of more than 30 percent and there are now 12 times more health care professionals in Venezuela than when Chavez came to power. Food is also subsidized through special Mission Mercal Stores and poverty has been halved. These changes, and the political defeats inflicted on the establishment forces that tried to unseat Chavez, have made the workers and the poor of Venezuela more confident. They see and sense that a better world is possible. And it is this, more than the changes in economic ownership, which have so profoundly unsettled Venezuela's traditional rulers. They fear that this growing confidence among ordinary Venezuelans will endanger their wealth and remaining power. When Chavez talks of Socialism, when he opposes US foreign policy, the Right fear that he will unleash an even more radical process than the 'Bolivarian Revolution'.

So can Chavez survive? Chavez's opponents have been defeated on every occasion when they have challenged him, but they are not finished. In 2007 Chavez lost a vote to extend his Presidential powers. Plus, in recent local elections Chavez was again victorious, but the opposition made gains; especially in important oil producing areas and in areas near Colombia from where many believe they get US aid. Chavez represents too big a threat for the establishment to let him go unchallenged for long. But on each occasion when Chavez has been threatened in the past it has been the mass mobilization of the Venezuelan workers and poor that have saved him. Faced with recession they will expect the Government to aid them: to adopt more radical policies that will prevent them from paying for the crisis, to defend the social welfare policies that have reduced poverty and to improve literacy and healthcare. Some workers, like those at the Invepal Paper Mill and Sanitarios Maracay, have already taken matters into their own hands by taking control of their factories and demonstrating with the aim of winning support from the Government for their action. Chavez's survival will depend on how he reacts to these developments: whether he embraces them as a deepening of the process of progressive change in Venezuela or whether he tries to limit this process. There are dangers either way. If Chavez embraces more radical change he will no doubt face intensified opposition from the Right. If he does not embrace more radical change he risks disappointing and demobilizing the very people who have saved him from the establishment on every previous occasion when he has been attacked. These are the choices that face Hugo Chavez and the Venezuelan people.

Timeline: Hugo Chavez's Revolution

1819: Simon Bolivar liberates the area including present day Venezuela
1982: Chavez establishes Bolivarian Revolutionary Movement (MBR200)
1989: 'Caracazo Revolt' against Neo-Liberal economic policies
1992: Hugo Chavez stages unsuccessful coup
1998: Hugo Chavez elected President
1999: new 'Bolivarian' constitution agreed by 71 percent of voters
2000: Chavez re-elected under new Constitution
2001: Fedecameras calls general strike
2002: Fedecameras calls second general strike; attempted coup defeated; oil strike starts

2003: oil strike ends; opposition calls for referendum to remove Chavez
2004: Chavez wins referendum
2006: Chavez wins another six-year term as President
2007: Chavez loses vote to extend Presidential powers
2009: Chavez supporters win local elections, but opposition makes gains

Student revolts

In recent years, hundreds of thousands of students worldwide have been involved in marches and college occupations over issues as diverse as the plight of the Palestinians, the war in Iraq and the imposition of student fees. They are the latest student generation to be involved in radical politics. Before them, Chinese students protested for democracy in Tiananmen Square in 1989. A decade earlier Iranian students had helped overthrow the Shah of Iran in 1979. And ten years before that there were mass student protests over the war in Vietnam. Here we examine how student revolts have changed our society.

Most student movements since the Second World War have been radical and progressive. But it was not always this way. Before the War, the University system, both in Britain and throughout the world, was for the wealthy elite. Only small numbers got to go to University at all and they were overwhelmingly the sons and daughters of the rich. Whatever their chosen topic, they were also being taught how to be the next generation of rulers. As such, whenever there was any social conflict or division, the majority of students would side with the political elite. This was the way it was in the British General Strike of 1926. The Government organized volunteers to scab on the strike by keeping the transport running; students were prominent, if not very effective, among the volunteers. In Germany in the following decade, students were as likely to support the Nazis as they were to oppose them. Indeed, students participated in the notorious 'Book Burnings' organized by the Nazi SA, as one American observer recorded:

> Here the heap grew higher and higher, and every few minutes another howling mob arrived, adding more books to the impressive pyre. Then, as night fell, students from the university, mobilized by

the little doctor [Goebbels], performed veritable Indian dances and incantations as the flames began to soar skyward.

There was little opposition to the Nazis from the Deutsche Studentenschaft, the student organization to which all German University students had to belong. Some of its members even tried to 'out-Nazi' Hitler's rival student organization. Nevertheless, there was opposition to the Nazis from a minority of German students. Hans and Sophie Scholl and their White Rose organization scattered anti-Nazi leaflets around Munich University, including in the main atrium of the University itself. They were caught by the Gestapo and beheaded in 1943. In the same year one of their leaflets that had been smuggled out of Germany was reproduced and dropped by Allied planes over Germany.

It was the post-War expansion of University education in the 1950s and 1960s that really transformed student politics. University was certainly not open to most working class children even after this expansion had taken place, but the number of working class students was larger and the number of middle class students, as opposed to students coming from the real elite, was also significantly enlarged. The fast-growing Capitalist economies needed a larger educated stratum of mangers, officials, technocrats, teachers and professionals. University education was expanded to meet this need. In 1940 there were just 69,000 students in Britain; that figure had doubled by 1954. Ten years later it had doubled again to 294,000 and in the next eight years this figure more than doubled again to reach around 600,000 by 1972. Students made up just one percent of their age group in 1950, but by 1972 they made up 15 percent of their age group. As they expanded, the Universities began to change character; education was no longer the leisurely amateur pursuit of a small highly privileged minority. Education became more standardized; it was a mass product, not a craftsman's product. Universities became more like factories designed to turn out this product.

One of the first and most significant student revolts of the post-War period came not in the West but in the Stalinist East where students were the instigators of the Hungarian Revolution of 1956. Opposition to the Government in Hungary first appeared as a Solidarity Movement with the political reforms that were taking place in Poland. There the thaw that began in the Eastern bloc after Stalin's death in 1953 had produced a reform-minded government under Gomulka. On 22 October, student meetings in Hungary called for a mass demonstration the following day 'in solidarity with our Polish brothers'. At first, the Government allowed the demonstration to take place; it even allowed for details to be broadcast on the radio. In Budapest, the walls, trees and hoardings were covered with the students' placards. Crowds formed around them discussing the coming demonstration. Then the Government changed its mind and withdrew permission for the demonstration; this only made it look weak and increased the students' determination. As the demonstrations began from different parts of the city the Government knew that it could not stop them; 100,000 were on the streets and more still were arriving. Later, after listening to speeches, some protestors toppled the statue of Stalin in the city park and then they headed for the radio station. Here they were met by 500 armed political police, the AVH. The police used tear gas, but the tear gas blew back in the face of the police. The crowd surged forward again; a police machine gun fired. Some demonstrators fell to the ground, but others fought back with stones and petrol bombs. And, because off-duty police and Home Guard officers were in the crowd, they had guns. The fighting spread throughout Budapest. Workers ran to their factories to gather their friends and to get weapons from the factory sports clubs. A revolution had started; workers' councils and revolutionary committees soon sprung up across Hungary. The Revolution was only halted by Russian tanks and the death of 20,000 Hungarians.

The next peak of student radicalism took place in the 1960s in the heart of Western Capitalism, the US. The Civil Rights Movement was a conflict between the black population of the US and the endemic racism of US society, especially in the Southern States. Here racist laws and racist attitudes born on the slave plantations before the American Civil War still lived on. In 1960 the US Supreme Court ruled in the case of Boynton vs. Virginia that is was against the law for there to be racial segregation in the restaurants and waiting rooms in terminals serving buses that crossed State lines. It was already supposed to be illegal on the inter-State buses themselves. The Freedom Rides that started in 1961 were designed to test the law. Increasing numbers of Freedom Riders took buses into the south, many of them students, and when they got there they organized Freedom Schools to compensate for the racist education system and voter registration campaigns to ensure that blacks were not terrorized out of exercising their democratic rights. Many white students also became part of the Civil Rights Movement, whose figurehead was Martin Luther King. The activists were attacked by police and by lynch mobs. They also did time in jail, but they kept coming. They went to live in black communities. One volunteer, Vivian Leburg, found herself sleeping on the porch 'next to a rifle I didn't even know how to use'. It was a political awakening that would feed into the coming anti-war movement and the Women's Movement. Above all it was a radical break from the conformity of 1950s America and, for many, from the middle class backgrounds from which they came. One woman wrote to her parents:

> Dear Mom and Dad... This letter is hard to write because... it is very hard to answer your attitude that if I loved you I wouldn't do this... I can only hope you have the sensitivity to understand that I can both love you very much and desire to go to Mississippi... I think you have to live to the fullest extent... or you are less than the human being you are capable of being... This doesn't apply just to civil rights or social consciousness but to all the experiences of life.

As the Civil Rights Movement gained in strength the new mood began to affect whole campuses, not just the minority from the colleges who went south. And students also began to raise their own issues. In 1964, the year of Freedom Summer in the South, the Berkeley Campus in San Francisco exploded into life. Student Mario Savio was addressing 6,000 students having just heard that he might be expelled for his part in a demonstration two months before; part of the crowd occupied the college. They were cleared by police who arrested 800 of them. As they sat in the cells, between 60 and 80 percent of the student body of 30,000 staged a strike. It was a sign of things to come.

1968 has become known as the year of student revolution. Certainly students were at the forefront of the battles of that year, but it would be quite wrong to imagine that they were the only force which made 1968 a watershed year in the history of the twentieth century. January 1968 saw an equally dramatic turn of events in Vietnam when the liberation forces launched the Tet Offensive, catching their US opponents by surprise and permanently altering the global perception of the US's ability to win the War. Also in January, the new leader of Czechoslovakia,

Alexander Dubcek, began a cautious process of liberalization. It became known as the Prague Spring. It was too much for the Moscow old-guard and in August a Russian-led invasion force entered Czechoslovakia to crush the reform movement. They were met by protests. In one of the most poignant student protests Jan Palach set himself on fire in the central square of Prague. Elsewhere, student protests went off like firecrackers around the globe: Poland, Mexico, the US, Germany, Italy, France, Brazil, Spain, Britain. In Berlin, 10,000 students held a sit-in to protest over the Vietnam War. In March, the University of Rome was closed for 12 days by an anti-war protest. The same month the Grosvenor Square Demonstration in London ended with 86 injured and 200 arrested. And again in March military police in Brazil killed a high school student who was protesting in favour of cheaper meals for poor students. This sparked a movement against the military Government of Brazil. In Madrid, the University was closed by protest for 38 days after a Catholic Mass was said for Adolf Hitler. Instantly, student leaders became, depending on your view, heroes or villains in the media: Dany Cohn-Bendit in France, Rudi Deutscke in Germany, Tariq Ali in London. No wonder the student slogan of the hour was 'We shall fight, we shall win, Paris, London, Rome, Berlin'.

Of all the student movements of 1968, however, it was the French students who showed both the strength and the limitations of 'student power' as it was being called. The French Student Movement was part of the global movement, concerned with Vietnam and civil rights, but it also had local origins. French universities were growing and overcrowded and their internal regimes were, like the French State, authoritarian. The French Student Movement had been building up for some time, although until May 1968 relatively small numbers were involved. It was the Minister of Education's decision to close the whole of the University of Paris and send in the riot police to clear protesters from the Sorbonne that escalated the protest. On 6 May, students were battling with riot police in the Latin Quarter of Paris. The rioting dominated the news; student protest had become a national crisis. On the 8 May, the leaders of the Paris Trade Unions joined the demonstrations.

Then came the night of 10 May, the 'Night of the Barricades'. As police tried to bottle up protesters in the streets around Boulevard Saint Michel, the protestors responded by turning the area into a police-free zone by erecting barricades of overturned cars, barbed wire and building materials. The Government ordered the police in and street battles lasted through the night. If the demonstrations had remained mainly student in composition, then that might have been the end of the matter, but now a crucial change in the balance of forces took place. The leaders of the major Trade Unions had been meeting that night. They listened, horrified, to the reports as they came in. Then they called a general strike for the following Monday (13 May). This general strike and mass demonstration marked the transition from a student uprising to a working-class revolt. The next day in Nantes at the Sud Aviation factory, where weekly symbolic strikes of 15 minutes to protest against the cut in hours and wages had been going on for months, young workers, under Trotskyist and Anarchist influence, refused to return to work after the 15 minute stoppage. They marched through the factory; they were feeling confident as a result of the biggest working-class demonstration since the liberation of France. The next day, at the Renault plant in Cleon, the young workers did the exact same thing. The day after that, the strike spread to all of the Renault Plants (six in total). That night, the main Renault Plant at Billancourt – the largest, most militant and historically important factory in France, employing 35,000 people – was occupied. A full-scale general strike was under way. Eventually, only the dissolution of the Government and fresh elections were able to end the crisis. But what the French students had shown was that, where they could link with other more powerful forces in society, student protest could become the beginning of wider challenges to the political elites. This pattern has been repeated time after time in very different circumstances ever since 1968.

In 1979 Iranian students were at the forefront of the struggles to overthrow the despotic, Western-backed Government of the Shah of Iran. But, as in France, it was only when workers, especially the critical oil industry workers, joined in the protest that the Shah had to flee the country. Again, as in France, the movement did not develop a leadership which represented the interests of either the students or the workers. In fact, the leadership of the Revolution fell into the hands of Ayatollah Khomeini, whose supporters, although long-time critics of the Shah, had neither been the ones who began the Revolution nor the main force that had rid the country of the old despotism. In 1989, students were involved in the Tiananmen Square democracy protests in China, but although the image of the lone student facing the tanks that finally crushed the demonstrations tends to give the impression that the protesters were mainly student or human rights activists, this is in fact not the case. Some 400 factories in China were also involved in the democracy protests and it was this, as much as the more publically visible protests in the capital, which terrified the 'Coca Cola Communists' who were trying to integrate China into the world market.

Today, as a new strike wave surges through China, protestors might recall the real lessons of 1989: protests can be powerful on the street, but more powerful still if they also have the weight of protest in the workplace added to them. Similar lessons are being re-learnt among students in the West. The last decade has seen more student protest than at any time since the 1970s. Students have protested over globalization, Third World debt, the wars in Iraq and Afghanistan, environmental issues, the conflict in Palestine, cuts to their courses and hikes in the fees that they are having to pay to go to college. Many have had to work their way through college in a way that their parents did not. In this harsh climate the most important enduring lesson of student politics remains relevant. It is easier for students than it is for others to begin a struggle, but it is harder for them to finish one successfully unless they find allies among wider layers of working people.

Timeline: student revolts

1950s and 1960s: post-War expansion of Higher Education
1956: students in Hungary protest against Stalinism
1960s: students support US Civil Rights Movement
1968: student revolutions in France, Germany, Italy, UK and US
1979: Iran Revolution
1989: Tiananmen Square protests
2003: students protest against war and globalization

CONCLUSION
The first decade of the twenty-first century

As the year 2000 dawned, with spectacular firework displays crackling through the air in capital city after capital city around the world, all seemed to be set fair for the defenders of the system. The world economy had successfully survived the economic crash in South East Asia in the late 1990s and, led by the so-called 'new economy' in the US, seemed set for another expansive burst; there had been wars in both Iraq and the Balkans, but both conflicts were concluded as the new century opened; the global challenge of climate change seemed to have been addressed with the signing of the Kyoto Protocol in 1997 (although the US were not one of these signatories); even the much-feared 'Millennium Bug' that some thought would crash computers around the world had failed to take effect. Yet, despite this optimism, the first years of the new century went on to be dominated by new wars, whilst the final years of the decade have been dominated by global recession and renewed fears of climate change. So what went wrong?

First, it should be appreciated that the optimists in the establishment had not been the only ones voicing their opinions as the new millennium approached. In the dying days of the twentieth century, the World Trade Organization had met in the US city of Seattle. A counter-protest had been organized against 'globalization', as it was then called, by a relatively small group of people who, some ten years after the fall of so-called Communism in Eastern Europe, were newly critical of free-market Capitalism. Some 40,000 to 50,000 took to the streets to protest at low-wage non-Union 'Mac-jobs', the destruction of traditional agriculture in the less-developed world, at poverty and at climate change. Those who protested were described as being 'anti-Capitalist' by the media; a new language was being born. This same

Conclusion 195

alliance – the Unions, the Left, NGOs, charities and churches – continued to protest throughout the coming decade, profoundly altering the terms of mainstream political debate. But although these voices from below were becoming more critical, it was still business as usual for the politicians, financiers and corporate leaders. This was despite the fact that with the new decade only two months and ten days old there was warning tremor in the financial system as on 10 March 2000 the 'dot.com bubble' collapsed. The ensuing stock market crash was nowhere near as serious as the current global slump, but it was a warning that even stocks based on the newest technological breakthroughs would not go on rising forever. It was a warning that was ignored.

The world of international relations was also facing its own tremors. Vladimir Putin was elected President of Russia, symbolizing the resurgence of Russian power from the pit into which it had fallen after the collapse of Communism ten years earlier. Russia's economy was recovering and it began to develop a more assertive foreign policy. But the Presidential Election that really altered the face of world politics came at the end of the first year of the century, when on 7 November 2000 George W. Bush – son of former President George Bush Snr., Texan oilman and the darling of the Republican Party's Right-Wing – was elected the 43rd President of the US. Bush followed his January 2001 Inauguration by appointing one of the most Right-Wing governments the US has ever seen. Vice President Dick Cheney, Secretary for Defense Donald Rumsfeld, Secretary of State Condoleezza Rice and many others beside, were all part of the Neo-Conservative Right. Many of these figures had been associated with a private institute called the 'Project for the New American Century' which, even under the Presidency of Bill Clinton, had been demanding that the US take a new more hard-line international policy. In their view, the end of the Cold War meant that the US was now free from the restraints that might be imposed by competition from another major power; put bluntly, it was time for the US to throw its weight around and to get its own way in the world. Now, thanks to George W. Bush, this group had the power to put this policy into effect. What they did not have was a motivating factor that would make such an aggressive foreign policy acceptable both in the US and around the world.

On 11 September 2001 an opportunity presented itself. That day, hijackers associated with Al Qaeda crashed two aircraft into the World

Trade Center in New York and a third into the Pentagon in Washington. A fourth hijacked airliner missed its target (most likely the Capitol Building in Washington) and crashed in Shanksville, Pennsylvania. In all, nearly 3,000 people died. The attack horrified millions of people around the globe. This sense of outrage gave the Neo-Conservatives their chance, as Condoleezza Rice recognized when she asked her staff, 'how do we take advantage of this opportunity?' The Bush Administration faced two problems after 9/11. First, the Taliban regime in Afghanistan actually offered to hand over Osama Bin Laden to the US in order to forestall an attack. This was simple enough for the Bush Administration to deal with; they brushed the offer aside and continued to debate the military options. Over this, however, they were divided. The hawks in Bush's Administration, like Cheney and Rumsfeld, wanted to bypass Afghanistan altogether and go straight in for an invasion of Iraq. Iraq was much more important, they argued, both strategically and because of its oil riches. But Secretary of State Colin Powell eventually convinced Bush that they could not go straight for an invasion of Iraq because Iraq had no link (there were no Iraqis involved in the 9/11 attacks and there was no Al Qaeda in Iraq) to the attacks on the World Trade Center. So, the attack on Afghanistan was agreed on as a kind of preliminary war, preliminary to the real aim of the Neo-Conservatives, the invasion of Iraq. The following month the air bombardment of Afghanistan began. In 2002, a land invasion of Afghanistan led by NATO troops ensured that the US won the already-existing Afghan Civil War for the Northern Alliance against the Taliban. This was a deceptively easy victory for the US; some ten years later, Western forces are still stuck in Afghanistan, the Afghan Government the West supports is universally condemned as being corrupt and the Taliban still have a presence in 80 percent of the country.

While the US was beginning the long 'War on Terror', both its allies and its opponents were making some historic decisions. Two of these events underlined a central paradox of the early twenty-first century: the mismatch between declining US economic power and its predominant military strength. On the first day of 2002, the Euro replaced the currencies of 12 of the EU's 15 member States. For the first time since the decline of the Pound Sterling, a currency to rival the US dollar on the world markets was emerging. Then, on 11 April 2002, the Socialist Leader of Venezuela, Hugo Chavez, was threatened by a Right-Wing military coup. A dramatic mass popular mobilization saved Chavez; it was a symbolic moment which showed that one cost of the 'War of Terror' for the US was a declining influence in its own backyard, Latin America.

Even in the West, discontent was growing. Activists from the global anti-war movement that was springing up met at a protest in Florence, Italy, to plan a worldwide day of action to try and stop the war against Iraq. The day agreed on was 15 February 2003. That day turned into the largest ever globally coordinated day of political protest. In hundreds of cities and towns in every continent of the world, protestors poured onto the streets to oppose the war in Iraq. In Britain, the two million who took to the streets officially created (according to the *Guinness Book of Records*) the largest ever political demonstration the country had ever seen. But the decision to go to war had already been taken, and George W. Bush and Tony Blair began the attack in March 2003. The following month, US forces seized control of Baghdad and by December 2003 Saddam Hussein had been captured. Yet, the attack on Iraq did not end terrorism. As the British Security Services had warned Tony Blair before the War, it simply made things worse, as evidenced by the 2003 Madrid Train Bombing which killed 191 people. The massive response on the streets of Spain forced the Spanish Government to withdraw its troops from Iraq and the US lost one of its most important European allies. Elsewhere the 'War of Terror' was strengthening the hand of the opponents and competitors of the US. On 14 March, Vladimir Putin was returned to power for a second time in the Russian Presidential Election. On 1 May, the largest expansion to date of the EU took place, with Poland, Lithuania, Latvia, Estonia, the Czech Republic, Slovakia, Slovenia, Hungary, Malta and Cyprus all joining.

Yet, despite these difficulties, George W. Bush – pitching himself as a 'War President' – succeeded in winning a second term in November 2004. Tony Blair had been second only to Bush as a proponent of the 'War on Terror'. Inevitably, the propaganda of war had demonized Muslims as the enemy abroad and this could not help but lead to them being demonized as the enemy within. The awful, but predictable, result of this demonization was brought home with terrible force on 7 July 2005 when suicide bombers attacked London's public transport system, killing 56 people. By the middle of the decade, the full effect of Bush's 'War on Terror' was beginning to emerge. In October 2006, North Korea performed its first successful nuclear test. In July 2006, Israel, encouraged by the aggressive turn in US foreign policy, invaded Southern Lebanon in an attempt to crush Hezbollah and the Lebanese Resistance. The month-long war was a disaster for Israel and its forces were decisively repulsed by the Lebanese Resistance. In Britain, there was a renewed burst of anti-war activity, with 100,000 people taking to the streets in protest at Tony Blair's refusal to back calls for a ceasefire. Eight Government Aides resigned over the issue and Blair was forced to promise that he would leave office within 12 months. *Fox News* reported Blair saying, 'I would have preferred to do this in my own way', and went on to announce that: 'Pressure for the Prime Minister to announce a departure date had intensified in recent weeks, fuelled by widespread anger at Blair's handling of last month's fighting between Israel and Lebanon-based Hezbollah militants.'

In April 2007, President Vladimir Putin announced that Russia would suspend the 1990 Conventional Armed Forces in Europe Treaty, which limited conventional weapons stockpiling in Europe. In July, Putin said that he would suspend Russia's participation in the Conventional Forces in Europe Treaty, a Cold War era agreement that limited the deployment of heavy weaponry. Further unintended consequences of Bush's 'War on Terror' were felt in Pakistan, where the war in Afghanistan was destabilizing the country. On 27 December 2007, Benazir Bhutto was assassinated in Rawalpindi just two weeks before a national election that she was widely predicted to win. In May 2008, Dmitri Medvedev, Putin's appointed nominee, took over as President of Russia; Putin remained as Prime Minister. In August, war between Russia and Georgia (backed by the West) broke out over the disputed South Ossetia Region of the Caucuses. Loud but ineffective protests emanated from the West, but Russia invaded Georgia anyway; the result was de-facto independence for South Ossetia.

The other growing rival to US world leadership, China, announced its own spectacular coming-of-age on 8 August 2008 when the Olympic Games opened in Beijing. It was obvious that a new power in the world system – resting upon rapid industrial growth and a savage repression of the population – was emerging, presenting the US with far bigger challenges than anything that had emerged from the 'War on Terror'. This fact was underlined by the sudden worsening of the economic crisis that had begun with the housing loan debacle of 2007. In September, Lehman Brothers – one of the biggest banks in the world – filed for bankruptcy. It was the catalyst for the crisis to become a global economic catastrophe, the worst slump since the 1930s. The IMF estimated that large US and European banks lost more than $1 trillion from bad loans between January 2007 and September 2009. These losses were expected to top $2.8 trillion by the end of 2010. Barack Obama inherited this disaster when he became US's first black President on 4 November 2008. The 44th President of the US, he had deeper crises to contend with than any previous Presidents, except Abraham Lincoln and Franklin Roosevelt.

The final year of the decade reads like a roll-call of problems that have been created by globalization and war in the last ten years. Israel tried to avenge its 2006 defeat in Lebanon by invading the Gaza Strip in the very first days of 2009 before Obama was inaugurated. Iran, strengthened by the US's struggles in Iraq and Afghanistan, advanced its own nuclear programme, although its Government did face sustained protests by a population whose faith in the regime is draining away. Meanwhile, the growing economic crisis has meant that US's dependence on China's dollar reserves has been made clear for all to see. Indeed, China, Russia and some other Oil States are now even talking of creating a new world currency to challenge the US dollar and, on 10 July, Russian President Dmitry Medvedev unveiled a potential world currency to replace the US dollar by pulling from his pocket a sample coin of a 'united future world currency' at the G8 Summit.

This new great power rivalry could not even be contained at the UN's 2009 Climate Change Conference, which was held in Copenhagen, Denmark, in December. The standing of the US in relation to this issue had already been undermined when they refused to sign the Kyoto Agreement, which came into force in 2005. Nature seemed almost to take her own revenge as Hurricane Katrina hit coastal areas from Louisiana to Alabama in 2005, killing at least 1,836 and doing severe damage all along the Gulf Coast. Unfortunately, the Copenhagen Conference only proved that many other nations were no better placed than the US to face the challenges of climate change and the Conference descended into farce as world leaders scuttled for their planes after failing to reach an agreement. President Obama blamed China and China blamed the US.

In some senses, the first decade of the twenty-first century ended just as it had begun. Millions of ordinary people were looking to their Governments to do something about climate change, just as they had looked to them at the end of the previous decade to address world poverty and climate change. Likewise, they still looked to them to prevent wars and economic disasters from occurring. In all cases, failure by the governing classes in response to these issues produced two characteristic reactions: some became demoralized and cynical, but millions of others became engaged and active, determined to change what their leaders seemed incapable of changing.

FURTHER READING

In this guide to further reading I have tried to include at least one book that either in whole or in part relates to each of the preceding essays. The latest book on any particular topic is not necessarily the best and so I have listed the most notable works of which I am aware on the basis that the Internet now allows much easier access to out-of-print work than was previously the case. I have usually referred to the edition which I consulted in writing the essays, but, where I am aware of newer editions, I have cited them instead. I have also included some works of fiction because the historian's job is not just to record the facts about the past, but also to recover the thoughts, feelings and emotions of those who shaped our history.

The outstanding radical history of the twentieth century is Eric Hobsbawm's *The Age of Extremes, The Short Twentieth Century, 1914–1991, New Edition* (Penguin, 1994). Hobsbawm's scope and ability to synthesize make this an essential volume. His judgments are often correct and always interesting. In part, Hobsbawm's book is required reading because it has relatively few competitors. Gabriel Kolko's *Century of War: Politics, Conflicts and Society since 1914* (New Press, 1994) is also a serious work of synthesis, though his *The Politics of War: The World and United States Foreign Policy 1943–1945* (Pantheon, 1968) is, though narrower in focus, the stronger book. John Terraine's *The Mighty Continent: A View of Europe in the Twentieth Century* (BBC/Hutchinson, 1974) was, like this book, the product of an accompanying TV series many years ago. It makes no claims to radicalism, but it is serious and well written and the illustrative material is still impressive. James Joll's longstanding *Europe Since 1870, Third Edition* (Penguin, 1983) and Peter Calvocoressi's *World Politics Since 1945, Seventh Edition* (Longman, 1996) can also be consulted. Paul Kennedy's *The Rise and Fall of Great Powers: Economic Change and Military Conflict from 1500 to 2000* (Fontana, 1988) starts its story in 1500, but the second half of the book concerns the modern era. The account, despite being asked to serve an unconvincing general theory, nevertheless repays careful reading. Patrick Brogan's *World Conflicts: Why and Where They Are Happening* (Bloomsbury, 1989) is now dated, but it is one of those invaluable works of factual reference which are usually undervalued. Likewise, Michael Kidron and Ronald Segal's *The State of the World Atlas: A Unique Survey of Current Events and Global Trends* (Penguin, 1995) conveys factual information in an original and usable manner. The first half of the century is covered in the last two sections of A. D. Harvey's *Collision of Empires: Britain in Three World Wars, 1793–1945* (Phoenix, 1992) and the single best general coverage of fall of European Colonialism is Brian Lapping's *The End Of Empire* (Paladin, 1985).

Marc Ferro's *The Great War 1914–18* (Ark, 1987) will guide readers through the First World War. The turbulent prelude to the First World War in Britain is nowhere more readably covered than in George Dangerfield's *The Strange Death of Liberal England* (Paladin, 1972). David Fromkin's *A Peace to End All Peace: Creating the Modern Middle East 1914–1922* (Penguin, 1989) is also essential reading. Another outstanding and gripping account of the crisis of the First World War and its aftermath is to be found in Richard Watt's *The Kings Depart: The Tragedy of Germany: Versailles and the German Revolution* (The Literary Guild, 1985) and a second is to be found in F. L. Carsten *Revolution in Central Europe 1918–1919* (Wildwood House, 1972). The German Revolution is also brilliantly recounted in Pierre Broue's *The German Revolution 1917–1923, New Edition* (Brill, 2005). Simply one of the best history books ever written, and certainly the best account of a revolution by one of its leaders, is Leon Trotsky's *History of the Russian Revolution* (Pluto, 1979). The most readable short account however remains John Reed's classic *Ten Days That Shook the World, New Edition* (Penguin, 2007). William H. Chamberlin's two volume *The Russian Revolution 1917–21* (Princeton, 1987) and Nikolai Sukhanov's *The Russian Revolution 1917: A Personal Record, New Edition* (Princeton, 1984) should not be missed either. The revisionist case about the Russian Revolution is debated by John Rees, Robert Service, Sam Farber and others in *In Defence of October: A Debate on the Russian Revolution* (Bookmarks, 1997). The whole period of War and Revolution can also be followed in C. L. R.

James' *World Revolution 1917–1936: The Rise and Fall of the Communist International, First Paperback Edition* (Humanities, 1993).

A readable account of the rise of Italian Fascism can be found in the late and much-missed Tom Behan's *The Resistible Rise of Benito Mussolini* (Bookmarks, 2003). The most authoritative and comprehensive modern account of German Fascism is Ian Kershaw's two volume study of Hitler, *Hubris: 1889–1936* (Penguin, 1998) and *Nemesis: 1936–1945* (Penguin, 2000). The causes of the rise of Nazism can be traced in Daniel Guerin's *Fascism and Big Business* (Monad, 1973). Ignazio Silone's masterpiece of fiction *The Abruzzo Triology* (Steer Forth Press, 2000) has never been bettered as, among many things, an account of the Italian peasantry's reaction to Fascism.

The rise of Stalinism and the economic underpinnings of the Cold War can be discovered in Tony Cliff's path-breaking study *State Capitalism in Russia, New Edition* (Bookmarks, 1996) and Mike Haynes *Russia, Class and Power 1917–2000* (Bookmarks, 2002). Roy Medvedev's *Let History Judge: The Origins and Consequences of Stalinism, Revised and Expanded Edition* (Oxford University Press, 1989) is a powerful account of tyranny and Michael Reiman's *The Birth of Stalinism: The USSR on the Eve of the 'Second Revolution'* (I. B. Taurus, 1987) tells how it arose. The psychology of those who resisted and those who capitulated to Stalin is brilliantly caught in Victor Serge's novel *The Case of Comrade Tulayev* (Journeyman, 1993).

No one who reads George Orwell's *Homage to Catalonia* (Penguin, 1975) will fail to grasp the meaning of the Spanish Revolution. But they would also profit from Felix Morrow's *Revolution and Counter-Revolution in Spain, New Edition* (New Park, 1976) and Ronald Fraser's remarkable oral histories contained in *Blood of Spain: An Oral History of the Spanish Civil War* (Penguin, 1979).

Angus Calder's account of the Second World War, *The People's War: Britain 1939–1945*, was first published in 1969 and it has subsequently run through many editions for the simple reason that it has not yet been bettered (Pimlico, 2008 is the current edition). A distinctive Marxist interpretation of the Second World War can be read in Ernest Mandel's *The Meaning of the Second World War, New Edition* (Verso, 2011). Olivia Manning's *The Balkan Trilogy* (Arrow, 1997) recreates in fiction the atmosphere in Europe during the rise of Fascism.

Oil is the commodity of the twentieth century and it has its classic studies in Daniel Yergin's *The Prize: The Epic Quest for Oil, Money and*

Power, Revised Edition (Free Press, 1991) and Anthony Sampson's *The Seven Sisters: The Great Oil Companies and the World they Made* (Coronet, 1988). A more recent study is Michael Klare's *Blood and Oil* (Penguin, 2005). The origins of the Israeli conflict with the Palestinians are briefly and effectively addressed in John Rose's *Israel: the Hijack State: America's Watchdog in the Middle East* (Bookmarks, 1986). A general history of the Cold War can be found in Martin Walker's *The Cold War and the Making of the Modern World, New Edition* (Vintage, 1994). Fred Halliday wrote *The Making of the Second Cold War* (Verso, 1986) before the most recent phase of Imperialist conflict disabled his clear-sightedness about great power rivalry.

Among the mass of books on the Vietnam War Christian G. Appy's *The Vietman War: The Definitive Oral History Told from All Sides* (Ebury Press, 2006) is a good place to begin. The events of 1968 are reliably retold in Chris Harman's *The Fire Last Time: 1968 and After, Second Edition* (Bookmarks, 1988). The memories of a leading participant are recorded in Tariq Ali's *Street Fighting Years: An Autobiography of the Sixties* (Collins, 1987). The rise of Solidarity in Poland is best studied in Timothy Garton Ash's *The Polish Revolution* (Coronet, 1985) and the fall of the East European States can be traced in Gwyn Prins (ed.) *Spring in Winter: The 1989 Revolutions* (Manchester University Press, 1990). The decisive battle of Margaret Thatcher's Prime Ministership – the miners' strike – is recalled in Seumas Milne's *The Enemy Within: The Secret War Against the Miners, Revised Edition* (Verso, 2004) and in Mike Simons and Alex Callinicos *The Great Strike: The Miners' Strike of 1984–5 and its Lessons* (Bookmarks, 1985). Meanwhile, the effect of Neo-Liberal economics on the politics of our era is laid bare in Colin Leys *Market Driven Politics: Neoliberal Democracy and the Public Interest* (Verso, 2001).

Peter Gowan's *The Global Gamble: Washington's Faustian Bid for World Dominance* (Verso, 1999) tells the story of the present crisis on US power with an emphasis on economic factors. In my *Imperialism and Resistance* (Routledge, 2006) I attempt to relate US economic decline to the era of the 'War on Terror'. Tariq Ali's excellent *Clash of Fundamentalists: Crusades, Jihads and Modernity* (Verso, 2002) and Alex Callinicos' *The New Mandarins of American Power: The Bush Administration's Plans for the World* (Polity, 2003) also provide valuable anatomies of Neo-Conservatism.

For an understanding of the slump of the 1930s, J. K. Galbraith's *The Great Crash 1929, New Edition* (Penguin, 2009) is a delight to read.

A more substantial account of the economic substructure of the long post-War boom is to be found in Michael Kidron's *Western Capitalism Since the War, Revised Edition* (Pelican, 1970). A still more general account can be found in Phillip Armstrong, Andrew Glyn and John Harrison's *Capitalism since World War II: The Making and Breakup of the Great Boom* (Fontana, 1984). The background to the recent crash is to be found in Robert Brenner's *The Boom and the Bubble: The US in the World Economy* (Verso, 2002) and the best accounts of the crisis as it unfolded is John Bellamy Foster and Fred Magdoff's *The Great Financial Crisis: Causes and Consequences* (Monthly Review Press, 2009) and Graham Turner's *The Credit Crunch: Housing Bubbles, Globalisation and the Worldwide Economic Crisis* (Pluto, 2008). I and others have attempted to analyze the crisis in its political and economic dimensions in Ozlem Onaran and Fred Leplat (eds.) *Capitalism: Crisis and Alternatives* (Resistance Books, 2011).

Peter Fryer has written the premier retelling of black people's history in *Staying Power: Black People in Britain since 1504* (Pluto, 1984) and an excellent account of the dynamics of immigration is to be found in Robert Miles and Annie Phizacklea's *White Man's Country: Racism in British Politics* (Pluto, 1984). Those who want to know more about Malcolm X should read his *The Autobiography of Malcolm X* (Penguin, 2001). David Garrow's *Bearing the Cross: Martin Luther King Jr. and the Southern Christian Leadership* (Vintage, 1988) is a reliable general history of the US Civil Rights Movement. The most advanced political movement of the era is described by participants in Dan Georgakas and Marvin Surkin's *Detroit: I Do Mind Dying* (Redwords, 1998).

Afghanistan's history can be read in *Taliban: Islam, Oil and the New Great Game in Central Asia* (I. B. Taurus, 2000) by Ahmed Rashid and in John K. Cooley's *Unholy Wars: Afghanistan, America and International Terrorism, Second Edition* (Pluto, 2000). Ireland's history is briefly but effectively summarized in Chris Bambery's *Ireland's Permanent Revolution: Second Edition* (Bookmarks, 1988). It can be supplemented by T. A. Jackson's *Ireland Her Own: An Outline History of the Irish Struggle for Freedom and Independence, Second Edition* (Lawrence and Wishart, 1991). Mao's China is dissected by Nigel Harris in *The Mandate of Heaven: Marx and Mao in Modern China* (Quartet, 1978). The critical account of *The ANC and the Liberation Struggle: A Critical Political Biography* (Pluto, 1997) is crisply delivered by Dale T. McKinley, a participant in the fight against South African Apartheid. Richard Gott's *Hugo Chavez and the Bolivarian*

Revolution (Verso, 2005) is sympathetic but realistic in its account of Latin America's most radical Head of State. Iran's development can be traced in Nikki R. Keddie's *Modern Iran: Roots and Results of Revolution* (Yale University Press, 2002), Ervand Abrahamian's, *Iran Between Two Revolutions* (Princeton University Press, 1982) and Assef Bayat's *Workers and Revolution in Iran: A Third World Experience of Worker's Control* (Zed, 1987).

Paul Mason's *Live Working or Die Fighting: How the Working Class Went Global* (Harvill Secker, 2007) is one of the few attempts to come to terms with the way in which older forms of struggle are being reinvented in the new global economy. Accounts of the student movement of recent years and of its precursors can be found among the essays in both Clare Solomon and Tania Palmieri (eds.) *Springtime, The New Student Rebellions* (Verso, 2011) and Michael Bailey and Des Freedman (eds.) *The Assault on Universities: A Manifesto for Resistance* (Pluto, 2011).

INDEX

1968 year 154–8; Chicago Democratic National Convention demonstrations 158; Czechoslovakia invaded by Russia 158, 191; French General Strike 61, 157, 192; global rebellions 106, 190–1; Robert Kennedy assassination 157; Martin Luther King assassination 157; Mexico City Olympic Games 158–9; Richard Nixon elected President 159; Northern Ireland Civil Rights protest 120, 158; student revolt Paris 61, 157, 191–2; Vietnam War 155–6, 159; Women's Liberation protest Atlantic City 158

1989 revolutions 174–80; Bulgaria 177; Czechoslovakia 177, 179; Eastern Europe 62, 174–80, 191; fall of the Berlin Wall 174–6, 177; Hungary 177, 179; Poland's Solidarity Revolt 175, 179; post-Cold War world 179–80; Romania 178, 179; Tiananmen Square protests 176, 192–3

Abyssinia 24
Adams, Gerry 124
Afghanistan 62, 77, 80–7; aid during Cold War 82–3; British invasion 1838 80–1; British invasion 1878 82; Civil War 1989 84; invasion by Russia 1979 84; US support for Mujahidden 84; US/NATO invasion 2001 75, 85–7, 196
African National Congress (ANC) 160, 162, 165–6
Ahmadinejad, Mahmoud 92–3
Al Qaeda 84–5, 195
Allied Forces: Cold War 56; First World War 10; Second World War 47–52
ANC (African National Congress) 160, 162, 165–6
anti-Capitalist protests 194–5
Arab Spring 2011 101
Arab–Israeli conflict 77, 95–102
armistice: First World War 10
asylum seekers 132, 133
Austria 21; Anschluss with Nazi Germany 40; Civil War 1934 24; declaration of war on Serbia 1914 7; First World War 7, 10
Austro-Hungarian Empire 7; collapse 19

Balfour, Arthur 20, 95
Balkan War 74–5
Bandung Conference 1955 59
Bass, Alfie 46
Battle of the Atlantic 1940–1943 47
Battle of Britain 1940 44–5
Battle of the Bulge 51
Battle of El Alamein 48
Battle of Jutland 10
Battle of Marne 10
Battle of the Somme 10
Battle of Stalingrad 48

Index

Battle of Tannenberg 7
Battle of Verdun 10
Benn, Tony 169
Berlin Wall 62, 174; fall 1989 174–6, 177
Bhutto, Benazir 198
Biko, Steve 163
Black Panther 152, 157
Blair, Tony 115, 116, 170, 172, 173, 197
Blitz, the 1940–1941 45–6
Blix, Hans 115
Blum, Leon 40
BNP (British National Party) 33
Bolivar, Simon 180–1
Botha, P. W. 163
Boxer Rebellion 65
Brandt, Willy 25
Brecht, Berthold 58
British Empire 48, 50; decline 40, 42, 96
British National Party (BNP) 33
British Nationality Act 1981 132
Bulgaria 177
Bush, George, senior 63, 114, 180
Bush, George W. 74, 75, 77, 115, 116, 195, 197

Cable Street battle 32
Callaghan, Jim 168, 169
Cambodia 107–8
Cameron, David 173
Carr, E. H. 3, 40
Carter, Jimmy 84, 89
Ceausescu, Nicolai 178
Chamberlain, Neville 41, 43
Chavez, Hugo: Venezuela Revolution 180–7, 196–7
Cheney, Dick 74, 78, 195, 196
Chiang Kai-Shek 66, 67
Chilcot Inquiry 110–11, 114
China: Communism 57, 66, 68; Cultural Revolution 68; market economy 68–9; military power 69; nuclear power 64; Opium Wars 65; rise to power 64–71; rival to US world leadership 198, 199; space programme 64, 69; Tiananmen Square protests 1989 176, 192–3

Churchill, Winston 43–4, 46, 50, 53, 54, 56, 129; Battles of El Alamein 48
Civil Rights Movement: United States 144–54, 156–7
climate change 199–200
Clinton, Bill 115
Cold War 3–4, 54–64, 72; aid to Afghanistan 82–3; nuclear missiles 55, 56, 60–1, 169; post-Cold War world 179–80; Space Race 59; Thatcher's 'Iron Lady' image 169
Communism: Cold War 56–64
Congress of South African Trade Unions (COSATU) 164
Cuban Missile Crisis 1962 55, 60–1
Czechoslovakia 21, 56–7, 61, 62, 75; Hitler invasion 1939 41–2; Prague Spring 1968 106, 156, 158, 191; Velvet Revolution 1989 177, 179; Warsaw Pact invasion 1968 158, 191

D-Day 50
Day Lewis, Cecil 25
De Klerk, F. W. 165
Dubcek, Alexander 191

Eastern bloc: Czechoslovakian revolt 61, 62, 106, 156, 158, 177, 179, 191; Hungarian uprising 1956 58–9, 176, 188–9; Poland's Solidarity Revolt 62, 175, 179; post-Cold War world 179–80; revolutions 1989 62, 174–80
East Germany: Cold War 57, 58, 174; fall of the Berlin Wall 1989 174–6, 177; post-Cold War world 179–80
economy: consequences of First World War 21–3; *see also* recessions
Edward VIII, King of England 42
Egypt 100–1
Eisenhower, Dwight 104, 146
Enigma Code 48
Estonia 21
the Euro 196

Falklands War 1982 168–9
Fascism 19, 21, 24–6, 40; Britain 31–3; Italy 21, 24–5, 27–8, 40, 49; rise of

26–34; South Africa 165; Spain 25–6, 36–8, 40
Ferdinand, Franz: assassination 7
Finland 21
First World War, 1914–1918 2–3, 7–11; consequences 18–26; economic consequences 21–3
foreign policy: United States 74, 75–7, 78–9, 99–100
France: First World War 7, 9–10; General Strike 61, 157, 192; German invasion 1940 44; Popular Front Government 1936 40; student revolt 1968 61, 157, 191–2; Vietnam colony 102–4
Franco, Francisco 25, 26, 35, 36–8, 40

Gagarin, Yuri 59
Galbraith, John Kenneth 105
Gallipoli campaign 10, 44
General Strike 1926 22–3, 44, 187
Germany: Austrian Anschluss 40; Cold War 57, 58, 175; consequences of First World War 20, 21–2; First World War 7–10; invasion of France 1940 44; Revolution 1918–1923 40; Second World War 40–54; *see also* East Germany; West Germany; Nazis
Goering, Herman 29–30
Gorbachev, Mikhail 62, 176, 177, 178
Gottwald, Klement 25
Great Britain: Afghanistan invasion 1838 80–1; Afghanistan invasion 1878 80–1; appeasement with Hitler 41, 42–4; Battle of the Atlantic 1940–1943 47; Fascism 31–3; First World War 7, 10; IMF austerity package 1976 168; immigration 126–34; miners' strike 1984–85 169–70; Munich Agreement with Hitler 1938 41, 42; nuclear missiles under Thatcher 169; Opium Wars 65; Palestinian occupation 95–6; pro-Nazi sympathies 42–3; public sector strikes 1979 168; Second World War 40–54; Tottenham and Brixton riots 1985 170
Great Depression 139

Great War *see* First World War, 1914–1918
Guernica 37
Gulf War 1991 74

Hamas 77
Healy, Denis 168
Heath, Edward 167
Hezbollah 76–7, 198
Hitler, Adolf 19, 23–4, 25, 26; rise to power 28–31, 40; suicide 52
Hitler–Stalin Non-Aggression Pact 1939 42
Ho Chi Minh 103
Holbrooke, Richard 78
Holocaust 52, 98–9
Honecker, Erich 175, 177
Hoover, J. Edgar 146
Hungary 21, 62, 75; East Germans cross border 1989 176–7; October 1956 uprising 58–9, 176, 188–9; October 1989 Revolution 177, 179
Husk, Gustav 177
Hussein, Saddam 91, 111, 113–16, 197

immigration: Great Britain 126–34
Immigration Act 1971 131–2
International Monetary Fund (IMF): 1976 austerity package for Britain 168
Iran: Middle East influence 76–7; nuclear threat 199; student revolts 91, 192; US Embassy in Tehran siege 1979 91
Iran–Iraq War 1980–1988 91, 111–12
Iranian Revolution 1979 73, 88–94, 192
Iraq: Iran–Iraq War 1980–1988 91, 111, 113; oil nationalization 111; origin of the nation 111
Iraq Inquiry 110–11, 114, 117
Iraq War 74, 75–6, 110–17; protests 197, 198
Ireland 117–26, 158
Irish Free State 21
Irish Republican Army (IRA) 119, 121, 122, 123, 124, 125, 126
iron curtain 55, 56, 174
Israel: formation of State of Israel 96–8; Lebanon invasion 2006 197–8;

Palestinian issue 77, 95–102; US aid 99–100
Italy: Fascism 21, 24–5, 27–8, 40, 49; First World War 10; Second World War 49–50

Japan: Hiroshima and Nagasaki bombings 52–3, 56; Pearl Harbour attack 46–7
Jenkins, Roy 123
Jews: anti-Semitism 32, 33; Hitler's persecution 28, 30, 52; Holocaust 52, 98–9; Russian Revolution 15, 16
Johnson, Lyndon 78, 105, 107, 151, 155, 159
Jones, Jack 25
Jordan 100
Joy, Magalia 87

Kara, Ahmed 85, 86
Kennedy, John F. 59, 61, 78, 105, 148, 150, 153
Kennedy, Joseph 46
Kennedy, Robert 146, 150, 156, 157
Kerens, Alexander 13–14
Khomeini, Ayatollah 89, 90–1, 192
Kim Il-Sung 57–8
King, Martin Luther 146, 147, 148, 152, 153, 156–7
Kinnock, Neil 170, 172
Kissinger, Henry 61
Kessler, Arthur 25
Korean War 58
Kornilov coup 14–15
Khrushchev, Nikita 58, 61
Kuwait 113–14

Laos 108
Latvia 21
Lawrence of Arabia 95
League of Nations 20: failure 24–5
Lebanese Resistance Movement 76–7, 198
Lebanon 99; Israeli invasion 2006 197–8
Lenin, Vladimir 13, 14, 16
Liebknecht, Karl 28
Lithuania 21
Luxemburg, Rosa 28

McCarthy, Eugene 156
McGuiness, Martin 124
Macmillan, Harold 129
Major, John 172
Malcolm X 148–51, 152
Mandela, Nelson 162, 165
Mao Zedong 57, 61–2, 66, 68
Marshall Aid 56, 57, 72
Medvedev, Dmitri 198, 199
Mesopotamia: First World War 10
Mexico City: 1968 Olympic Games 158–9
Middle East: collapse of Ottoman Empire 19; first Gulf War 74; First World War 10; Iran's influence 76–7; US foreign policy 74, 75–7, 99–102; *see also* Iran; Iraq; Palestine
military power: China 69; United States 72–3, 74
military weapons: First World War 9
Miners' Union 22; NUM strike 1984–85 169–70
Mosley, Oswald 31, 32
Mubarak, Hosni 101
Munich Agreement 1938 41, 42
Mussolini, Benito 19, 21, 24, 25, 40, 49; invasion of Abyssinia 24–5; rise of Fascism 27–8

Nagy, Imre 58, 59, 176
Nasser, Gamal Abdel 48, 59, 99
National Front 32–3
National Union of Miners *see* Miners' Union
Nazis 19, 26; Operation Barbarossa 1941 46; rise to power 28–31; student support 187–8
Nenni, Pietro 25
New Labour 142, 170, 172
Nixon, Richard 61–2, 68, 107, 158, 159
North Africa: Battles of El Alamein 48
North Atlantic Treaty Organization (NATO) 3, 57–8, 72; Afghanistan invasion 75, 85–7, 196; Balkan War 74–5; enlargement 75
North Korea 57–8, 197

Index

Northern Ireland 120–6, 158; Civil Rights protest 1968 120, 158
nuclear missiles: China 64; Cold War 55, 56, 60–1, 169; Cuban Missile Crisis 1962 55, 60–1; Hiroshima and Nagasaki bombings 52–3, 56; Pakistan 86; Thatcher's government 169

Obama, Barack 71, 75–6, 199; foreign policy 78–9; Middle East foreign policy 75–7
Official IRA 122
oil: Iraq 111; Venezuela 181, 182–6
Opium Wars 65
Orwell, George 25, 26, 35, 38–9, 56
Osama bin Laden 77, 196
Ottoman Empire: collapse 19; Palestine 95

Paisley, Ian 120
Pakistan 77; Afghanistan war spread to 86
Palestine 20, 77, 94–102; British occupation 1917 95–6; partition 96; Zionist immigration 96
Parks, Rosa 145
Passchendaele: First World War 10
Pearl Harbour 46–7
Picasso, Pablo 37
poison gas: battle at Ypres 10
Poland 21, 75; First World War 10; Hitler invasion 1939 42; Solidarity Revolt 62, 175, 179
Potsdam conference 55
Powell, Colin 114, 196
Powell, Enoch 32, 130–1
Priestley, J. B. 46
Provisional IRA 122, 123, 124
Putin, Vladimir 195, 197, 198

racism 32, 127, 129–31; Apartheid South Africa 160–7; US Civil Rights Movement 144–54, 156–7
Ratner, Harry 45
Reagan, Ronald 62, 74, 84, 140, 169, 178
recessions 135–44; global 2008 77–8, 135, 139–43, 198–9; South Sea Bubble Crash 1720s 135–7; Wall Street Crash 1929 23, 137–9
refugees 133
Rice, Condoleezza 74, 78, 195, 196
Robeson, Paul 37
Romania 178, 179
Rommel, Erwin 48
Roosevelt, Franklin D. 46, 48, 50, 53
Rumsfeld, Donald 74, 115, 196
Russia: Afghanistan aid during Cold War 82–3; Afghanistan invasion 1979 84; Battle of Stalingrad 48; Civil War 1918 16; Cold War 56–7, 58–64; Cuban Missile Crisis 1962 55, 60–1; First World War 7–8, 10, 11–12, 15, 19; Hitler–Stalin Non-Aggression Pact 1939 42; Hungarian uprising 1956 58–9, 176, 188–9; invasion of Czechoslovakia 1968 158, 191; Nazi invasion 1941 46; Perestroika 62, 176, 178; Second World War 48, 49, 50, 53, 55–6; space programme 59; twenty-first-century-politics 195, 198
Russian Revolution 1917 10, 11–18

Sadat, Anwar 100
Scargill, Arthur 169
Second World War, 1938–1945 39–54; United States' entry 1941 46–8
Selassie, Haile 24
Shah of Iran 88–90, 192
Sinn Fein 119, 124, 125
South Africa: Apartheid struggle 160–7; Fascism 165; public sector strikes 2007 166; Sharpeville massacre 1960 162; Soweto Uprising 1976 162
South Sea Bubble Crash 1720s 135–7
space programme: China 64, 69; Cold War Space Race 59; Russia 59
Spain: Civil War 1936 25–6, 34–9; Fascism 25–6, 36–8, 40
Sputnik 59
Stalin, Joseph 11, 16, 18, 50, 53; Berlin Rising 58; Hitler–Stalin Non-Aggression Pact 1939 42
Strategic Arms Limitation Treaty 1972 62

student revolts 187–93; Czechoslovakia 1968 191; global revolutions in 1968 190–1; Hungary's October 1956 uprising 188–9; Iran 91, 192; Nazi opposition 188; Paris 1968 61, 157, 191–2; Tiananmen Square 1989 176, 192–3; US Civil Rights Movement 146, 152–3, 189–90; Vietnam War 106
Suez Canal 48, 59, 99
Swastika 28

Taliban 84–5, 86, 196
Tambo, Oliver 165
Terreblanche, Eugene 165
Thatcher, Margaret 62, 140; elected prime minister 1979 168; election victory 1983 168; election victory 1987 170; Falklands War 1982 168–9; 'Iron Lady' image 169; miners' strike 1984–85 169–70; poll tax 170–2; Tory leadership 1975 168
Thatcherism 167–74
Tito, Josip Broz 25, 57
Trades Union Congress (TUC) 22–3
Trades Unions: attack by Thatcher 168, 169–70; Poland's Solidarity Revolt 62, 175, 179; South Africa 163, 164, 165–6; *see also* Miners' Union
Treaty of Brest-Litovsk 10
Trotsky, Leon 10, 13, 14, 15, 16, 18
Truman, Harry 56
Turkey 21; First World War 8
Tyndall, John 33

United States: 9/11 attack on World Trade Center 85, 195–6; Afghan Mujahidden support 84; Afghanistan aid during Cold War 82–3; Afghanistan invasion 75, 85–7, 196; aid to Israel 99–100; Civil Rights Movement 144–54, 156–7; Cold War 54–64; Cuban Missile Crisis 1962 55, 60–1; economic power post-Second World War 71–4; economic recession 77–8, 198–9; First World War 10; foreign policy 78–9; Hiroshima and Nagasaki bombings 52–3, 56; Iraq War 74, 75–6; League of Nations 20; Middle East foreign policy 74, 75–7, 99–102; military power 72–3, 74; Pearl Harbour attack 46–7; Second World War 46–53, 71–2; Space Race 59; twenty-first-century politics 195–7; Vietnam War 59–60, 61, 72–3, 102–10, 155–6, 159

Venezuela: Chavez's Revolution 180–7, 196–7
Versailles Treaty 20, 21
Vietnam War 59–60, 61, 72–3, 102–10, 159; My Lai Massacre 106–7, 156; Tet Offensive 61, 155, 106–7, 155
von Braun, Wernher 53

Walesa, Lech 175
Wall Street Crash 1929 23, 137–9
Warsaw Pact 3, 57; invasion of Czechoslovakia 1968 158, 191
West Germany: Cold War 57, 174; fall of the Berlin Wall 1989 174–6, 177
Western Front: First World War 9–10
Wilhelm II: abdication 10
Wilson, Harold 168
Wilson, Woodrow 20
Wolfowitz, Paul 74, 115

Yalta conference 53, 55
Ypres: First World War 10

Zhivkov, Todor 177
Zionism: Arab–Israeli conflict 77, 95–102